SIMPLICITY OF LIFE AS LIVED IN THE EVERYDAY

Sister Kathleen Storms, SSND

UNIVERSITY
PRESS OF
AMERICA

LANHAM • NEW YORK • LONDON

Copyright © 1983 by
Sister Kathleen Storms, S.S.N.D,
University Press of America,™ Inc.

4720 Boston Way
Lanham, MD 20706

3 Henrietta Street
London WC2E 8LU England

Library of Congress Cataloging in Publication Data

Storms, Kathleen, Sister, 1946-
    Simplicity of life as lived in the everyday.

    Bibliography: p.
    1. Simplicity—Religious aspects—Christianity.
2. Storms, Kathleen, Sister, 1946-   . I. Title.

BV4647.S48S76   1983   248.4'82   83-16812
ISBN 0-8191-3601-8 (alk. paper)
ISBN 0-8191-3602-6 (pbk. : alk. paper)

Co-Published by arrangement with the
Institute of Formative Spirituality,
Duquesne University

dedicated to all who search to

    simplify their lives . . .

iv

ACKNOWLEDGMENTS

To the many people who have helped to weave the fabric of my life, I lovingly and gratefully dedicate this study.

I wish to extend special gratitude to my parents and family who first helped me to begin to unfold my life by their example of simplicity. I am also grateful to my community, the School Sisters of Notre Dame of the Mankato Province who have encouraged me through this writing and in the sometimes painful search for simplicity in religious life.

I also deeply appreciate the guidance and direction I have received from Father Adrian van Kaam, CSSP, and Dr. Susan A. Muto, who have continued to unfold the science of formative spirituality enriching the spiritual lives of many.

TABLE OF CONTENTS

A SEARCH FOR SIMPLICITY

PART FOUR
THE VOWED CHRISTIAN RESPONSE
TO THE CALL OF SIMPLICITY

PART FIVE
THE NOVICE'S MOVEMENT TOWARD SIMPLICITY

GENERAL INTRODUCTION TO THE UNIVERSITY
PRESS OF AMERICA SERIES ON THE CREATIVE
FORMATION OF LIFE AND WORLD

General Editors: Adrian van Kaam, Ph.D.
                  Susan Muto, Ph.D.

    Humanity is faced with a crucial epoch in its for-
mation history. Side by side with the growth of the
human and physical sciences, we are faced wtih a new
critical awareness of the formation traditions of past
and present cultures. Now, as never before, we enjoy
the potential availability of a more complete and better
integrated knowledge, empirically validated, of the
foundational principles of the formation of human life.
Until recently the various world populations had to
respond to the new demands placed on their historical
development on basis only of the limited experience of
their own generation. Or they could depend only on one
or the other form tradition restricted to their own culture. Neither were they sustained by the numerous
insights and findings of the humanities, the human and
physical sciences, and the scholarly studies about the
great formation traditions with their corresponding
philosophical and theological reflections, presently
available to us.

    The disclosure of this new possibility is exciting
but at the same time an awesome challenge to the human
mind and its scholarly effort. It confronts humanity
with the task, never possible or necessary before, to
integrate on a foundational basis the relevant contri-
butions of different fields of knowledge and experience
with the consonant formation of human life and world.
At the same time, it sparks the never-dying hope of the
human race that some day we may attain the art and
discipline of living together in peace and mutual affirmation while deeply respecting all people's rights to
their own consonant form traditions.

    The time of a monolithic cultural formation tradi-
tion, that uncritically and exclusively gave form to
the life of one specific population, is behind us. To
the art and discipline of human formation applies also
what has been said over and over again: the world has
become a global village. This does not mean that the
continuous formation of life and world should be homo-

genized. On the contrary, it poses the challenge to
profit from all differentiated sources of formation
wisdom and knowledge in order to arrive at universal
principles of a distinctively human formation of our
life. At the same time such a universal science should
leave room for the specific articulation of such principles and empirical observations in terms of the
different formation traditions to which people on this
globe are committed. Neither should this science fall
into the trap of a false irenicism. It should foster
critical dialogue between the various formation traditions in this specific area of concern. The purpose
of such dialogue would not necessarily be to come to
unity beyond the foundational formation principles but
foremost to help people to establish more clearly their
own identity as belonging to their own specific formation
traditions. It should enable them to disclose what is
best and most congenial, compatible and compassionate
in those traditions.

        The world is becoming one. The break-up of the
formative hegamony of Europe in the periods after the
last two world wars was a necessary condition. It
paved the way for dialogue between our ways of form
giving to life and world. This facilitating condition
has not yet been fully utilized. We still have many
enclaves of formation. But even these last centers of
provincialism are gradually permeated by new directives
and forms of life. An increasing mixture of populations,
each with their own form traditions, contribute to this
widening of consciousness. The immediate result,
however, is that many people are faced by a bewildering
number of options.   To them, it may seem difficult to
relate them to their own personal life direction and to
the limited understanding of their own formation traditions. In a world of increasingly complex formation
directives, coming from so many sciences and traditions
unfamiliar to us, we find ourselves often confused about
how to give form to our own life and that of our children
or students.

        Contemporary world formation is dynamic and fasci-
nating. Many are its enthusiastic projects. While such
tentative efforts are valuable, they are often short on
the age-old wisdom of the classical formation traditions
and the well-tested knowledge of the empirical sciences.
We may be fascinated by the newness of many formative
ideas. We may follow them blindly without sufficient

appraisal of their deeper meaning for our human life
and its distinctive unfolding. We become so adept at
reacting that we forget how to respond personally to
such new directives out of an inner at-homeness with
our own experiences, experiences that should be appraised
in the light of universal human formation knowledge and
wisdom. We may run excitedly after any new formation
movement to gain the approval of its charismatic leaders.
The problem is that we may betray the unique wisdom of
our own experience and of our formation tradition. They
should penetrate, appraise, and, if necessary, transfi-
gure these directives. We take on new patterns of living, yet we do not try to make them consonant with our
own values. We go along with what is popular thought-
lessly, enchanted by the media, bewitched by the sophis-
tication of our peers.

Compelled by our need to give form to lives that
have to be lived in new world situations, we forge
ahead, often in directions that cannot really fulfill
our deepest aspirations because they may be dissonant
with our inner direction. Lost in such movements, we
may lose the concrete sense of a unique life call. The
more empty we feel, the more anxiously we search for
fulfillment. We may rush after any project that seems
to promise an instant solution to our quest for a meaningful, distinctively human form of life.

Our present-day world on the road to unity may seem
like a jumble of life styles and forms. Still this confusion is also a promise of opportunities for personal
living. Choices that were not available in former periods
of history can be pondered now. It enables us to create
a richness and variety of empirical life forms undreamt
of before. We are on the threshold of a pluralism of
life forms, mutually respected, somehow unique, yet rooted
in universal formation principles in which we recognize
each other as belonging to the same species. To be sure
the security of conformity is lost. Many of us are under-
standably pained by this loss. We gained, however, in
potential creativity and openness to pluriformity. A
uniform national formation may be dead, but its demise
has given rise to the art and discipline of human formation itself as a source of formative wisdom and creation.
This is more alive than ever.

We foresee that global formation wisdom will slowly
be established. It will spread over the nations, trans-

figuring countless cultural styles and forms, enfleshing itself in myriad ways in this planet on its path to unity in diversity. Paradoxically, creative formation of life against the background of a universal and unifying knowledge has become a much more personal responsibility. No longer is it possible for one closed-off country to offer by itself alone sufficient guidelines for the authentic formation of each unique human life. Rather persons in dialogue with their own unique preformation and with the foundations of the form traditions to which they belong must find out what is involved in the unique formation of their own life, their formation should not only be congenial with their own being but compatible and compassionate in regard to the people and to the global and local situations that co-form their existence.

The purpose of this series of books within the science of foundational human formation is to serve this dialogue. Sometimes this science is called foundational formative spirituality. In this connection the terms "spirit" or "spirituality" have no dualistic connotations. They only indicate the distinctively human aspect of life and its formation as a whole. Research in this field, insofar as it has developed today, is of two main kinds. First of all: basic research in the universal and general foundations of all human formation. Secondly, students or practitioners in this field may be interested in the dialogue between the results of this foundational research with one or more specific formation tradition. This second complementary kind of research is called "articulation" research. This term refers to the fact that this research attempts to articulate the general findings in terms of one or the other formation tradition. The publications in this series will restrict themselves in the area of articulation research to mainly an attempt to articulate the universal findings in terms of the Christian formation tradition. The reader should be aware, however, that a similar articulation can take place in relation to other form traditions. Most of the publications will illustrate this feasibility by a brief application to some aspect of a formation tradition other than Christian.

The publications in this series will direct themselves to various dynamics of human formation. The topics will be initiated by an analysis of the concrete human experiences underlying a specific formation event. Subsequently, it will be shown how this experiential description and analysis gains in objectivity, amplification and depth of meaning when placed in critical dialogue with emerging insights in literature, the sciences, formation traditions and contemporary experience. Each study intends to be of some assistance to readers who like to grow in insight in the art and discipline of formation. It hopes also to be enlightening for those who are trying to find their own form of life in this age of transition. Each study may help us to answer such basic questions as: How can I find my way as a creative human being in the new, wide open situation of a world that is breaking down and formed anew at the same time? How can I give a meaningful form to my life and my situation in a unique yet communal style now that there is no longer a uniform, popular code to tell all citizens or members of a community in minute detail how to arrange their lives?

The science of distinctively human formation can be seen as a discipline that guides this search for our communal and unique form of life. The science analyzes formative directives and dispositions that will enable us to be more open to our own form potency. It investigates how we make ourselves ready for their unfolding, how they can affect us beneficially.

The focus of this approach is on the conditions, structures and dynamics of our daily formation. It wants to facilitate the disclosure and unfolding of our best possibilities. This new field of study tries to establish the necessary and sufficient conditions for a distinctively human formation of our life and world. It explores from this perspective special and personal ways of formation, experiences, exercises, deviations, failures and successes, abstracting in this way the essentials. It attempts to lay the basis for a foundational formation wisdom of humanity. It assists people in finding practical and particular solutions to their formation questions in the modern world without betraying the fundamental conditions of their own formation traditions.

This approach also takes into account the functional, social, and physiological problems that may hinder the free disclosure of our human life direction. Similar hindrances may delay or obstruct the full permeation of our formation by this increasingly disclosed direction. The humanities and the human sciences contain many findings and insights regarding such problems. They propose

effective means of coping with them. The science of
formation integrates--and if necessary, reforms and
reformulates--such insights along with those found in
the great human formation traditions into a synthetic
understanding of basic human formation.

The science of formation is in this way profoundly
practical. It refers to what effects a real change in
human life. It contends that such a change will affect
in turn people's formation of the world in concrete ways.
Superficial changes affect mainly the emotional, functional or external periphery of human existence. Change
in depth leads to a lasting inner conversion which will
be echoed in one's practical formation of the world.
The science of formation tries, therefore, to disclose,
describe and apply the principles of the process of a
profoundly practical change of human life on basis of the
potential knowledge and wisdom now available in principle
to humanity. In this way it wants to be of help to con-
temporaries who go through transition crises in a rapidly
changing world in which they and their children have to
live their life.

The science of formation builds on a theory of the
development of human life in relation to this newly
available knowledge, affecting as it does our own formation, that of others, of the immediate situation and that
of the global community. During the past 20 years of
developing this new science, the results have been most
gratifying. The vast majority of M.A. and Ph.D. graduates
after study and preparation in this new field, have re-
ported spontaneously on profound changes they experience
in their own life and in that of people entrusted to
their care as specialized formation counselors, consul-
tants, teachers, or as parents or practitioners in the
helping professions. The studies presented in this series
have been written by men and women who for a prolonged
period of time have participated in the unfolding of this
new discipline at the international graduate Institute
of Formative Spirituality at Duquesne University. It is
our hope that this series will enable the reader to
participate in the results of this new field of study.
Their subsequent reflection will deepen their awareness
of the dialogue to which each person today is called as
an active participant in a newly emerging global community.

--The Editors

FORWARD

This reflection by Sister Kathleen Storms on
simplicity of life addresses the yearning for wholeness
all people share. As we progress towards the year 2000,
ordinary existence appears increasingly complex. Too
many computers . . . too much technology . . . information overload--these are frequent complaints. Thus our
hearts long at times for plain, uncomplicated, simple
patterns of living.

The science of formation refers to this experience
as the longing for consonance. It is rooted, among
other things, in our innate poverty or simplicity of
spirit, in the fact that we are essentially an incomplete
species, earthbound yet in search of the eternal. We
want all the parts of our lives to sound harmoniously
together.

The author offers us in this text a personal,
thorough exploration of this most common formative
experience. She echoes in a unique way the universal
longing for simple, wholesome, consonant living. She
deals delicately with the tissue of dispositions surrounding simplicity, such as obedience, respectful love,
openness, reverence, wonder, and humility.

Following the methodology of the science of formative
spirituality, she traces her theme across universal,
distinctively human lines; against the horizon of explicit
religious openness to the Holy; and into the faith and
formation tradition of Christianity as revealed in the
scriptures and as articulated by the great spiritual
masters. Along the way she discloses several key obstacles to simplicity of spirit and suggests facilitating
conditions that can correct and possibly reverse these
deforming abberations. This practical sensitivity enables
her to apply her findings to a major formation segment
of the population: vowed religious in initial and ongoing
formation.

Crucial to her study is the integration of relevant
topical insights from both remotely and proximately
directive sciences like philosophy, theology, psychology
and sociology. She manifests that respectful presence
to the auxiliary sciences typical of the formation
expert. Whether one is an ordinary reader or a scholarly

academician, this text is bound to be enriching and
challenging.

Simplicity is not a disposition confined to monas-
teries; it is an essential component of the consonant
life. It guards us from the impulsive, hectic, overly
exalted, ambitious pace that depletes our presence to
self, others and God. The author convincingly demon-
strates the truth of T. S. Eliot's oft-quoted phrase from
Four Quartets, "A condition of complete simplicity/
(Costing not less than everything)."

The price we pay to live in detached, gracious
simplicity may be high, but, as we learn from Sister's
words, the reward is infinitely great. To reach blessed
simplicity is to taste on earth something of that peace
and joy that will be fully ours only in eternity.

We, therefore, thank Sister Kathleen for the time
she took to prepare this text and proudly include it in
our University Press of America series on the creative
formation of life and world. May it lead each of us to
ponder the call to simplicity in our own lives; may it
help us to foster this formative goal in the lives of
all those entrusted to our care.

                              --The Editors
                              Adrian van Kaam, Ph.D.
                              Susan Annette Muto, Ph.D.

PREFACE

Simplicity is a difficult concept to describe or to define. And yet, almost everyone has some notion of the meaning of this term. We use simplicity to describe a pleasing architectural design, a room decor, a style of furniture, or a work of art. It seems most often that we say something is simple when there are no extraneous parts, when everything contributes to an integrated whole. No one aspect seems to protrude or demand our total attention.

In times of natural disaster or monetary crisis, many people seem to be drawn to a type of simplicity. They are forced to "do without." Paradoxically, they often discover that their lives are far more rewarding now than in prosperous times. Others consider simplicity to be a virtue to be striven for within a religious context. Frugality becomes a "doing with less" in the name of simplicity.

Perhaps the most difficult simplicity to describe is that which is attributed to certain people. Because of the profundity and uniqueness of each person, the quality of simplicity evidenced in a person is difficult to describe without distorting its deepest meaning. However, we may ask, what words would we use to describe a simple person? Are there certain traits that seem to characterize a simple person? Is it really possible to be simple in our complex modern society?

Life today is characterized by uncertainty and constant change. The way I did things yesterday may not be the acceptable thing today. The cry is often heard: why can't life be simple! Why do we have to be caught up in a race that seems to have no purpose or goal? Being "caught up" seems to make my life un-simple as I encounter the difficulties of trying to relate to others, appreciate the beauty around me, or even live my own life. I may find that I am "caught up" in time schedules, meeting other's expectations of me, or living in the present with one eye fixated on past failures, while the other eye is anticipating the future.

My intent in this study is to develop throughout in five parts the ongoing movement toward self-simplification in the everyday. This movement seems to begin with a slowing down to see, resulting in a moment of awakening. The gifted moment of seeing clearly the scattered motion of my life fills me with an awareness of the need to let go of those things that keep me from living out of the true self I am called to be. These perceptions seem to draw me to surrender freely in the ongoing movement toward the center of my life where I am most in touch with who I really am, and can thereby respond most freely to the complexities of daily life.

My research will be limited to the discovery of those hidden factors that keep me from living simply within the complexities of my life and world. I will not do a detailed study of the person, who because of some lack (intellectual, cultural refinement, or monetary) is said to be simple. Nor will I dwell on examples of persons who have already reached a high degree of simplicity. My main research will focus on those individuals who desire to simplify their lives; the factors that make this movement more difficult; and finally, the surrender necessary to come to full human and spiritual living within the complexities of daily life. I will also present means by which the process of self-simplification will be a way of spiraling close to the true self I am called to be from all eternity.

INTRODUCTION

Struggling to find the relationship that numbers have to each other in a math puzzle, or trying to find the answer to a riddle can be a frustrating experience. I try many different ways to find the hidden pattern buried somewhere beyond my immediate comprehension. The tendency is to say, "Are you sure all of these numbers are correct? They can't be related!" No matter how hard I try, I cannot see the pattern. If by chance I discover the pattern I am ecstatic over the experience. Suddenly everything seems so clear and simple. At times I need the help of another because I cannot discover the pattern on my own. I either try too hard or I am blinded to some small clue. With the aid of another, I become aware of how the elements of the puzzle fit together. I wonder how I could have been so blind when now I see the relationship so clearly.

Rapoport* says that our quest for simplicity stems from a conviction that beneath wide dissimilarities there are regularities to be discovered. We, in yearning for wholeness and oneness with all that is, become convinced that there can be a clarity, a simplicity of relationship in our world--if only we can discover that hidden pattern.

If we look at the Latin root of the word simplicity, we discover it comes from simplex. Plain, straightforward, uncomplicated, or without fold are several of its meanings. The final meaning--without fold--fascinates me. When something is without fold there are no hidden aspects, no underlying parts. An object is clearly recognized for what it is because the whole of it can be seen. If I see a folded up bundle of cloth, I am not sure what it is. It may simply be a table cloth. But it could also be a few yards of material to make a dress or it could be material already fashioned into something to wear. The bundle could also be concealing a flaw or a change in pattern. I can only discover what it is by unfolding it and allowing the object itself to reveal its meaning for me in all its simplicity.

Looking at these few brief examples of the search for what I see as simplicity may give me some notion of how I can experience it in my own life. However, if I try to apply these principles immediately to my own life,

I may run into difficulty. I am not static thing or a collection of hidden relationships waiting to be discovered. I am a complex being--complex because of the many factors in life that make me what I am. My family background, inherited traits and childhood experiences are only a few of the factors that make me more than a math puzzle or riddle to be solved.

As I move through life experiences, I am affected in my own unique way because of these underlying factors, but I am more than the sum of these relatively limited, somewhat understandable influences. I am constantly becoming more, emerging beyond these initial factors. In meeting and growing beyond these relatively static factors I realize that I cannot control all my life experiences or the world in which I live. I cannot control the weather. Neither can I control others' reactions to me nor pattern their reactions according to what I want. I cannot (beyond a certain limited degree) control or regulate the happenings of my day. I may never know when the telephone will ring, or when someone will come to my door shaking up the plan of my work, prayer, or recreation schedule. I cannot control my body or simply understand how it functions for me. A sudden headache or an attack of the flu thwarts the free flowing use of my body. All of these factors, which are beyond my control, make it difficult for me to discover and apply to my life underlying regularities or factors that would make it simple.

Because of the influences of my world, my bodily influences and my own personal way of responding, my life as lived is not simple, not controllable, not predictable beyond a certain limited degree. My life is not static but an ever changing dynamic, growing, emerging into something new for me. How then can I simplify my life? How can I live a relatively anxiety-free, uncomplicated life when I know that I live in a world that is ever changing, in a body that is often unpredictable, and through a personality that is not completely clear and translucent for me? Somehow I need to live out the conviction Rapoport spoke of earlier--that is, I need to experience that beneath wide dissimilarities, there are underlying, ordering regularities to be discovered. Somehow I need to "unfold the cloth" and discover that meaning. I need, in other words, to discover that core of meaning deep within me that gives sense and direction to my life, despite the complexities I cannot deny or ignore.

Description of a Lived Experience

The summer is quickly drawing to a close. I am
exhausted and yet pleased about the good experiences I
have had with my students. All the effort seemed worthwhile as I could see the students respond enthusiasti-
cally to what I had to present to them. There were a
few painful moments, but the accomplishment of the
summer as a whole was good.

This end also signals a new beginning. One school
year flows after another. Somehow before I begin again,
I need to take the time to come to a revitalized life
after the exhausting, intense schedule of the past weeks.
I look forward to this time of year when there is a lag,
giving me time to catch my breath before again pursuing
the tasks ahead. Because this is a slower paced time
for me, I like to take a week of just "going into my
own woods" to find what direction my life is taking. I
choose a traditional conference retreat at the Mother-
house as a means of attaining the quiet I need to take
a closer look at myself and my situation.

Slowing down after the hectic pace of the summer is
not as easy as I had anticipated. I am too exhausted
physically to really get involved in the effort to slow
down. It has been much easier to keep up the fast,
almost automatic pact I had become accustomed to in
trying to meet the demands of my work. My mind churns,
actively engaged in reliving the events of the past
weeks. I cannot force these memories to be quiet.

The August temperatures are typically high and the
air is humid. No matter how hard I try to concentrate
on the words of the speaker, my mind wanders. It would
be far more inviting to be at the lake than sitting here
in this stuffy conference room.

Somehow through the thick fog-like layers of pre-
occupations and distractions, the words of the retreat
master begin to penetrate my previously sleepy awareness. I don't remember the exact words he used, I only
remember being struck by desperate questions as though
by a thunderbolt. Where is my life going? There seems
to be no substance, no direction. The whole of the past
year flashes through my mind as one constant maze of
activity directed nowhere. I see flashes of the then
meaningful activities as only adding several more

complications to my life. It seems as if the activities I have been involved in were merely agreed to by me; I had only conformed to the decisions of others, I realized that I had not freely and willingly agreed or conformed totally. I merely appeared on the surface to be happily moving through life tasks, while within I was struggling with meeting these demands. I'd been "caught up" in mere appearances, automatically pacing myself to the desires of others and the image of my ideal self I had set up.

All I wanted to do was to throw off the baggage of senseless activity and false conformity. I found I had been wasting my energy trying to meet every demand, trying always to be accepting of every situation and task I had been called to do. I clearly realized that I had been directing my life by the desires of others, without the thought of making these desires mine. I said "yes" to their request, but not totally. Something inside me fought back, saying "NO". All of a sudden I clearly saw that my life was slipping by, becoming ever more bogged down with half worked out promises. I found I was buried deep under a mountain of pretences and false conformity.

Somehow the words of the retreat master penetrated through to let me see for the first time the clutter surrounding my life. The sudden flash of awareness prompted me to ask the question: How can I simplify my life? How can I truly live my life instead of the surface self I had been conforming to, for so long a time?

Reflection on the Experience

Questions and more questions seem to color my life. But there seem to be no easy answers. I cannot look at my life and say, "I want it to be clear and simple." Life just isn't that way. The retreat experience brought me to a new realization of my life. I could see no direction, no clear precise road that I was walking on. The whole of the past year seemed like a maze of activity, one hinging on the other but not really related. I seemed to be answering "yes" to the call of every situation without really making the response totally my own.

Before long I realized that all my "yes's" are not consciously given. I say yes to keep from rocking the boat, to keep from upsetting the smooth flow of what

others expect from me. My responses become automatic.
My life is not simply and clearly lived out. I conform
to the desires of others, tucking my own ideas into the
background. It is more important for me to appear open,
kind and generous than for me to express my own desires
or to really make their desires mine.

Suddenly the flash of insight occurs during the
retreat: I haven't been living my life but have directed
and guided it into doing what others wanted me to do.
I appear to be so agreeable, so conforming that I soon
lose the direction of my own life. Taking some distance
in the retreat, I see a view of the direction my life
has taken--no direction really, but a sporadic orientation that others' desires have forced me to take in
conforming to them.

My immediate response is to tear loose the baggage
that has accumulated in my life. I want my life to be
simple. I desire to throw off the complexities welded
to me by my own response to others. I have allowed my
blind Yes-saying, my own indecision, to prevent my ever
being in a situation fully on my own. I have over-
stressed availability and surrender to the other
outwardly, while being pulled apart inwardly by not
totally and sincerely feeling the good and true "yes-
response."

My life at this point seemed to be pulled apart by
the many and varied calls made upon me. But I know I
cannot throw off, all at once, the accumulation of half
worked out promises and false conformity. I cannot
constantly or forcefully manipulate my life to strive
for the simplicity that I desire, for in the striving
in the here and now, I again lose sight of the whole.

I, too, am convinced that beneath wide dissimilarities there are underlying, ordering regularities to be
discovered. How can I become loosened from the surface
self I have become to discover the pearl of my life
buried deep underneath? How can I move to the center
of my life, from which I can then work through the complexities of my life and my world? How can I affect a
world when I have no sense of my life's direction?

In light of the above description of experience,
the components in our search for simplicty appear to be:
slowing down to see; a moment of awakening; awareness of
a need to let go; and finally, working through to the

center of life. These components will be explored in the successive Parts of this study in order to understand and concretize some of the means by which a person may discover the need to simplify life and then begin the endless journey to that goal.

Implicit in each Part of this study is that the movement toward simplicity is never finished, never fully achieved, never concretely graspable. At times life seems clear and translucent; at others, diffuse and multi-faceted. Both may be gifted moments in helping each person to move further on the road to a more complete simplicity. By living out of the conviction that beneath wide dissimilarities there are underlying regularities to be discovered, ambiguities and diffusion can be lived with.

*Rapoport, Anatol.   "The Search for Simplicity," Main Currents in Modern Thought, XXVIII: 3 (Jan.-Feb., 1972), 79-84.

PART ONE

SEARCH FOR SIMPLICITY

INTRODUCTION

Throughout all time, humanity has been searching
for understanding, explaining and verifying that which
was believed to be true in order for us to live in a
world that was not totally threatening, mysterious or
foreboding. Scientists and philosphers have attempted
to understand their world by trying to uncover hidden
patterns and meanings. Scientists such as Linneaus
and Einstein worked out of the premise that the world
was created in an orderly, systematic way. They claimed
that the maker of creation used simple laws in order
to encompass the vast complexity of the created world.
This premise they named the Principle of Simplicity.[1]

Not only the scientist who desired to understand
the nature of the world, nor the philosopher who
desires to explain clearly the world of man, but also
every person has the need to come to understand the
common underlying principles that will make one's world
more understandable and livable. But with the vastness
and complexity that is there in nature, in events, in
other people and most especially in oneself, each
person would almost have to be a god to come to full
understanding and knowledge. Each person is limited;
therefore I cannot come to this full knowledge, even
though this may be my greatest desire and security.
To compensate for my limitedness, I often turn in upon
myself rather than being open to the fullness of my
life situation; this compensation makes it even more
difficult to arrive at a basic understanding and
acceptance of my limited world.

The purpose, then, of this first part of this book
is to propose ways in which each of us can come to
accept our limitedness, can see our place in the whole
reality as it is, and respond out of the true self
each of us is called to be. In other words, I will
propose ways in which the Principle of Simplicity may
become a lived reality as I come to understand who I am;
as I discover that core of meaning deep within me that
gives sense and direction to my life despite the complexities of my self and world.

1

CHAPTER I

SLOWING DOWN TO SEE

Going to the annual county fair had been something I looked forward to as a child. I was especially drawn to the Midway by the captivating music of the merry-go-round. The up and down motion of the horses accompanied by the fast churning in circles was an exhilarating experience. But I also remember it being a frightening experience. I remember with a child's eye trying to find Mom and Dad in the crowd of onlookers as we circled round and around. Everyone seemed to blur into one mass of changing color--I could not find them. I could not focus on them because the constant circling motion pulled them out of my sight. I recall clinging to the horse, not really enjoying the last few rounds, eager to again find my parents. Even though the ride was great fun, I was glad to jump off the merry-go-round and run to them on wobbly feet.

The fast pace of activities, the complications that develop around my life, can be likened to the experience of the blurred vision of the child on the merry-go-round. Activities come so quickly; people are met only in a hurried way; things and events are not clearly seen. I cannot perceive clearly where they are heading or direct my response to them. I seem to be going up and down, circling around rapidly within immediate involvements with the whole of my life appearing as a blur. I cling to the "horse" of my self image, that being the only clearly perceivable self within my grasp.

I too need to jump off the merry-go-round to perceive clearly, to slow down, to stand on my own two "wobbly" feet to see the direction my life is taking, to again focus my attention in the direction I find I am called to, to discover the self that I have somehow lost. The time of retreat was for me a time of slowing down to see what I could not grasp in the hectic automatic pace of the past year. For another, the slowing down to see could have taken place during a vacation away from the family; it could have been seeing for the first time the beauty of each child a mother has called her own. No matter the time or place of the slowing down experience, aspects of life come into focus where they can be questioned, reflected upon, or accepted as a gifted moment.

2

In this first chapter I will show that there is a
need to slow down from the hectic, merry-go-round pace,
to see clearly, as though for the first time, the
direction of my life. In so doing, I will first consider ways in which we may become "caught" in the
routinized way of life, cutting out the possibility of
finding meaning and happiness in that life. Then I
will present means by which we may distance ourself
through reflection and the meditative way of life, in
order to develop a new way of sensing in everyday
situations, thus opening us to the possibility of
living more simply in the everyday.

BEING "CAUGHT" IN THE EVERYDAY ROUTINIZED WAY OF LIFE

Alfred Schutz[2]
Stock of Knowledge at Hand

    From the very day of birth until the last breath
is breathed, each person is involved in a world with
others, preceded by others and sure to be followed by
still others. Because of the time, place, civilization,
country and situation into which we are born there are
certain experiences, certain acceptable ways of doing
things. This heritage of others surrounding our lives
is called by Schutz the framework out of which we
meet the world and become conscious of others within
that world. He refers to it specifically as our "stock
of knowledge at hand."[3]

    Schutz further states that all interpretations of
this world are based on previous experiences of it
handed down by parents, siblings, and teachers. This
stock of knowledge functions as a framework out of
which the world can be met without a conscious awareness of the processes being performed. For example,
after years of practice in dressing myself in the
morning I no longer need to consciously direct all my
attention to lacing my shoes or buttoning my dress--
chores which once took intense concentration and
co-ordination of the pudgy little fingers unaccustomed
to this task. In other words, this common stock of
knowledge developed as habit through interaction with
others, frees the person from conscious thought on how
to perform a certain task enabling the person to cope
with a broader spectrum of the world all around,
instead of merely focusing on the slight task of, say
for example, tying a shoe.

3

Because of a mutual, shared fund of appropriate
actions, I may walk with a friend down a busy downtown
street carrying on a conversation; neither of us needs
to concentrate our attention solely on placing one foot
in front of the other, stepping up and down at the
curbs, or consciously noting the changing color of the
street lights. Because of the common stock of knowledge of our present world, I may move through the
world complacently, not questioning or wondering about
the everyday affairs of this world. I expect the
changing weather, night and day, the coming of spring
and the falling leaves of autumn. The happenings of
the world become familiar and therefore less frightening. The experiences in relating with others also
becomes less frightening as each person learns what is
acceptable behavior and that others are most often
naturally friendly and of good will.

In summary Schutz states: To this stock of
experiences at hand belongs our knowledge that the
world we live in is a world of well circumscribed
objects with definite qualities, objects among which
we move, which resist us and upon which we may act.[4]
This stock of knowledge, increasing over a life time,
has the possibility of making a person more in touch
with a greater portion of the world in which one lives.
But, on the other hand, a person may rely too heavily
on this stock, living one's life complacently, totally
embedded within this framework, not allowing for a
free responsiveness to new experiences. Schutz gives
further insight into this phenomenon which he terms
natural attitude.

Embeddedness in the Natural Attitude[5]

Schutz describes the natural attitude as it relates
to the world of everyday life. He states that the world
of everyday life is the scene and object of man's actions and interactions. The world is governed by
practical and pragmatic motives of continuing to cope
with life. The world in this sense is not the private
world of a single individual but an inter-subjective
world common to all of us. Actions and interactions
are thus based on common sense, the same common sense
holding true for all situations and all individuals
within those situations. Because of past experiences,
the person knows how to cope with certain present
situations without any real thought or feeling involved.
All answers appear to be a practical answer to the
question: what is the most practical solution for me?

4

Being embedded in this natural attitude of living purely by common sense, means the person is motivated purely by habits which were established because of once pleasant experiences related to these practical solutions. Interestingly, the difficulty does not lie in the fact that the person is directed by habit and common sense solutions, but, the problem lies in the attitudes the person adopts towards these circumstances. In other words, the person may merely go through the motions and actions of a meaningful response without really finding meaning therein. For this person, each response is simply patterned after a former response that seemed acceptable. There seems to be no recognition of the minute nuances that makes this occurrence different from all others, or this individual person uniquely different from all others, within the same type of experience. Meaning is based on practical solutions without thought or care for the unique circumstances surrounding this situation, to make it different from all others. All solutions seem "cut and dry" without concern about the final outcome as long as it seems practical and common sense.

In the realm of work there seem to be no difficulties with this concept. The practical solution seems to be necessary for functional purposes. But in the more personal domain of interpersonal relationships and in the world of the everyday, remaining purely with this one finite province of meaning, that is, seeing only with eyes focused pragmatically, cuts out the possibility of experiencing a segment of the world that is not pragmatic or practical. For instance, what is practical about an unimpressive little wild flower peeping its head up in the dew-filled morning sun? Or what common sense solution can one give to a child who has just seen his kitten crushed by a passing car? Needless to say, the pragmatic common sense solution at times falls short of the meaningfulness innately rooted in the most ordinary of circumstances. Following will be Emmanuel Levinas' formulation in regard to grounding all experiences in the world in which one lives and not merely in remembered past experiences that no longer touch one's life directly.

Emmanual Levinas[6]
All Living is a Living From...

According to Levinas all living is a living _from_ the world. Consciousness of a world is a consciousness

5

through the world. For a person to be a body is on
the one hand to stand (se tenire), to be in control of
ourself in that world, and, on the other hand, to
stand on the earth, to be in the world and thus to be
encumbered by one's bodily pact with that world. Only
momentarily can one transcend this rootedness in the
objects of the world. Hence, I may find myself
existing in a world of alien things and elements which
are other than me but not necessarily negations of that
self. In living from that world of objects, one takes
precedence over the objects found around oneself. From
early infancy each person learns to manipulate and
control these objects to one's own advantage. One
learns the manipulative art either as a member of a
group, say for example one's family, or simply as a
person alone. Therefore, there is a strong tendency
in all individuals and groups to maintain an egocentric
attitude and to regard other individuals either as
extensions of the self, or as alien objects to be
manipulated for the advantage of the individual or
social self. This magic circle of the self, Levinas
has termed the natural atheism of the self, meaning
that each person would naturally choose oneself before
others or objects in one's world. But because of a
person's pact with the world as an embodied being, the
world continuously disturbs and breaks up the magic
circle, calling one to an involvement in the world
greater than a particular individual's limited powers
of manipulation. In an effort to maintain this pact
with the world, the person struggles to hold on to
what has already been conquered while at the same time
needing to give in to one's instinct to discover, to
venture anew, to see with new eyes, hear with new ears,
and sense with a new touch. A healthy tension between
the opposing pulls of manipulation and openness to the
new is what strengthens this pact with the world.
Difficulty only arises when the circle of natural
atheism becomes so closely knit around the person,
that one can no longer be open to the surging power
within, which urges a person to broaden and enhance
that world. This powerful control, developed because
of an instinct for self preservation, places each
person in a defensive, calculative stance, only
allowing for the penetration of these aspects of one's
world that can eventually be controlled.

     In summary, the pact with the world that Schutz
speaks about in acquiring a stock of knowledge at hand,
and the living from that Levinas speaks about, are

necessary conditions for a wholesome relationship
with the world. The difficulty arises, however, when
the person becomes totally absorbed and embedded in
the attitude that does not allow anything beyond the
pragmatic and common sense to enter one's world as
has been noted in what Schutz terms the <u>natural atti-
tude</u>. Persons also naturally tend to draw the world
around one egocentrically, opting only for those
aspects of the world that will place one in a better
limelight. Levinas speaks of this process as the
<u>natural atheism of the self</u>. Keeping in mind that
each person again unconsciously levels and categorizes
one's world to make it more understandable, controllable,
and predictable, I will next present the scientific
theory of simplicity to show how we can come to a
false simplicity through tight classifications.

Lewis S. Feuer[7]
<u>Scientific Principle of Simplicity</u>

     The scientific principle of simplicity as spoken
of by Feuer stresses that as biologically rooted
organisms, persons can only cope with what is verifiable. The verifiability seems to be a natural phenomenon, for if one proposes in any way to control one's
environment, to plan for life in the future and struggle with the obstacles continuously faced, a person
must confront the behavior of things insofar as one
can learn about them through confirmable sequences of
events.

     Along with the verifiability of nature, the
principle of simplicity states that for every given
problem, the simplest solution should be searched for.
The greatest scientists of the world, such as Einstein,
believed that the world was governed by simple laws.
To allow people to deal more effectively with one's
environment, the principle which was adopted as a
scientific code was strictly adhered to. The basically
pragmatic principle allows us in our short duration on
earth to come to an elementary understanding of the
world in which we find ourself rooted.

     However, the principle of simplicity has a double
effect. While making the world more graspable
intellectually, it also may prevent an individual
searcher from delving more deeply into the unverified
strata of life. Strict adherence to this principle,
when translated into the daily life of an individual,

7

may blind an individual to the mystery within which one is embedded and surrounded. If a person only allows that which is verifiable and graspable to enter one's consciousness, the person closes out a large portion of one's environment that cannot fit under this classification. This person may, so to say, "smother" under what is known and can grasp as true while the new, the surprises of nature, the exciting unpredictableness of people are never experienced.

One more glance at how individuals may become entangled in a routinized, closed view of the world needs to be researched. Here I will present Martin Heidegger's findings in the area of thinking. While Heidegger points out that both calculative and meditative thinking are necessary and good, I will merely show how calculative thinking, when it becomes the dominant mode, may eliminate the element of surprise from life. Later on I will concentrate on meditative thinking and how it allows persons to be more in touch with life and, in a sense, to "see" more of life.

Martin Heidegger[8]
Calculative Thinking

The present age is characterized by a certain type of scientism in which everything encountered is analyzed, dissected, categorized and classified. According to Heidegger, calculative thinking computes ever new and more economical possibilities. It never stops racing from one prospect to the next. Calculative thinkers never stop to ponder, to collect, to contemplate the meaning which reigns in everything that is. Impulses are fed computer-like into the mind and are automatically slotted where they hold the most advantage for the individual. The mind never rests, the senses are never stilled from their anxious readiness to classify and categorize. Learning is equated with an increasing ability to rapidly sort the whole array of input efficiently and accurately. This type of thinking is of great advantage in the business world where success is based on quick witted, efficient output.

Calculative thinking is also essentially a waiting for something which interests us or can fulfill our needs. When we wait in this human way, our goals, ideals and needs are involved. Pragmatically speaking, this type of thinking seemingly makes the world more con-

trollable, predictable and stable. Influxes that do
not fit the present classification system are denied a
place or slotted in a special categorical niche of
"unclassifiables."

The difficulty with this type of thinking lies, not
in the fact that calculative thinking is wrong or
unnecessary, but, in the fact that the free flowing
influx of unpredictable data cannot be acknowledged;
nor can deeper meanings, which do not fit these limited
existing classifications, find entrance. In reflection
on lived experiences I will show how this type of
thinking, along with the other theory presented by
Schutz, Levinas and Feuer, may limit my participation
in the world in which I live.

REFLECTION

Stock of Knowledge at Hand

Watching a young child explore his newly discovered
world convinces one that this world is shared and learned with others. As the child incessantly asks "Why?"
and, "What is that?" the world slowly unfurls and
becomes meaningful for that child. Alive curiosity
seems limitless as it searches and discovers new
meanings each day. Slowly its world expands as the
child recognizes more than one's mother, crib and
favorite stuffed animal. Daddy, brothers and sisters,
and strange new shiny objects captivate its attention
and interest. The young person becomes an ever expanding storehouse for new knowledge, broadening experiences
and keener skills. The familiar gleam on the face of
a young child speaks of the endless curiosity to learn,
to discover and experience the new.

When I was a child the annual trip to the county
fair was looked forward to with great expectancy. I
had become familiar with the excitement of meeting
friends and neighbors who had come to show the fruit of
their labors and to renew friendships. The pungent odor
of the warm hay in the animal barns, the shared stories
of time past, the aura of excitement surrounding award-
showings filled the air. Popcorn, cotton-candy, ham-
burger and french fry scents mingled deliciously in
the air above the midway. The barking of the carnival
men persistently persuaded the fair-goers to try their
luck. This conglomerate mass of experiences were all

9

coupled together, giving "county fair" the meaning
it has for me. The merry-go-round was only one
infinitesimal part of this whole experience, but, as
has been shown, to the eyes of a child it was a most
impressive segment.

My world, as teacher, is also based on a stock of
knowledge acquired through interaction with others.
My parents, brothers and sisters, students and associates have all aided in forming, expanding and educating
me to pass this information on to others. My interaction with the students that summer before the retreat,
the relationship I have with those students now, the
very setting of the retreat itself have become familiar,
confirming the bondedness I have with the world.

Natural Attitude

The phrase "I've grown accustomed to your face...,"
from the popular musical My Fair Lady, epitomizes the
familiarity each person feels with one's world. I've
grown accustomed to the morning sun rising in the east,
the constant change of the seasons and most especially
to the notoriously cold winters of Minnesota. The
setting of my room with its unique location and view
of the city is now taken-for-granted. Others in the
house are approached in a carefree familiarity. Social
niceties are performed without the least thought as to
their inner meaning or appropriateness. Tasks in the
classroom are carried out in a complacent--"I know it's
the right thing to do" attitude. This familiarity and
at-homeness with the world is substantive to function-
ing effectively in it. But what so often happens is
that the world is taken for granted, leaving many of
the common daily experiences meaningless. The bus ride,
or the walk to work in the morning, can become so
routine that I may fail to notice the new coat of paint
on the house next door or enter wholeheartedly into
conversation with other riders. My tasks as teacher
may be performed routinely; my response to the students,
without meaning. I may become so entangled in the web
of routine responses that I no longer find meaning in
them. Because of my sleepy, almost tranquilized involvement, I may move robot-like through the many events of
the day. At day's end I may look back over what has
happened and nonchalantly try to recall the more or less
meaningful events. To my amazement, I am not able to
remember specifically even the most obvious happenings.
I realize that my world is clouded over by routine

responsiveness. I continue to function in that world but without personal meaning and without truly effecting an aliveness to these situations. The everyday no longer holds the brilliant beauty it once possessed. Everything seems to be "old hat."

All Living is a Living From

Levinas has said that all living is a living from. The world around us continually calls us forth, nourishes us, and holds us its captive. But because of the human ability to select and choose, there exists a tendency to cut out a part of that world from actually making an effect on life. Experiences that become routine no longer seem to find their rootedness in the world. Only when this routine is disturbed does it again re-establish its rootedness. For example, I may be driving to work and am suddenly shaken into consciousness by the flash of a young doe leaping across the road in front of me. The car I am driving binds me more closely to it. I feel the strain of the steering wheel in my hands as I try to bring the car under control. My foot rests heavily on the brake, my heart seems to be pounding against the back of the seat. The incident calls me back to where I am, leaving me firmly rooted in the world. But, for the most part, I will again fall back into a sleepy taken-for-grantedness.

Natural Atheism of the Self

Besides taking the world for granted, individuals naturally have the tendency to draw all things in a closely knit circle around oneself. Each person searches to find what will give one the most advantage, which objects can be manipulated, which people will be befriended to fulfill ones own needs. This tendency is thwarted by the world that sometimes upsets routine, becomes unpredictable or will not be controlled. The child on the merry-go-round illustrates this beautifully. The child is perfecltly secure until it can no longer find one's parents. The frightened child then panics, searching wildly in the rainbow of colors until all is "right" again as they are discovered.

Scientific Principle of Simplicity as Related to Calculative Thinking

11

Another way in which an individual may become caught in the routinized way of life is by the pragmatic leveling of incoming stimulation into categorized slots. If this is the case, the person reacts automatically to others' actions by one's own motivations. For example, I may conform to the desires of others out of fear of reprisal. I may automatically impute the same motivation to another, while the other may be free in motivation and I am not. Or I may feel that someone is angry at me because I would have been angry if someone had treated me as unjustly. All of these responses are unconsciously automatic, eventually leaving the individual with the feeling of being unwittingly caught in the clutches of reactivity.

In the following section I will present means by which one's response may become less routinized as the art of distancing oneself is learned through reflection and the meditative way of life. As in the example of the child needing to jump off the merry-go-round, a proper distance is necessary to allow life to be filled with meaning. This process of distancing and reflection will also give further insight into one prerequisite for simplifying life: slowing down to see.

DISTANCING SELF THROUGH REFLECTION AND THE MEDITATIVE WAY OF LIFE

David Bidney[9]
Persons as a Self-Reflecting Animal

"Psychologically, man is a problem to himself because he alone has the ability to reflect upon himself and his experiences."[10] Because of each person's innate ability to reflect upon self, each of us is plagued with two basic questions: what does it mean to be human? and what ought one be or become? Individuals are caught in the conflict of being a part of nature, being governed by the rules of nature, and yet striving to rise beyond them. Self interest coupled with a desire for self-satisfaction conflicts with one's ability to transcend the self-protective limits of nature. Bidney expresses this dilemma well when he says:

> Man is not only a part of the order of nature but also a being who, through his self-reflective intellect and creative imagination, is able to transcend the cosmic order of nature

12

> by setting up for himself norms of
> conduct which do not apply to the
> rest of nature.
>
> . . . .
>
> Man's dilemma lies in the fact that
> he is trying to do the apparently
> impossible, namely, to be a part of
> nature and yet in a measure,
> independent of it, to be an active
> participant in the drama of nature
> and yet a spectator at the same
> time.[11]

In other words, human beings are primarily self-
reflecting animals because each person can stand apart
from self to reflect upon the kind of person one is,
who the person wants to become, and how that individual
already relates to his or her world. Human beings
alone are capable of reflection and self-consciousness.
Secondly, persons also are gifted with a rationality
that allows one to experience with others and communicate these experiences intelligently and meaningfully.
And thirdly, individuals are uniquely gifted with an
imagination that allows one to sense and find meaning
in a realm outside of a biologically rooted world. A
quest for meaning is enhanced by one's capacity for
reflection as a person seeks to understand the import
of one's conduct as well as one's origin.

In the foregoing section we saw our bondedness to
nature as calling us forth. In this section we see
that individuals, because of their ability to reflect,
have the capacity to transcend the binding laws of
nature which relegate actions and interactions to the
natural and animalistic sphere. In the following
section we will consider ways in which we may live
reflectively, waiting upon the world to reveal its
deepest meanings.

Martin Heidegger[12]
Meditative Thinking

In contrast to the calculative thinking presented
earlier, Heidegger speaks of meditative thinking.
Meditative thinking tends to transcend reference to
pragmatic human affairs. It remains receptive to
whatever may be revealed by persons, events, and things
as they come into focus in everyday experiences. It is

13

a stance of receptivity, of openness to whatever may
happen. It is a non-defensive letting things be.
Without being passive, meditative thinking annulls the
will. Such thinking hospitably does not plan what or
who will receive a gracious welcome. It learns to
wait patiently for whatever is to come. It is the
practice and delicate art of biding one's time like
a farmer who patiently awaits the sprouting seed.

The analogous term of "waiting" describes the
process of meditative thinking. According to Heidegger,
"In waiting we leave open what we are waiting for. [13]
Because waiting releases itself into openness. . ."
To wait in this sense calls one to be attentive, to
be alert but without anything special in mind.
"Waiting upon" frees one to wonder in awe, to be ready
for the unexpected. In waiting upon, one does not
attempt to fuss about to make things right. Instead,
it is a stilled waiting. . . for surprises or no
surprises. . . for the unpredictable or the common-place.
It is not governed by set anticipations. Whatever may
happen could be experienced as sheer joy. Waiting upon
unbinds the shackels of false hopes for there are no
hopes at all. It is simply a being there, a letting
the world tell its own meaning.

Waiting upon denotes a center out of which the
scattered surprises may find a grounding and rooting.
In the same vein as Heidegger, Levinas speaks of
meditative thinking as a dwelling.

Emmanual Levinas [14]
Dwelling and Interiority

Of necessity people need to discover concretely a
place for meeting and moderating the incredible forces
of the world. Individuals need to find some way of
organizing life to prevent a total bombardment by the
world. In answer to this dilemma, Levinas differentiates existing and dwelling. To exist is to be placed
in the world to receive its onslaughts. To dwell is
not the simple fact of being cast into existence; it is
a recollection, a coming to oneself, a retreat home
with oneself as in a land of refuge, which answers to a
hospitality, an expectancy, a human welcome. [15] Individuals thus abide in the world by being "at home" with
themselves. Circulating between what can be seen,
and what is not sense-perceptible in the calls of the

world, one is always bound for the interior, of which
one's home is the vestibule. A person discovers one's
inwardness and interiority by dwelling at home with
oneself. A person may thus find a healthy distance from
the world and yet a real involvement in that world
because one moves about from an inward haven. As a
result a person may maintain the proper distance from
a world to which a person is open. The world will then
not overcome the person while waiting for what the
world has to offer.

REFLECTION

Slowing Down to See: Distancing Self through Reflection
and the Meditative Life.

      William James aptly describes the condition of
life today by the use of the German word "Zerissenheit
--torn-to-pieces-hood."[16] The boundless activities
of a normal day from rising before the crack of dawn to
settling down again to rest my weary body late at night,
all have the possibility of pulling me off center. I
have the tendency of being overly involved with one
sector of my life while totally ignoring another. My
vision becomes myopic as I move in too close proximity
to any one task without distancing myself somewhat from
the experience.

      I need to find the delicate balance of moving apart
and becoming involved. Anne Morrow Lindbergh maintains
that a woman must consciously encourage those pursuits
in life which oppose the scattering forces of today:
quiet time alone, contemplative reflection on the
events of the day, any creative action that aides the
individual person in remaining whole amidst the pursuits
of life.[17]

      One needs to step aside and reflect. The numerous
events of the day may tend to fall domino-like if they
are lived through and then forgotten. I need to gently
reconstruct the events of the day to see them in clear
perspective. The conversation with a good friend on the
telephone, the hectic end-of-the-year day at school,
the quiet moments alone before I fall off to sleep seem
to take on a proper perspective. Neither the painful
moments, nor the delightful experiences override the
effect of the other.

15

I need to discover that center within me, where I am at home with myself, the self that I am meant to be. Only then can I wait patiently upon what gift the day may graciously grant me. "Only when one is connected to one's core," stresses Anne Morrow Lindbergh, "is one connected to others."[18]

One is most oneself, when one is alone with oneself in one's own corner of the world. Slowing down to see, also happens best there. When I am alone, I am not overly concerned about playing the role of good teacher, concerned mother, or whatever my role in life may be. When I am alone, I may re-collect and sort out what is really happening in my life, what direction it is taking. In solitude I am less pragmatic. I let the world reveal its many splendors.

Let me digress for a moment back to the initial retreat experience. Then, I did not value the rewards of proper distance and solitude. Only when I distanced myself from the role of teacher and fulfiller of other's needs, did I perceive clearly, although painfully, how much of my life was slipping through my hands unnoticed. I needed to do something, but what? The privileged gift of being able to reflect upon the whole of my life was not accepted. I could not fall back on that. "Waiting upon" life's revelation was a whole new concept to me, who always waited for certain hoped for events to materialize and certain predicted desires to be fulfilled. I did not sense that I needed to be at home with myself before I could see the real meaning of all my experiences. Waiting seemed fruitless. Nothing seemed to be happening. Little by little, during the retreat experience I began to grow in patience. I could wait without really waiting for anything.

In the following section, Alfred Schutz offers insight into what he calls wide-awakeness. Individuals are brought into wide-awakeness by a disturbing "shock." Here we will see how the deeper meanings of the everyday may catch hold of our attention as the "shock" is experienced.

Alfred Schutz[19]
Wide-awakeness

According to Schutz, wide-awakeness denotes a plane of consciousness of highest tension finding its roots

in an attitude of full attention to life and its consequences. Attention a la vie, attention to life, is
the foremost regulative principle of our conscious life.
This wide-awake stance clearly defines the realm of
the world that is meaningful for an individual; it
enunciates an unending flowing stream of thought; it
directs persons to live either within present experience, directed toward the objects of our language, or
turn about-face in a reflective attitude to past
experiences and question their meaning. Wide-awakeness
functions best in the realm of the world in which
attention is turned wholly to the NOW moment. Because
we live most of our days embedded in the natural attitude, we are not ready to quickly abandon this familiar
outlook. As a consequence, we need to experience a
specific shock which breaks through that one restricting
finite province of meaning, and shifts the accent of
reality to another plane. Schutz lists some possible
shock experiences:

> . . . the shock of falling asleep as
> the leap into the world of dreams; the inner
> transformation we endure if the curtain of
> the theater rises as the transition into
> the world of the stage play; the radical
> change in our attitude, if, before a
> painting, we permit our visual field to
> be limited by what is within the frame as
> the passage into the pictorial world; our
> quandry, relaxing into laughter if, in
> listening to a joke, we are for a short
> time ready to accept the fictitious world
> of the jest as a reality in relation to
> foolishness; the child turning toward his
> toy as the transition into the play-world
> . . . [20]

The "shock" of wide-awakeness brings deeper meaning to
the present moment. It also allows for the past
experience to acquire greater meaning as it is reflected
upon in the present NOW. The experience becomes
acutely meaningful only as we can re-construct the
happening and become aware of the new plane of meaning
other everyday happenings take on. The "shock" into
wide-awakeness may be pleasant, indifferent, or
entirely uncomfortable. In the following reflection I
will present "shocks" that made the everyday more
meaningful for me.

REFLECTION

One warm spring day I decided it would be a perfect day to do all my necessary shopping, preparing
for the summer months ahead. Toward the end of the
day my morning enthusiasm and freshness began to wilt.
I decided to make one last stop before I headed home.
The shop was small and really nothing spectacular but
it had just what I needed. I had sought for and found
all I wanted from the dusty crowded shelves. I set my
packages down on a nearby desk and waited for the
cashier to return my change. I began to notice the
few other people in the shop. Seated facing me was a
retarded young man. He rocked back and forth gently,
talking and smiling to himself. He looked at me as I
was watching him. Suddenly, he stopped rocking. He
looked me straight in the eye and said quite clearly,
"A smile on your face and in your heart." I was
dumbfounded. I didn't know how to respond. Did he
know what he had said? Stupidly I continued to smile
back at him. I could say nothing. Time seemed to stop.
What should I do? I needed to get away from there.
Impatiently I received my change from the cashier,
clumsily placed it in my purse, hurriedly picked up my
assorted packages, quickly walked toward the door. At
the door I was greeted by one of the other clerks,
"Did you know Joe was trying to get your attention?"
"Yes," I answered, "and he did."

Once I finally got into the street, I could stop
and slowly review what had just happened. Why did he
say that to me? What was I doing? Why couldn't I say
anything in response to him? Why did his remark catch
me so off guard? His few simple words forcefully struck
me. For some time I could only replay again and again
what had happened. Gradually a feeling of joy crept
over me. Why was I fortunate to have been the recipient
of so great an experience and why did this effect me so?

I had been sleepily going about the routine of a
normal shopping day, intent upon finding bargains and
the "just right" articles. I was existing in a shopping
day world. Suddenly I was shocked into a profound wide-
awakeness. The comment of this young man threw me off
my feet. At first I was stopped still; then I experienced a great joy. His comment lifted the face of the
day, making it more than an ordinary shopping day. I
experienced a new surge of energy. The faces of the
people I passed on the street no longer appeared

anonymous. I discovered something special in each.
The glum faces of those caught in a worried frown,
those filled with sheer determinism, and the face all
smiles after falling upon a terrific bargain. I became aware of the brightness of the sun that afternoon.
Had it been that bright all day? I could hardly
contain myself. I needed to share with someone the
experience in the tiny shop. I knew I would find open
ears when I arrived home.

This experience happened many years ago now, but
it still seems as fresh as yesterday. Shockingly, it
removed the blinders from the ordinariness of the day.
The brilliance of so simple an experience moved me
deeply. The very unexpectedness of the experience
transformed that day into a real holiday.

However, the "shock" into wide-awakeness does not
always occasion such a pleasant enlivening experience.
Other experiences of wide-awakeness may engender a
painfully beautiful experience of a life that's
deepening. Recall again the "flash of insight" I
experienced during the retreat. The flash seemed to
make me the sole spectator on a rerun of "This Is Your
Life." I was brought painfully face-to-face with the
sleepiness of my involvement with life. There I could
sense the sporadic movement and meaningless of the
past year. I sadly acknowledged what I had missed,
the people I had ignored unknowingly, the possible
meaningful experiences that held no meaning for me.

The quiet beauty of the everyday slowly began to
penetrate. I could see and appreciate the uniqueness
of others, the ability to share experiences with them,
and the renewed capacity to meaningfully say yes and
no. I could face the future with new eyes, being
totally myself, waiting upon whatever happening the
everday might bring. Just as the pearl of the oyster
can only begin to grow if it is disturbed by the tiny
grain of sand, so too, can I begin to grow to a greater
awareness of who I am as my complacent common sense
self is disturbed. Little by little I need to be
reawakened to the whole of my life, to return to that
childlike simplicity of saying, "Yes, I want to be
reawakened to all the areas of my life."[21]

The "shock" into wide-awakeness experienced so
forcefully in both happenings recorded here, convinces
me I need to see more clearly the fuller meaning of my

19

life. In the following section I will explore various
means by which a person may develop new ways of sensing
in the ordinariness of everyday life, thereby continuing on the path to renewed awakeness in all areas of
life.

DEVELOPING A NEW WAY OF SENSING IN EVERYDAY LIFE

Gabriel Marcel[22]
Ingatheredness

Balancing my life as it actually is, against the
life I would have to lead to be fully myself, can only
be done by drawing my life as it is, inward. Marcel
says there can be no contemplation without a kind of
inward re-collecting of one's resources, or a kind of
"ingatheredness." In these moments of ingatheredness
I make contact, "I take my stand or, more accurately,
equip myself to take my stand towards my own life."[23]

Thus the role of ingatheredness essentially is to
draw me nearer to myself, while at the same time
making it possible for me to more deeply participate
in all of reality. Ingatheredness potentially allows
me to be more myself as I participate with others in
the situations of everyday life. It means imbibing
all the circumstances as fully as possible. Only then
can I draw myself closer to my true being. Only then
can I participate fully with the landscape of the world
outside me.

Evelyn Underhill gives us further insight into the
notion of ingatheredness. She refers to it as recollection. I will especially dwell on what she calls the
essence of recollection: developing the simple eye
and simple ear.

Evelyn Underhill[24]
Recollection as Developing the Simple Eye and the
Simple Ear

Evelyn Underhill pleads with us to stand back from
the vague and purposeless reactions in which we
dissipate our vital energies. She says: distance yourself from ambition and affection, likes and prejudices
that are constantly fighting for your attention. Still
your consciousness from "frittering" to and fro. Then

you can with a certain detachment and calm, scrutinize
your world and the possibilities in store for you there.

No matter how scattered and meaningless life may
seem, there is at the center a stillness which no one
is able to destroy. Out of that center a person
disciplines and simplifies one's life. One withdraws
one's attention by turning inward in recollection.
One can then say a first deliberate "no" to the claims
of the world of appearances. The world is thus sensed
as being far richer and yet far simpler than one would
suppose.

Seeing from this tranquil center aids in the
development of the simple eye. All things are synth-
esized and find a unity just as all colors do in white
lights. Learn to be in touch with that center in
which you are most yourself--then the world will reveal
its unspeakable beauty. The eye loses its complexity
as it focuses without intent upon the sunset, the landscape, and other individuals. There is no hindrance
in the simple eye, no blind spot preventing the full
perception of the seen and the unseen magnificence of
all creation. Now turn this purified gaze back upon
yourself.

Uncover the simple ear which discerns the celestial
melody in which all music is resumed. Hear the gentle
whisperings coming from the noisy world. Be still
and hear the sound of quiet, the language of silence.
Listen attentively to the deepest center within. Then
communicate with the world.

From a psychological point of view, Ernest Schachtel examines what he calls perceptual modes of presence.
Here again will be stressed the basic differences
between self-centered and other-centered perception.

Ernest Schachtel[25]
Allocentric and Autocentric Perceptual Modes

The two basic perceptual modes are designated as
the subject-centered, or autocentric, and the object-
centered or allocentric modes. The main difference
between the two lies in the emphasis. In auto-centric
perception there is little objectification. What is
felt, sensed, or desired is directed by pleasure or
unpleasure. Allocentric perception, on the other hand,

is characterized by complete openness, profound interest and receptivity, a full turning toward the object being perceived.

The autocentric mode is basic to a child. The child goes about the discovery of the world, hungrily searching for everything to fulfill one's own needs. In the autocentric mode, one is in the tension of expectancy. The ear is cocked for particular sounds, hopefully or fearfully, whatever the case may be. The eye strains for any perceptible change in gesture, movement or facial expression. The person is only open to hear or see what fulfills immediate needs.

The allocentric mode is basic to an artist or a wise man. Objects are viewed over and over again, which makes possible a direct encounter with the object as a totality, not merely a quick registration of familiar detail. The perceiver turns toward the object with one's entire being, affirming the object in its totality. Then only will the object reveal itself.

True love of the object being viewed is not blind. It affirms the object in its totality. It does not presuppose or foster a blindness for the limitations or shortcomings of the object. True love in this sense sees more than hatred.

The perceptual shift between autocentric and allocentric modes continuously goes on, now more one, now more the other. One soon discovers that to remain more in the allocentric mode requires a discipline and a suffering, a "staying with" when attention and pleasure calls elsewhere. Evelyn Underhill speaks of this turning toward again and again as involving a discipline and a suffering.

Evelyn Underhill[26]
Slowing Down Involves a Discipline and a Suffering

Try to slow down to sense more deeply and you will discover over and over again, the tendency to drop back into "former", "easier", ways of sensing. For the surface self, left for so long a time in control of the whole life, has grown strong and "cemented itself like a limpet to the rock of the obvious."[27] Freedom has been exchanged for apparent security, building up a defensive shell of fixed ideas and set responses. Only

22

slowly as the person ascends the mountain of self-knowledge can the summit be reached wherein all of life is united. Then can the heart of one's true self groove a path deeper and deeper into the heart of reality. The path will become obscure, the true self deeply hidden. All one can do, is continually try to discover that path again, slowly dropping the cares that now bind one to a lesser reality.

REFLECTION

Pause for a few moments. Sit down in an easy chair and just allow yourself to be. Do nothing; think of nothing. Just sit still with your arms resting lightly on the arms of the chair. Allow your muscles to relax. Become as comfortable as you can. For five minutes let the world take care of itself.

The five minutes seem to be endless. The ticking of the clock can almost be heard in every fiber of my being. My mind wants to race on, thinking about what needs to be done yet today. My fists are clenched, my neck muscles are taut. Remaining quiet for these few minutes is not easy. I cannot relax my muscles, much less my mind, that wants to race on and on. I try closing my eyes and stopping my ears. Nothing seems to work. Slowly the clock ticks on and on.

It is extremely difficult to slow down my body from actively moving about from one task to another. It is even more of a hardship to slow down my mind with its motives, intentions, needs and desires. My body needs to be about something constantly, my mind never stops to recollect itself and find meaning in all the racing about. I cannot command my body to relax, my mind to gather up the real meaning of all the happenings surrounding it. There is just too much going on, too much that needs to be taken care of.

No wonder I found slowing down at the beginning of the retreat such a chore. I blamed the August heat and humidity for making it so difficult. Everything outside of me received the blame for the failure in slowing down. I didn't accuse myself of being too patterned in racing about to see clearly where my life is going. I needed to step aside in this retreat so that the scattered calls of my life as teacher and organizer could be gathered together into a meaningful

23

whole. My eyes and ears were strained. All my senses
were intent on absorbing more and more. Where does it
all stop? where does life acquire meaning?

I discovered during the retreat that I needed to
step aside more often. Once a year for a week was a
great start. But I soon realized that minute retreats
during the day were even more beneficial. They open
every moment to meaningfulness. Take the time to enjoy
a joke, study the face of a friend, view the intrica-
cies of a flower. Be open to the conversation that
went awry, the good intention that turned sour, the
accident that seemed to spoil your day. Try to see
people, events and things as they really are, not as
you would like them to be. Gently allow your eyes to
be cleansed, your ears to be unstopped. Slowly become
"turned on" to life and its meaning without set purpose.
Discover what you can do in your home, on your job and
in between to acquire the art of slowing down. Maybe
today it will be to walk slowly and deliberately.
Tomorrow it may be to eat your meals slowly, savoring
both the conversation and the food. Consciously become
aware of your feelings, responses and habits. Come
in touch with your life where it is really lived.

Summary and Transition

Throughout this chapter I have considered the
necessity of slowing down to see. These considerations
were based on our innate tendency to become "caught"
in the routinized way of life; our need to distance
ourself through reflection and the meditative way of
life; and the ongoing development of new ways of
sensing in everyday situations.

In regard to the first thematic, we saw how we
develop a stock of knowledge about the world through
interaction with others. And we saw how this stock
may be a help or a hindrance in being in touch with
the world of the everyday. It is a help insofar as it
acquaints us with a broader spectrum of the world. It
is a hindrance when this stock of knowledge is accepted
in the natural attitude of: what is in it for me?
Living in this attitude may eventually lead to a self-
centered, closed existence based on sheer pragmatism.

In the consideration of the second thematic of
our need to distance ourself through reflection and
the meditative way of life we discovered that human

beings alone are self-reflecting. We are able to
distance ourselves objectively, using rationality and
imagination to give and find meaning. By discovering
a center in which we are at home with ourselves, we
may live meditatively. Through meditative reflection
all people, events and things are seen in perspective
and acquire meaning.

And finally, in the third section we developed
the theme of developing a new way of sensing in everyday life. Here we spoke of the ongoing necessity of
seeing with simple eyes and hearing with simple ears.
Development of perceptual abilities will allow us to
be more in touch with the deeper realities of life.

In concluding this chapter on slowing down to
see, I shall present Cardinal Cushing's "Prayer for
Our Times":

> Slow me down, Lord: Ease the pounding
> of my heart by the quieting of my mind.
> Steady my hurried pace with a vision of
> the eternal reach of Time. Give amidst
> the confusion of the day, the calmness
> of the everlasting hills. Break the
> tension of my nerves and muscles with
> the soothing music of the singing streams
> that live in my memory. Help me to know
> the magical restorative power of sleep.
> Teach me the art of taking minute vaca-
> tions,...of slowing down to look at a
> flower, to chat with a friend, to pat a
> dog, to read a few lines from a good
> book. Remind me each day of the "Fable
> of the Hare and the Tortoise," that there
> is more to life than increasing its speed.
> Let me look upward into the branches of
> the towering oak and know that it grew
> slowly and well. Slow me down, Lord,
> and inspire me to send my roots deep
> into the soil of life's enduring values,
> that I may grow towards the stars of
> my greater destiny.

Getting more in touch with my life by slowing down
to see the meaning of life, I realize that my life has
become complicated by ego embeddedness in daily life.
I discover I need to look with new eyes on my situated-
ness. Let us then consider what in my life is not simple, what I've clung to that I now need to let go of, to
make my life more simple.

ENDNOTES

[1]For a further explanation of the Principle of
Simplicity and its influence on the thinking and explor-
ations of man, especially in the areas of science and
mathematics, see Lewis S. Feuer, "The Principle of
Simplicity," Philosophy of Science, XXIV (1957),109-122.

[2]Alfred Schutz, Collected Papers I (The Hague:
Nijhoff, 1967), pp. 207-233.

[3]Ibid., p. 208.

[4]Ibid., p. 208.

[5]Ibid., p. 208-210.

[6]Emmanuel Levinas, Totality and Infinity, trans.
Alphonso Lingis, Duqnesne Studies, Philosophical Series,
Vol. XXIV (Pittsburgh: Duquesne University Press, 1969),
pp. 11-19; and Charles Maes, Unpublished Class Notes,
Center for the Study of Spirituality of the Institute
of Man, Duquesne University, Pittsburgh, Fall, 1972.

[7]Lewis S. Feuer, "The Principle of Simplicity,"
Philosophy of Science, XXIV (1957), 109-122.

[8]Martin Heidegger, Discourse on Thinking trans.
John M. Anderson and E. Hans Freund (New York: Harper
Torchbooks, 1966), pp. 7-29, 45-73.

[9]David Bidney, Theoretical Anthropology (New York:
Columbia University Press, 1953), pp. 3-22.

[10]Ibid., p. 3.

[11]Ibid., p. 9.

[12]Heidegger, loc. cit.

[13]Ibid., p. 68.

[14]Levinas, op. cit., pp. 152-174.

[15]Ibid., p. 156.

[16]William James as quoted by Anne Morrow Lindberg,
Gift from the Sea (New York: Pantheon Books, Inc.,
1955), p. 56.

26

[17]Ibid., p. 56.

[18]Ibid., p. 44.

[19]Schutz, loc. cit.

[20]Ibid., p. 231.

[21]Charles Maes, Unpublished Class Notes, Institute for Formative Spirituality, Duquesne University, Pittsburgh, Fall, 1972.

[22]Gabriel Marcel, The Mystery of Being, Vol. 1 trans. B.S. Fraser (Chicago: Henry Regnery Co., Gateway Edition, 1960), pp. 154-169.

[23]Ibid., p. 168.

[24]Evelyn Underhill, Practical Mysticism (new York: E. P. Dutton and Co., Inc., 1943), pp. 29-55.

[25]Ernest Schachtel, Metamorphosis (New York: Basic Books, Inc., 1959), pp. 81-84, 213-248.

[26]Evelyn Underhill, op. cit., pp. 56-73.

[27]Ibid., p. 63.

CHAPTER II

THE AWARENESS OF A NEED TO LET GO

INTRODUCTION

Seeing so clearly my need to slow down gave me the desire to peel off quickly and completely the accumulated layers of embeddedness that, like layers of old paint, keep me from seeing the finely-grained unique self underneath. But I knew the process of letting go had to be done slowly and gently to discover the true self underneath. The pride system that has taken years to develop cannot just be put aside. I must slowly discover the ways in which living out of my true self has become hidden and disguised, and then I must again allow my life to become meaningful and inner directed. Gently the layers of a false self-image need to be acknowledged and then replaced by a living out of the true self I am, as limited as I may discover it to be. In the letting go process, I must own the self I truly am, see it and listen to it, as if for the first time.

The guiding question for this section of my study of simplicity is: What in my life is not simple? To begin the exploration of the various ramifications of this question, we will need to look at the meaning of the world simplicity. Etymologically, simplicity means "without fold." When something, e.g., a piece of cloth, is without fold we mean that there are no hidden aspects. An object may be clearly recognized for what it truly is, with all its beauty, as well as its flaws and shortcomings. Similarly, someone who is said to be simple appears to be open, honest, sincere, true to self, hence, without fold, without a pretentious presentation of self in interaction with others in the world.

In exploring the question of what in my life is not simple, I need to discover the ways in which my life has become unsimple, that is, folded up into itself. First, I will dwell on the personal, social and cultural factors that may cause one's response to be unsimple. Then I will consider factors in my life that need to be accepted with responsibility to again "unfold", to simplify life. And lastly, the recurring obstacles to simplifying one's response to life will be explored.

29

FACTORS IN LIFE THAT MAY CAUSE ONE'S RESPONSE
TO BE UNSIMPLE

To begin this research in response to the question
of what is unsimple about my life, I will explore
aspects of Adrian van Kaam's thought, especially in
regard to personal factors at the beginning of life
that may cause one's response to be unsimple, that is,
may cause it to be folded up into itself.

Adrian van Kaam[1]
Initial Defensive Uncongenial Life Style

When an individual is newly born, the child lives
in a kind of paradise; has a vague feeling of omnipotence; and only needs to cry and basic needs of
warmth, nourishment and security are automatically
answered by the mother. A child feels totally safe
and contented. At a very early age, the child begins
in a vague sort of way to awaken to a whole beyond
oneself, mother and father. This awareness of whatever
it is that transcends one's immediate world makes the
child different from an animal who will never be
capable of reacting beyond mere instinct.

Contrary to what one might expect, this awareness
of a beyond is not pleasant. The child experiences
smallness and therefore powerlessness, lostness,
aloneness, and vulnerability. The child experiences a
feeling of no longer being one with mother and yet
wants to feel safe, protected and totally with her.
To cope with this utter helplessness the child cannot
fall back on the animal's instinctual reactivity.
Instead, the child develops a reactive pattern based
on what has been learned as acceptable behavior from
parents and peers. Adrian van Kaam says that this
social reactive pattern forms the hard core of the
initial life style of the child.

The initial fundamental life style is a defensive
style of life, formulated to protect the child from
being overcome by ontological anxiety as experienced in
complete powerlessness and vulnerability. Through trial
and error one learns what behavior is acceptable, what
behavior fulfills needs. This defensive life style is
said to be uncongenial because it is not in tune with
the unique and individual makeup of the person. The
defensive system becomes increasingly more elaborate
to meet the expanding anxieties of the child's world.

30

Even what seems to be attractive cannot be coped with,
so the child begins to repress pristine, innocent
openness to the beauty of things. Since the protective
system remains imperfect, anxiety keeps seeping through.
Consequently, most children go through a period of a
fear of the dark, and fear of being left alone. They
seem to need fairy tales, witches and goblins to give
an object to the sheer horror experienced, making it
easier to cope with basic anxiety.

REFLECTION

The county fair was a pleasant experience for me
as a young child. The fun and games of the whole day
were looked forward to with great anticipation. I
held no fear for all the strangers I would meet there;
I was with Mom and Dad and my older brothers. But
suddenly while circling around the merry-go-round I
became terribly frightened. Where were mom and dad?
I couldn't find them. I was alone. I searched
anxiously for them in the passing crowd but to no
avail. When music stopped and the horses stood still,
I spotted them again and ran to them on wobbly feet.

Visiting with my family I often observed a niece
or nephew exerting his or her own uniqueness. One
child may find security in staying close to mother.
Another may be much more contented roaming about the
house exploring and discovering anew. Each child reacts
differently in similar situations, depending upon what
each had discovered fulfills personal needs the best.
For one child it might be stubbornness and pouting; for
another to be kind and sweet, to experience the craved-
for love. The more a child's experience expands, the
more elaborate and complex a defensive system is developed. Repression of whatever would reinstate initial
dread, unconsciously denying whatever will not fit into
a neat little system and protecting self from a feeling
of total lostness, may waken a child in the middle of
the night, panting with fear for no apparent reason.
Out of fear of being left behind, another child may
refuse to take off one's coat or let mother out of sight.
Still another may blindly adjust to parental demands
to keep safe from punishment.

This defensive initial life style thus inhibits
full growth. In effect its main function is protection
of the pride system and the child's idealized self

image. In the following section I will explore aspects
of Karen Horney's thought with particular concentration
on the unconscious folding up of one's life as a protective defense through interaction with others. To
be stressed here is that what was begun as a child's
defense against powerlessness and vulnerability may
become a reactive way of life.

Karen Horney[2]
Experiencing Inner and Outer Conflicts

        Because each individual exists in a particular
situation, with unique ways of responding to these
situations, and because of the cultural demands placed
on each person to respond in a particular way, a
person often experiences conflict. These conflicts
may be inner conflicts: a person may not be able to
live up to the expectations of others, or oneself, or
may feel entirely different about a situation than the
rest of one's associates--what response should be
given? Should I give in to the group's expectations or
should I live up to my own convictions, accepting the
consequences of such? Conflicts may also arise within
the situation in which one lives: meeting constantly
changing moods of people, events and things often
catches each of us face to face with inconsistent,
imcompatible and conflicting values.

        The person who is unable to meet the conflicts
discovered in oneself (at least somewhat satisfactorily),
is said to be neurotic. We may say then, that everyone
in some particular aspects of life has the tendency to
respond neurotically when not able to sort out the
conflicts that will be met naturally. Therefore, we
will look at the means by which conflicts are not met
realistically, and the effect these means have on
complicating and "folding" life.

        Instead of meeting the conflicts in the best way
one can with limited potentialities, the neurotic
person makes many attempts to negate, to do away with
conflicts by creating a feeling of unity, of oneness,
of wholeness. This longed for unity within oneself is
prompted by the necessity of having to function in life,
which seems almost impossible when one is continually
being pulled in different directions under the constant
threat of being pulled apart. Therefore, one's reactions to conflict are not merely determined by
situations, but more importantly by one's needs within

32

these situations. In response, then, individuals
often turn in upon oneself to protect the semblance of
security felt to safeguard oneself from further hurt
within these situations.

Need to Feel Safe--Protected

According to Horney's theory, every person yearns
for security and when this is denied, basic anxiety is
experienced, which drives one to protect and increase
any security felt." An individual knows a need to
depend upon self and yet has never built any confidence
in self; the person knows others are needed, and yet
feels that they are the cause of personal difficulties.
In an attempt to protect oneself against these disturb-
ances, a series of defenses are built up. These
defenses form a protective system designed to prevent
or forestall further hurt to an already injured pride.
Places and situations in which one's pride is in
danger of being injured may be avoided. Actually,
this person is saying it is far safer to renounce,
withdraw, or to resign than to take the risk of exposing
one's pride to further injury.

The pernicious character of neurotic pride lies
in the fact that pride supposedly protects the person
from hurt, where in actuality it renders one extremely
vulnerable to a far deeper hurt, that is, the covering
over of real responses. For the person caught in the
clutches of this false pride, genuine feelings, awareness and strengths are diminished or hidden almost to
a vanishing point--because they really don't "protect".
Pride censors all true responsive feelings, only
allowing those feelings to surface that feed into the
aggrandizement of this false pride. The person
necessarily becomes rigid, losing the spontaneity
genuine feelings would allow. This false pride then
acts as a political tyrant making demands without
regard for the individual's psychic, biological, cultural or situational conditions. Appearance becomes the
guiding criterion, governing the image a person presents
in life situations.

Idealized Self Image

The dictates of false pride again protect the
person from hurt. Because this pride is false, it

33

does not truly protect the person as intended, what
image one wishes to create, what seems acceptable to
one's culture. This image is in effect something
"out there" that needs to be protected from harm while
the real self is the person "in there" who is smothering underneath while being kept from responding spontaneously to the demands of the situation. In living out
of our idealized image of the self we would like to be,
Horney further states that "we cannot suppress or
eliminate essential parts of ourselves without becoming
estranged from ourselves."[3] The person lives within a
hazy cloud, oblivious to the fact of being caught in
the spider's web of living one's image, being completely
blinded to the real self buried under the inevitable
pretenses and rationalizations involved in living out
of the idealized self. Although a self-inflated image
is obvious to others with whom one works and lives, the
neurotic person is unaware of the somewhat bizarre
conglomeration of characteristics portrayed in
protecting oneself. The person who lives merely out
of the idealized image of oneself, is set in motion by
the push and pull of others, (or what is interpreted
as such) and becomes driven instead of being the driver.
One's capacity to determine a path in life is weakened.
This person needs others to verify an image and therefore becomes exceedingly dependent upon people, whether
it be blind rebellion, blind craving to excel, or
blind need to keep away from others. All of these
complicated forms of dependency inhibit the spontaneous
expression of true feelings and the actualization of
genuine ideals. For in an idealized image, the dynamic
quality of genuine ideals is bound. The absolutely
perfect image is lived out within the bounds of feelings
that are programmed to meet the needs of this image.

In summary, Horney states that the consequence of
this neurotic development of an idealized image is

> alienation from self, unavoidable unconscious
> pretenses, and also unavoidable unconscious
> compromises due to unsolved conflicts, the
> self-contempt--all these factors lead to a
> weakening of the moral fiber in the nucleus
> of which is a diminished capacity for being
> sincere with oneself.[4]

In effect, freedom of choice becomes frustrated in the
living out of this idealized image. All responses are
regulated by what the person should have done, should

wish, feel or respond in the future, and should be in
the present situation. Horney terms this dictation
by "shoulds" the "tyranny of the should."[5]

The Tyranny of the Should

In an attempt at molding oneself into a perfect
image, almost godlike being, the neurotic holds before
oneself an image that is completely flawless and without limitation.

Whenever the person responds to a situation,
where a perfect response is not known, the person is
whipped into shape, trying to remove the difficult
"flaw" as quickly as possible. Because the "shoulds"
direct appearances, they always contribute to some
sort of disturbance in human relations. The person
becomes hypersensitive to any type of criticism because
it points out the flaws that should not be there. The
person becomes as easily hurt by the criticism of one's
image as if it were the real self because the person
is no longer sure what is real, or what is only real in
imagination. The "tyranny of the should" is most
devastating when the person is faced with contradictory
"shoulds" The resulting anxiety is severe because the
perfect choice cannot be made. The end result of
living merely by the dictates of the "shoulds" is
impaired spontaneity of feelings, wishes, thoughts and
beliefs, even further smothering the real self and
its capacity for growth. The effect of living merely
from the "shoulds" eventually leads to a constant
feeling of indecision and strain, the sum total of which
is merely living in pretenses--of love, fairness,
interest, honest, and modesty to name only a few.
Ironically, these pretenses, instead of actually allowing the person to feel loving, kind and interested in
others, merely produce feelings of guilt and fear
that they may be found out or criticized. Continuing
to live under the false notion of perfection, the
person becomes more strict, cautious, circumspect, and
controlled. The effort to bridge the gap between an
idealized self and a real self by the use of pretenses
and "shoulds" merely serves to widen it. As Horney
concludes, "even though godlike in his imagination, he
still lacks the earthy self-confidence of a simple
shepherd."[6]

Conclusion

As a result of an unrealistic meeting of the conflicts we necessarily face in life, a false protective system may be formed which often safeguards the person's image instead of a real self. In effect, this whole process may close the person in upon oneself, not allowing for a spontaneous, dynamic, sincere meeting of conflicts, even in a limited way. The person becomes closed in upon oneself, complicating life because of the rigid, static, pretentious response adhered to in order to stay in tune with an imagined self.

Horney assures us that the real self which is the original force and praxis of individual growth and fulfillment can be uncovered when freed of the crippling shackles of neurosis. At bottom, says Horney, this uncovering consists in no more and no less than plain simple honesty about oneself and life. It is unfolding the real self with its capacity to wish and to will, to expand and to grow. It is an owning of the limited self as it is; taking the responsibility this entails. It is a saying yes or no without fear or guilt. It is, in fact, leading again to a sound sense of wholeness and oneness, the precious commodity so earnestly protected from the beginning.

REFLECTION

In these reflections on Horney's theory, let us dwell on and consider how life may become folded up upon itself in striving to meet the demands of life; and how the protective pride system complicates life instead of simplifying it. For the most part I will use the somewhat universal experiences of Anne Morrow Lindberg, recorded in Gift from the Sea,[7] as an explicitation of how life becomes complicated. We then will see on the one hand, how reactions to these complications in life make it more difficult to grow in simplicity. I will, on the other hand, propose ways by which we may realistically respond to these experiences to simplify life.

Experiencing Inner and Outer Conflict

Turning the empty channeled whelk slowly in her hands, caressing the spirals that slowly wind into the center, gazing in through the open door searching for

some faint spark of life inside, Anne slowly begins
to also look at her own life.

> My shell is not like this, I think. How
> untidy it has become! Blurred with moss,
> knobby with barnacles, its shape is
> hardly recognizable any more.[8]

In looking at her life as contrasted to the simple
channeled whelk, she has discovered that it has become
covered with moss and barnacles, not allowing the
pearly beauty of her inner self to shine through.
The moss and barnacles of human life are different
from those which may accumulate on the shell of a sea
creature in that they cannot be removed simply by
breaking off the barnacles and brushing away the moss.
Each person needs to look cautiously at what has
accumulated on life; what can carefully be removed;
and which complications need to be accepted and lived
with as a real part of one's chosen life.

Reflecting on her life, Lindbergh realizes that,
"The life I have chosen as wife and mother entrains a
whole caravan of complications."[9] Meeting the needs of
family, cooking and caring for their every need;
patching torn clothes, hurt little fingers and bruised
knees; relating to the children, husband, neighbors,
salesmen who come knocking at the door during the
busiest moments of the day, parents, friends, and
so on..., almost force one to be a "quick change artist"
in carrying out the duties of wife and mother. Life
becomes complicated by the car that won't start, the
child who is sick, the husband that needs to be rushed
to the airport, the birthday cake that needs to be
baked. Life becomes complicated even further because
of the desire to be the most concerned mother, the
most supportive wife and the best homemaker. At times
one is asked to be wife, homemaker and mother all at
the same time. Limitations in time, energy and talent
often make this impossible.

Even though my life is different from the life of
Anne Morrow Lindbergh, I too may say that the life I
have chosen to live entrains a whole caravan of
complications. There is a whole array of demands
embodied in people, events and things that call for my
undivided attention. I want to meet the expectations of
others, appear whole, without agitation in the varied
events that color each day, and give the needed atten-

tion to the things that need to be done. In other
words, I want life to be simple, predictable, and
without conflict. Looking back over one day, or even
one hour will convince me that life without conflict
is illusory for as soon as one part of my life seems
to be under control, another segment seems to be in
conflict. But as Horney has assured us, it is not the
amount and type of conflict that determines our life
but the manner and attitude with which we approach it.

Tyranny of the Should--Protection for My Idealized Image

I can try to work through the conflicts as best
I can with the limited time, space, and talents that
are mine at the present moment. When I am not able to
meet these conflicts I may try to deny their existence
by merely finding my security and safety in those things,
events and relationships which are not threatening.
One way of hiding these conflicts may be to become over-
active and unduly concerned for those areas of my life in
which I now am in control. But as Anne Morrow Lindbergh
discovered in her own life, suddenly the spring is
dried up and the well is empty from constantly
performing unnecessary errands, compulsive duties and
social niceties. Instead of working through the
demands made upon me, my actions are guided by the way
I should be. Each request seems to pull me off center
because I fail to look at them realistically in light
of the whole. The images of best mother, most
supportive wife, most generous committee member, and
most concerned teacher call for energies I may not
possess. These images may soon pull me in many
directions, fragmenting and dissipating the energies
I do own.

Returning again to the channeled whelk in its bare
simplicity and sublime beauty, I may find a clue, a
means of removing the "barnacles and moss" of the way
in which I might now respond to the necessary complications of life. It may, as it were, teach me the
gentle art of simplification of life by shedding the
"folds" of pretentious cares and concern, uncovering
genuine feelings and realistic goals.

The Art of Shedding

Speaking of the channeled whelk covered with
barnacles and moss, one automatically thinks of shedding

something that can be seen, something that visibly
covers over the pearly treasure underneath. Perhaps
is speaking about life, the outward shedding may be
the place to begin. Anne Morrow Lindbergh refers to
this exterior shedding as the physical shedding of
clothing or shelter. It is, in a sense, making do with
less. However, she discovered that the outward shedding mysteriously pointed to a deeper kind of letting
go--a letting go of the hidden motivation that underlies
the cover up. She describes this in the following way:

> ...one needs less anyway, one finds suddenly.
> One does not need a closet-full, only a
> suitcase-full. And what a relief it is!...
> One finds one is shedding not only clothes
> --but vanity.
> ....
>
> Washable slipcovers, faded and old--I hardly
> see them; I don't worry about the impression
> they make on other people. I am shedding
> pride.
> ....
>
> I find I am shedding hypocrisy in human
> relationships. What a rest that will be!
> The most exhausting thing in life, I have
> discovered, is being insincere.[10]

Vanity, pride and hypocrisy are all means that are
used to cover up true self-respect, wholesome pride
and unfeigned sincerity. The more I find myself caught
up in the binding pretensions of these false attitudes,
the more complicated and unbearable conflicts in life
appear, and finally, the more out of touch I become
with my real self.

Conclusion

Once more we pick up the channeled whelk as a
symbol of the simplified life. We need to do that
again and again to unfold continaully the complexities
that tend to clutter life with false ways of responding.
Each person needs to do that for oneself, to discover
and recognize the shell for what it is without
minimizing or exaggerating what one sees. Each person
alone can take the responsibility to cleanse the
shell of "barnacle and moss" by accepting the consequences of her actions and decisions. Each person

alone can uncover her real difficulties in life and bear
the burden and the joys this entails. Life will then
be viewed with different eyes, seeing more clearly the
challenges of life as stepping stones to a fuller life.

After considering the personal factors that may
contribute to making my life unsimple, I shall present
social factors that set the framework for further
complication of life. First I will take a brief look
at the thought of George H. Mean in setting the
foundation for self becoming a social self.

George H. Mead[11]
The Social Self and Roles

From observing the play of children, Mead concluded
that it is when a child in play is able to assume
different roles, that the child becomes aware of self
and of others in mutual social interaction. One cannot
become a self-conscious, responsible, moral self without
contact and interactions with other human beings.
Interaction, actions and conversations influence the
course of one's subsequent action in future roles.

The self constitutes and alters society just as
much as society influences and molds the individual.
The self is what it is first, because of its own nature;
and secondly, because of the community's action upon
that individual. At best then, society and self are
twin-born. On the one hand, self arises where the
individual has the ability to take the attitudes of
the group for its own; and on the other hand lays
upon oneself responsibilities that go with community
life. One learns to "take the roles of others", to
see oneself in their place and reflectively see oneself
as others see. This ability to "get into" the experience of the other, to experience from the other side,
and then come back upon oneself is to "take on the role"
of another. The more roles we thus assume as children,
"the wider will become our sympathy, the more sensitive
and realistic will be our social responses, the more
loving will be our attitudes."[12]

Erving Goffman furthers our understanding of the
formation of a social self when he speaks of the
presentation of self in everyday life. He has employed
as a framework the metaphor of the theatrical performance
to give interesting insight into the roles people play.

Not only the child growing to be a social self resorts
to roles, but often adults "play" roles to set the
stage for their own advantage.

Erving Goffman[13]
Presentation of Self in Everyday Life

Each person is present to and interacts with others
in the day-to-day world in a unique way. His performance
indicates and projects the situation surrounding his
actions. Goffman labels as "front" that part of a
person's presentation which functions regularly in a
general and fixed manner to define the situation for
onlookers. A "front" may be employed intentionally
or unwittingly to meet the changing circumstances in
which he must act in some form or another. In so doing,
he sets the stage, demanding others to value and respect
his actions as being sincere. And while he is acting
in one situation, he disclaims any other role for the
time being.

But, as is soon discovered, many crucial facts lie
beyond the time and place of the interaction. Attitudes,
beliefs and emotions often remain concealed. The
difficulty in this concealment lies in the fact that
attitudes, beliefs and emotions are often incorrectly
ascertained. One can only grasp the sincerity of an
action by discovering the "proof in eating the pudding."
A person may wish others to think highly of him, or to
think that he thinks highly of them, or to obtain no
impression at all. He may merely wish to ensure
sufficient harmony so the interaction may meet his
expectations. In other words, an individual constantly
employs protective and preventive practices to avoid
further embarrassment brought on by situations that
did not "pan out." This initial protection commits
an individual to what is proposed, requiring one to drop
all other pretenses. Thus, when an individual appears
in the presence of others, there is usually some reason
to mobilize activity so that an impression may protect
or be conveyed. Motives for doing so may be as varied
as the people involved in like situations.

REFLECTION

For a few moments let go of your grown-up stance
toward life. Picture in your mind any three-year old

41

absorbed in play. There you may discover the child struggling into dad's old work boots, or into mom's prettiest new dress. Actions seem to show that the child instinctively knows the proper way for a mom or dad to be. In a grown-up voice the child may give commands to the crew under him; or she may show all the care and concern of a mother as she bathes and feeds her favorite doll. You may be lucky enough to glimpse the child playing the role of family doctor, curing all sickness with a generous dose of "M and M's"; or being nurse, propping up pillows and giving a drink to imaginary patients. Today the role may be mother or dad; tomorrow cowboys and Indians. Roles change as quickly as attention spans, dressing and redressing to be properly fitted for the new game. As parent you may even encourage children to "play school", or to "play house" to help time pass on a rainy day.

Not only children but also adults play roles according to the dictates of the situation and the desired impression. An adult may adorn oneself with "fronts" to be in tune with the social demands of the present situation. "Teacher look" may be put on to warn the students that it's time to get serious about their school work. When attending a ball game, the teacher drops the familiar stance of teacher and becomes "spectator". Our fictitious adult may attend a symphony, again becoming someone different because the circumstances call for different behavior. Without thought or much concern one automatically adapts to the changing circumstances of life.

However, there are more subtle and impressionistic changes that complicate life more than the mere conformity to acceptable role-changes mentioned above. To clarify what I mean by these complicating subtleties, place yourself once more in the role of teacher. Ask yourself the following questions: What impression do you usually try to convey to your students, deliberately or habitually? Do you find yourself being a stern, somewhat distant disciplinarian? Or, are you the teacher who is always "with it", keeping up with whatever is new in the changing world of your students? Or are you the kind of teacher who tries to be yourself with the students, allowing them to be themselves? In other words, what type of impression to your everyday actions convey to the group you relate with day after day?

When I reflect upon the great awakening during my
retreat I discovered that my life had unknowingly
become complicated by the very way I reacted to my
students, other teachers and the many others I related
to in my day-to-day world. To my alarm I discovered
that I was merely living out the impression of the
"good teacher," "kind and gentle person," "don't rock
the boat type." I lived the "front" unwittingly,
keeping hidden the responses that were really my own.
I realized that my life became so small because I lived
in the impressions I wanted to make on others. Spontaneity, ease and real gentleness were not part of my
repertoire. I had lost touch with these ways of being
in a situation, not allowing them free play in my well
structured, protective stance. I could not be myself
because I did not know myself. Little by little I'm
catching myself playing the role of giving a "good
impression." Ever so gently I hope to unfold this
well protected life, to live my life as it ought to be
lived with the gifts I have received.

In the following, final section on the factors in
my life that make it unsimple, I shall present various
cultural components that may contribute to the further
folding up of my life.

Erich Fromm[14]
Our Cultural Dilemma

All desires and strivings of human beings seek to
find and answer the questions of basic existence. All
cultures provide a patterned system in which certain
ways are predominant in answering this strived-for
satisfaction. In every center of culture the same
insights have been discovered largely without any mutual
influence from any other culture. In times past needs
were objectified in gods. Today, idolatry is masked,
says Fromm, in the deification of the state in authori-
tarian countries, and the deification of the machine and
success in our own culture. The all-pervading alienation
brought on by the one-sided emphasis on technique and
material consumption has caused us to lose touch with
ourselves and with life. Fromm exhibits a deep understanding of our cultural dilemma when he says:

The tendency to install technical
progress as the highest value is linked up
not only with our overemphasis on intellect but, most importantly, with a deep
emotional attraction to the mechanical,
to all that is not alive, to all that is
man-made. This attraction...leads even
in its less drastic form to indifference
toward life instead of "reverence for
life." Those who are attracted to the
non-alive are the people who prefer "law
and order" to living structure, bureaucratic
to spontaneous methods, gadgets to living
beings, repetition to originality, neatness
to exuberance, hoarding to spending. They
want to control life because they are
afraid of its uncontrollable spontaneity
...They often gamble with death because
they are not rooted in life.[15]

In summary, we today have easy access to all the
ideals of the past, so we are not in need of new
knowledge. The unfolding of our life today, the
evolution of each person's heart does not require more
wisdom but new seriousness and dedication in searching
for answers to the overpowering condition of today's
culture.

"Age of Anxiety", indicates Viktor Frankl, distinguishes the disease of our time. The four symptoms
of the collective neurosis, typifying our culture, as
Frankl sees it, will follow.

Viktor Frank[16]
Age of Anxiety

Although previous centuries probably had more
reason for anxiety because their basic needs were often
not met, it is doubtful whether the collective neurosis
experienced today was as prevalent then. Viktor Frankl
has defined the neurosis of our time according to four
symptoms.

First, he maintains that modern humanity's planless,
day-to-day attitude, stemming from experience of war,
has forced humanity into a state of anomie. We may ask
ourselves the question: Why plan for the future when
the end seems to be so near?

Secondly, humanity harbors a fatalistic attitude
toward life. Planned actions are considered impossible.
People drift through life feeling the impotent result of
many conditions beyond one's control. Freedom is
disavowed to do the best one can with the conditions
life has dealt.

The third symptom is collective thinking. People
abandon themselves as free and responsive beings as
they try to submerge themselves in the masses. People
literally drown as they deny their own personalities.
To them only conformity to the ways of the group is
important. People have no worth apart from that group.

Lastly, the fourth symptom is fanaticism.
Individuals ignore the worth of the values and person
of other people. Only one's own opinion seems valid.
Blindly each person adheres to one's own opinions
which are actually meaningless because the opinions
held are the group's opinions, not one's own.

Ultimately all four of these symptoms trace back
to denial of freedom and shirked responsibility. Since
one cannot point to specific causes for unrest, days
are spent in tense anxiety. Life appears meaningless
and without hope. People keep themselves busily occupied attempting to evade their own plight.

REFLECTION[17]

"I am very busy with matters of consequence!"
The Little Prince was greeted with these words as he
made the rounds of the planets. From the king on
asteroid number 325 clear through to the seventh planet,
earth, he sensed the "smallness" of the world of people.
Each one seemed to reduce the problems faced to a false
simplicity by ignoring complicating factors. Each
seemed to strive to cope with anxieties by reducing one's
world to controllable factors, denying whatever didn't
seem to fit the pattern one had set for life.

The king saw all people as subjects. He fundamentally insisted that his authority should be respected.
To make that respect possible, he made all his orders
obviously and ridiculously attainable. There was no
thought of making orders meaningful. Being bored here,
the Little Prince ventured on to the second planet where
a conceited man lived. When the Little Prince received

45

no response to his innocent questions he reasoned,[19]
"Conceited people never hear anything but praise."
The next planet was inhabited by a tippler who continued
to drink all the while the Little Prince spoke to him.
When questioned on why he continued to drink, he con-
fessed, "I drink to forget that I am ashamed of drinking."[20] The fourth planet belonged to a businessman.
He, too, was concerned with matters of consequence with
no time for idle dreams in his life. The Little Prince
conversed with the businessman about watering his flower
and cleaning his three volcanoes, "It is of some use to
my volcanoes, and it is of some use to my flower that I
own them. But you are of no use to the stars..."[21] In
reply the businessman opened his mouth but found nothing
to say because he, too, knew deep in his heart that what
the prince had said to him was true. On the very small
fifth planet he found a lamplighter and a lamp. His
work of lighting and extinguishing the lamp each minute,
although somewhat ridiculous, held more meaning for the
Little Prince than for all the others because "he is
thinking of something else besides himself."[22] On the
last planet before he reached earth, the Little Prince
visited the large planet of the geographer. What the
Little Prince thought to be a worthwhile profession
turned out again to be more concerned with "matters of
consequence." In his reductionistic attitude the geographer informed the Little Prince that only what is
eternal and not ephemeral is of importance. So in the
eyes of the geographer only mountains, rivers, and
oceans were important; the Little Prince's rose meant
nothing to him.

The fantasy-filled journey of the Little Prince
very simply brings me back to reflect again upon life
in our cultural milieu. Only what is functional, what
fulfills the growing needs of humanity seems to be of
importance. What one does is more important that what
one is in this technological thinking. Life can become
small, closed in upon itself if one exists only in the
world of "What I can do." To uncomplicate, to unfold,
to simplify my life, I need to seriously search out and
find the best answer for me in coping with the demands
of our present technological world, while at the same
time not losing my freedom or unique response to those
demands.

It is easy for me to blame the world "out there"
for the complications I experience in life. I can live
in the "Age of Anxiety" complacently saying, "This is

the condition of my life." I can unthinkingly exhibit
the symptoms spoken of by Viktor Frankl. I may delude
myself into living one day at a time, without plan for
the future, as a mere rationalization to the meaningless
and anomie I experience in my own life. I may also
disavow the freedom I have been dealt, drifting through
life like sand being tossed about by the waves of the
sea. I may further complicate my life by becoming deeply
submerged within the role of life I presently live, not
being open to and responsive toward the new possibilities
opening up all over.

As further protection I may close in upon the myopic
opinions I now have, without turning out and seeing the
worth of the thinking of everyone else around me. Yes,
it is easy to "cover over" the freedom and responsibility, the hurt and the joy of unfolding and simplifying
life as best I can by accepting what I can, and change
what needs to be changed in my own attitudes. Present
day culture in the Western World has brought with it
many difficulties, but it has also brought far greater
gifts than any era has ever experienced. It is now my
responsibility to <u>take</u> the responsibility to do the
little I can, to <u>remove</u> the bindings this culture holds
over me and seriously uncover ways of living my true
self within that culture. Hendrik Ruitenbeek speaks
about the loss of simplicity of life we face in our
culture today because of mechanization. He also proposes an escape route from the stereotyped difficulties
we face today--namely, the return to spontaneity.

Hendrik Ruitenbeek[23]
<u>Loss of Simplicity of Life</u>

"Apparently," Ruitenbeek states, "our relationships
have lost what I would call the <u>simplicity of life</u>"[24]
We can only consider the complexities that surround us.
Adults only tend to their problems and the young are
cognizant only of their alienation. Life has become
so encapsulated that people seem unable to sense a
desire or willingness to discover life anew, to share a
broader world than that of immediacy. Our inability to
meet life as an experience of potentialities excludes
the possibility of controlling our technology. We are
no longer in command of our lives.

Ruitenbeek approaches us with extremely provocative
questions: Are we irretrievably imprisoned in a
mechanistic culture? Is it inherent in the structure

47

of our contemporurury culture that people should move in
mechanistic ways? Is the earth that we touch a part
of ourselves, or has it become just a thing to walk on,
like a pavement? Are we being driven, or driving ourselves into exile from the unity of nature?

Ruitenbeek proposes spontaneity as a way to recap-
ture the lost simplicity of life. In so doing, he
immediately differentiates between compulsive and
spontanious behavior:

> Indeed, without control, there can be
> no spontaneity. For the spontaneous person
> can see his world and his life in perspective.
> He feels free to relax and appreciate exist-
> ence as an ever-unfolding surprising yet
> manageable enterprise. He does not need to
> live by formula. In a rigid and mechanistic
> existence the individual does not feel free
> or even cannot be spontaneous. The spark of
> life, the potentialities of new departures
> have disappeared from his horizon. Yet
> often he tends to look back, at least to fancy,
> when life was much less mechanistic and more
> spontaneous.[25]

But our culture no longer seems to believe in the aliveness of things, and consequently, is deaf to the ever-
unfolding entreaties of things.

Ruitenbeek cites an example given in the diary of
Jean Cocteau, of returning to his childhood neighborhood. To him nothing seemed the same. He couldn't
sense any of the delightful experiences he had treasured
in his mind over the years. He decided to do an experi-
ment in which he bent down, closed his eyes, and let
his finger trace the wall at a height which had been
natural in his childhood days. Immediately there
appeared what he had vaguely expected. The familiar
memories again took shape and form. He again began to
feel the splintering picket fence, the faint scent of
the dampness under the porch, the weight of the school
books tied with a leather strap resting on his shoulders.
He found himself returning to his childhood world where
nothing remained devoid of his benevolent touch. He
discovered he could return for those few brief moments
to life in all its simplicity.

REFLECTION[26]

David O'Neill realistically portrays a practical
means of returning to the sense of simplicity Rutenbeek
says we have lost. Wonder O'Neill is awefilled
reverence for the everyday:

> Wonder happens to me when I let myself
> be open to the full reality of things. It
> is like going through a door. I open this
> door and I go beyond the meaning of the
> ordinary "real world" where we live on the
> surface of being busy and being practical.
> This new world of wonder doesn't take away
> the everyday world; it gives it all an extra
> dimension of meaning for me--the meaning
> of wonder. I approach reality now with
> awe and with reverence. For I see beyond
> the surface of things to a mystery which is
> rich and fascinating.[27]

Perhaps it is impossible for everyone to return to
childhood haunts as Ruitenbeek suggests. Instead you
might invite a young friend to walk with you through a
garden. Become aware of your responses to the child,
his questions and the surrounding beauty. Test out
the spontaneity of your responses in light of what
Ruitenbeek terms the "loss of simplicity of life."

What then do you say to a child when you meet a
flower? Do you say to the child: oh it's just a flower;
it's nothing really important; there is nothing that
you can really do with a flower? Do you try to impress
the child with all your knowledge about it; its name,
genus and species; what it is used for; where it grows
best? Or, when you meet a child, and together you meet
a flower, do you talk to the child and the flower? Do
you make up stories about the flower? Do you allow the
child to question you? Does the child feel free enough
with you to ask why a flower has to stand still in one
place all the time; why it is white instead of red or
blue, or even brown; why it smells the way it does;
why it doesn't talk or cry or eat. Can you enter the
undiscovered world with a child and talk to the flower
about how pretty it is? Can you "bend down" to the
level of the child and stay with him as long as he needs
to, to really get to know the flower, to allow the
flower to speak to him?

Do you take the child and questions about the flower seriously? Do you feel silly talking with a child about a flower? Are you really interested in being with the child in that world, or are you merely pretending to be there, hoping the child will soon tire of this nonsense. How do you feel when someone "catches" you being yourself with the child and the flower?

Now ask yourself another set of questions: Can you be just as much yourself back in your adult world of the office, the home or school? Can you, or do you, give as much time, as much of yourself to your work, the people you work with and your job? Is the humdrum day-to-day world of the everyday meaningful for you, or is it filled with worry, fears and expectations that keep you from being spontaneously yourself? Can you let go of these concerns and worries and still fulfill your job? Can you speak out on issues that seem to belittle peoples, and the rights they have? Be not deaf to the cries for real meaning that are meant to be heard from a world at the brink of destruction. Allow the spark of life to come to full flame in an otherwise mechanical existence.

Summary: Factors in Life That May Cause One's Response to be Unsimple

In this section I have tried to explore several factors that tend to complicate life, namely, the personal, social and cultural factors. Because of these conditioning aspects, various reactions on the part of individuals occur, such as, an individual's reaction to the ontological experience of lostness, aloneness and vulnerability. These reactions tend to develop whole defensive systems through interaction with others. One's life may become closed and protective through both the initial defensive life style and the ongoing defensive style the person has adopted.

Furthermore, this study has been broadened to include extensions of society that may further compli-cate one's response to life, especially in the areas of role playing and total existence within a "front." We searched the cultural factors that may influence one's presentation in life in a culture that tends to be purely mechanistic.

In conclusion, each person has the option to respond or not, to the leveling brought on by personal, social

and cultural factors. Each factor was therefore
presented with the hope of ascertaining how one's
response to life may become needlessly complicated.
Life may always seem complicated and unpredictable,
but one's response to life need only be a living out
of the self each individual is uniquely called to be.
Flowing from the complicating discoveries found here,
I would like to concentrate on means to unfold, to
simplify life, and the responsibility a person must
take to move in that direction.

FACTORS IN LIFE THAT NEED TO BE ACCEPTED
WITH RESPONSIBLITY TO AGAIN "UNFOLD",
TO SIMPLIFY LIFE

William Luijpen[28]
Accepting What is Given in Life

An important initial step in simplifying one's
response to the unpredictable complications of life
is the acceptance of the limitations found there and
the possiblities hidden within these limitations.

Through reflection an individual will find oneself,
in a sense, "fixed." One is "already" a particular body,
and "already" involved in a particular world. An
individual finds oneself as American, worker, talented,
humorous, emotional, handicapped, etc. These determin-
ants which constitute what one already is, identify
situation or facticity. Although certain possibilities
are excluded because of a "fixed" past, there is no
facticity which does not include any possibilities
whatsoever. One is not blindly determined and inescap-
ably crushed upon oneself. A person, as subject,
experiences a freedom, a being-able-to-be, although
limited, giving oneself the elbow room and leeway to
grow beyond what one presently is. Each person always
remains unfinished, an oppositional unity of "already"
and "not yet". This freedom allows the person to reach
beyond the facticity of existence toward the fulfullment
of a possibility not yet reached. Because of the complex
set of motivations guiding all actions, no one can claim
to know whether another's action is free or determined.

Therefore, the subject's involvement in a situation
means for that person an affirmation as annihilation of
one's situation. "There is no reality to which man
cannot consent to some extent; at the same time, there

is no reality to which man can fully and definitely consent. No reality is the 'be all and end all' for man as having to be."[29] All response to life situations involves a yes or no, based upon the limited freedom each person as subject holds.

REFLECTION[30]

Through uncontrollable circumstances Oscar Wilde found himself imprisoned, numbered among the riff-raff of the city. He could have become embittered by these unhappy events, but as we shall see through reflection on his journal, De Profundis, he slowly grew through the humiliations and hardships to face the past, live in the present, and be open to the possibilities of the future.

The paralyzing immobility sanctioned by a prison cell; the regulating of all circumstances patterned on a monotonous routine of eating, drinking, sleeping and working made each day dreadful. Some men grew in bitterness, others began to ponder the details of their past life that resulted in their present circumstance. Oscar Wilde found himself reflecting on his past:

> Desire, at the end, was a malady, or a madness, or both. I grew careless of the lives of others. I took pleasure where it pleased me, and passed on. I forgot that every little action of the common day makes or unmakes character, and that therefore what one has done in the secret chamber one has some day to cry aloud on the housetops. I ceased to be lord over myself. I was no longer the captain of my soul, and did not know it. I allowed pleasure to dominate me. I ended in horrible disgrace. There is only one thing for me now, absolute humility.[31]

His living of humility did not become a bitter enterprise. He gradually came to discover more of himself as he faced what he had never faced before. He used to protect himself from suffering and sorrow of every kind. He hated them both. He had resolved to ignore them and in the process he also ignored his freedom and the pain that accompanied it. He found himself caught by his past, now experiencing the excruciating pain of suffering that had not been accepted all along. One day he spoke with a woman of this very problem:

> I remember talking once on this subject
> to one of the most beautiful personalities
> I have ever known: a woman, whose sympathy
> and noble kindness to me, both before, and
> since, the tragedy of my imprisonment have
> been beyond power and description; one who
> has really assisted me, though she does not
> know it, to bear the burden of my troubles
> more than anyone else in the whole word has,
> and all through the mere fact of her exist-
> ence, through her being what she is--partly
> an ideal and partly an influence: a sugges-
> tion of what one might become as well as a
> real help towards becoming it; a soul that
> renders the common air sweet, and makes
> what is spiritual seem as simple and natural as
> sunlight on the sea: one for whom beauty
> and sorrow walk hand in hand, and have the
> same message.[32]

Because of the example she gave, he could accept his past, and be open to the possibilities of the future. He had to live with himself. He found he could transcend the bindings of the past. He became aware of his freedom to say yes to all the past; no to the present situations that threatened him; and yes to a future still held as possibility.

Oscar Wilde not only accepted the responsibility for his past; he also accepted the freedom of choosing his response to the future. His life became simplified. He found himself more in touch with life and discovered that the prison walls chained him much less than his own responses toward the situations of life. He learned that saying "yes and no" meaningfully were never fully mastered as time and situations kept him fluctuating between past, present and future:

> One can realize a thing in a single
> moment, but one loses it in the long hours
> that follow with leaden feet. It is so
> difficult to keep "heights that the soul
> is competent to gain." We think in
> eternity, but we move slowly through time;
> and how slowly time goes with us who lie
> in prison, I need not tell again, nor

of the weariness and despair that creep
back into one's cell, and into the cell
of one's heart, with such strange insist-
ence that one has, as it were, to garnish
and sweep one's house for their coming,
as for an unwelcome guest, or a bitter
master, or a slave it is one's chance or
choice to be.33

Experiencing the present, after letting go of the
comfortable past, entails a time of suffering the
letting go, of releasing oneself from the bonds of
slavery to a former self, van Kaam speaks of this
necessity.

Adrian van Kaam[34]
Period of Mourning

A person as bodily existence, expresses a mode of
existence by behavior. One's behavior becomes a manifestation of a hidden design in life etched in words,
movements and gestures. A person may discover that
present behavior is incompatibale with one's project
of existence. A person may catch contrary reactions to
one's own project, necessitating a letting-go. In the
beginning of taking on a new mode of existence, the
older familiar ways continue to creep in trying to gain
a foothold.

The work of mourning, a dying to a part of self,
helps one to cope with the modes of existence a person
has given up, but are strongly woven into the tapestry
of one's life. The individual remains vulnerable for
a time, but the person who neglects the task of mourning
altogether, remains weak until a stand is consciously
taken to face squarely what has to be given up, how life
needs to be changed.

REFLECTION

Forced by his stay in prison, Oscar Wilde faced
the sorrow and pain of beginning a new life, discovering
where his life had become selfish, incompatible and
dissipated. He initiated the journey to self-discovery
by confronting the sorrow and pain:

Truth in art is the unity of a thing
with itself; the outward rendered expressive
of the inward: the soul made incarnate:
the body instinct with spirit. For this
reason, there is no truth comparable to
sorrow. There are times when sorrow seems
to me to be the only truth. Other things
may be illusions of the eye or the appetite,
made to blind the one and cloy the other,
but out of sorrow have the worlds been built,
and at the birth of a child or a star there
is pain.[35]

The pain of being born anew, of coming to a
simplicity of life, began for Oscar Wilde as he accepted
the pain of discovery. He did not look on pain as the
gloomy stripping of self but as the birth into someone
new:

It is the last thing left in me, and the
best: the ultimate discovery at which I
have arrived, the starting point for a
fresh development. It has come to me right
out of myself, so I know that it has come at
the proper time. It could not have come
before, nor later. Had anyone told me of it,
I would have rejected it. Had it been
brought to me, I would have refused it. As
I found it, I want to keep it, I must do so.
It is the one thing that has in it the
elements of life, of a new life, a Vita
Nuova for me. Of all things it is the
strangest; one cannot give it away and
another may not give it to one. One
cannot acquire it except by surrendering
everything that one has. It is only when
one has lost all things that one knows that
one possesses it.[36]

No one could prepare him for the surrendering of
his former ways, no one could force him to give up that
which he did not realize was hampering him. The awareness came through self-discovery, through facing his
life as it glared back at him in the prison cell. Again
he realizes that this awareness is only a beginning.
The road to full awareness, the road to the simplicity
of a fresh beginning is only a start in becoming fully
oneself:

Nothing seems to me of the smallest
value except what one gets out of oneself.
My nature is seeking a fresh mode of
self-realization. That is all I am
concerned with. And the first thing that
I have got to do is to free myself from
any possible bitterness of feeling against
the world.[37]

Accepting one's limitedness without bitterness
calls for courage. Rollo May presents courage as being
the necessary virtue one needs to practice every step
along the way to becoming a person in one's own right.
Courage is necessary because it is not humanity's
prerogative to accept suffering.

Rollo May[38]
Courage to Face Oneself

"Courage, whether the soldier's courage in risking
death, or the child's in going off to school, means the
power to let go of the familiar and the secure."[39]
Courage is the mortar that binds together the little
hour-to-hour decisions that function as brick, in
building the person into one who acts with freedom
and responsibility. It is the capacity to withstand
the tension which arises as one achieves freedom. With
courage one may continue to grow, to discover oneself
fully, with all one's strong points and limitations.
Courage is simply the virtue of being oneself. One may
then give oneself with greater equanimity. It preserves
the person's inner freedom instead of defiantly protecting an outer transitory freedom.

REFLECTION

Oscar Wilde's future seemed unpredictable and in a
sense frightening. He knew that his literary career
might be at an end because of the prison term; he found
he no longer belonged to the same social class. His
former life held no allurement for him, for he had
discovered himself.

But were things different; had I not a
friend left in the world; were there not a
single house open to me in pity; had I to
accept the wallet and ragged cloak of sheer
penury; as long as I am free from all

resentment, hardness, and scorn, I would be
able to face the life with much more calm
and confidence than I would were my body
in purple and fine linen, and the soul
within me sick with hate. And I really
shall have no difficulty. When you really
want love, you will find it waiting for you.[40]

The courage to accept life where it is, without striving
to make it meet one's needs and expectations, is needed
constantly to face the little things during the day
that may force one back into a former way of being.
Minute by minute, day by day, each challenging happening
necessitates courage.

Before concluding this chapter on the awareness of
a need to let go, we will look briefly at obstacles
that may quietly steal in upon one's best efforts to
simplify responses to life. Because of the sublety with
which these obstacles appear, it is most important that
one be aware of their implications.

POSSIBLE OBSTACLES TO SIMPLIFYING ONE'S RESPONSE TO LIFE

Adrian van Kaam[41]
Introspectionism

Adrian van Kaam distinguishes two kinds of self
presence: transcendent and introspective. In transcendent self presence the person is able to find oneself
to be a part of the ever-unfolding plan of the universe.
Transcendent self presence does not allow the person to
wall oneself within an inner world nor evade the shared
everydayness where demands have to be met, things done
and promises kept.

The other type of self presence is introspective.
Here the person dwells on oneself as closed off from
the rest of the world. When introspection is absolutized,
the person can no longer be aware of the world beyond
oneself, not centered on oneself. An individual often
becomes mesmerized by all the limiting dimensions of
one's person, life and situations. In this sense introspectionism makes one's self and its urgency for self
realization central, involving one in a futile battle
against time, and real or imagined competitors. The
real world is cut off by this self perfecting ego.
Inevitably, one feels misplaced in the world, becomes

disgusted with life and the meaninglessness of it all.
One no longer experiences the interwoveness with other
people, with nature, history, culture and cosmos. One
of the major drawbacks of introspectionism is the alienation of the person from the context, horizon and
integrity of the whole as it reveals itself in simple
everydayness.

Fixation on Immanence or Transcendence[42]

The two basic strivings of all human beings are
immanence and transcendence. The striving of immanence
inclines a person to become at home with oneself, to
get things well organized, situated and in a harmonious
flow. Life in immanence becomes centered, not scattered.
In the transcendent striving, one needs to go beyond the
"hominess" with oneself, become open to new experiences,
new awakeness, new involvements. Immanence allows for
the incarnation of new experiences; transcendence keeps
the individual open for the newly unfolding revelation
of oneself and one's world. Both of these human strivings are necessary for individuals to remain in touch
with one's world, but not fixated upon it or upon
oneself.

While both immanence and transcendence are necessary, there arises a danger when striving for one is
totalized to the exclusion of the other. In total
immanence the person becomes fixated and closed up
within one's small world, self and life situation as
they are. In absolutized transcendence the person
never comes to a settling down period, never develops
roots in search of ever expanding horizons. The
finely tuned interplay between immanence and transcendence calls the person to fuller growth while at the
same time allows one to interiorize and make one's own
the expanding discoveries about oneself.

Falling Back into a Post-Personal, Routinized Way of Life[43]

At any time an individual may fall back again into
the initial defensive life style of a child. This
especially happens during acute stress situations when
the higher motivations and strivings cannot be relied
upon. The defensive style is more readily available
to automatic behavior.

A person may also return to an automatic routinized way of life. van Kaam speaks of the automation
of what was once a personal response but no longer
remains such--a post personal response. What had become
meaningful and personal through higher aspirations,
social norms and ideals, effective adaptation and
custom no longer seems to be creative, spontaneous and
alive. What was begun as meaningful activity becomes
automatic and robot-like. In appearance the actions
remain the same. But inwardly the person who lives
a post-personal response finds no meaning for he is
truly not in the situation as fully as he once was when
the response was new, alive and creative.

REFLECTION

Although there may exist many other obstacles to
continued self-simplification, the three presented here,
namely, introspection; fixation on immanence or transcendence; and falling back into a post-personal routinized way of life, seem to be most devastating because
they creep in unawares, causing the person to again
become fixated upon some complicating factor in life.

The awareness of a need to let go as a means to
unfold is only a faint beginning along the road to
self-simplification. The actual letting go becomes a
life-long task because I am never fully in control of
my life. I can never "unfold" all my responses. For
just as I master one area of my life, another becomes
complicated. I may again become closed in upon myself,
introspectively forcing the newly discovered limitation
of myself, life situation, or others to find a place
and meaning in my small world. To make my life
predictable and controllable, I may fail to sense and
experience everything as part of the plan of the whole
universe. No wonder meaninglessness becomes my main
preoccupation.

I may also fear to transcend my present way of
being. I may be fearful of change, of being more myself,
of finding acceptance still among those with whom I've
always lived. I may fear giving up the defenses that
have become a way of life for me. I may still fear
being vulnerable. And even though my greatest desire
may be to be simple, I could fear that the most,
because it costs the most. I may often discover the
"old ways" returning. I may accept this limitation as

part of the plan for my life or I may allow it to make my life self-centered, meaningless, and complicated again.

The process of self-simplification is a slow, gradual process costing greatly, but rewarding just as abundantly. It always calls me to something greater, calling me to become more myself, more in touch with others and the world around me. Even though it will never be fully achieved, I hope that the awareness that it is never finished will guide me into a life-long effort to find my life simplified.

Summary and Transition

This chapter was begun by sketching the personal, social and cultural factors that may influence my response, making it unsimple. Each of these factors was presented as a way in which it may have an influence on my life. Ultimately, however, the complication of my life rests in my response to those factors.

Secondly, in this chapter we included the search for what was needed to be accepted with responsibility to again "unfold". Chief among those factors presented were: the acceptance of facticity of self and world as limited because people are incarnate, limited by their own bodies and place in the world; and the inherent possibilities within these limitations. Here we also stressed the realization that a period of mourning, a period of pain and sorrow is necessary to embody a new way of life. Above all, courage was described as a necessary means to achieve a simplification of life.

In the final section, the obstacles to simplifying one's response to life were studied. Once I have become aware of these obstacles to self-simplification they do not have as strong a hold on me. I realize I have a choice in responding to these demands. Through constant reflection on these obstacles, in light of the whole, I may discover how I respond and what I need to let go of, to simplify my life. Through the process of letting go, I sense the need to live more deeply than on the level of the mere surface self which locks me into appearances. The process of "letting go" and "unfolding" is never finished, never fully achieved. But there is a core, a center in my life that calls me to continued emergence and unfolding. My response will be simple if it is in

60

tune with the ever emerging, newly discovered self that
I am, and in tune with the life situation in which I
find myself. In the following chapter we will look at
some means by which my life may become simplified as I
work through to the center of my life, my true identify
as a unique and individual person.

ENDNOTES

[1] Adrian van Kaam, _In Search of Spiritual Identity_ (Denville, New Jersey: Dimension Books, 1975), pp. 156-159.

[2] Karen Horney, _Neurosis and Human Growth_ (New York: W. W. Norton and Co., 1950), pp. 64-175; _The Neurotic Personality of Our Time_ (New York: W. W. Norton and Co., 1937), pp. 26-28; _Our Inner Conflicts_ (New York: W. W. Norton and Co., 1945), pp. 96-114; and Peter Anthony Bertocci citing Karen Horney in _Personality and the Good_ (New York: David McKay Co., 1963), p. 61.

[3] Karen Horney, _Our Inner Conflicts_ (New York: W. W. Norton and Co., 1945), p. 111.

[4] Karen Horney, _Neurosis and Human Growth_ (New York: W. W. Norton and Co., 1950), p. 151.

[5] Ibid., p. 65.

[6] Ibid., p. 86.

[7] Anne Morrow Lindbergh, _Gift from the Sea_ (New York: Pantheon Books, 1955), pp. 21-35, 39-50.

[8] Ibid., p. 22.

[9] Ibid., p. 25.

[10] Ibid., p. 31-32. (Italics not in the original.)

[11] George H. Mead, _Mind, Self, and Society_ citied by Paul Pfuetze, _The Social Self_, (New York: Bookman Associates, 1954), pp. 78-103.

[12] Ibid., p. 86.

[13] Erving Goffman, _The Presentation of Self in Everyday Life_ (Graden City, New York: Doubleday Anchor Books, 1959), pp. 1-30.

[14] Erich Fromm, _The Revolution of Hope Toward a Humanized Technology_ (New York: Harper and Row, 1968), pp. 1-57; and _The Sane Society_ (Greenwich, Conn.: Fawcett Publications, Inc., 1955), pp. 298-306.

[15] Erich Fromm, _Revolution of Hope Toward a Humanized Technology_, op. cit., pp. 44-45.

[16]Viktor Frankl, The Doctor and the Soul trans. Richard and Clara Winston (New York: Random House, 1955), pp. ix-xxi.

[17]The following reflection will be based on an interpretation of Antoine de Saint Exupery, The Little Prince trans. Katherine Woods (New York: Harcourt, Brace and World, 1971), pp. 28-74.

[18]Ibid., p. 28.

[19]Ibid., p. 48.

[20]Ibid., p. 52.

[21]Ibid., p. 57.

[22]Ibid., p. 61.

[23]Hendrik Ruitenbeek, "Mechanization Versus Spontaneity: Which Will Survive?" Humanitas, II, 3 (Winter, 1967), pp. 261-269.

[24]Ibid., p. 265 (Italics in the original).

[25]Ibid., p. 264.

[26]The following reflection is based on David P. O'Neill, What Do You Say to a Child When You Meet a Flower? (St. Meinrad, Indiana: Abbey Press, 1972), pp. 18-27.

[27]Ibid., p. 18.

[28]William Luijpen, Existential Phenomenology, trans. Henry J. Koren (Pittsburgh: Duquesne University Press, 1969), pp. 187-203, 234-237.

[29]Ibid., pp. 236.

[30]All the reflections in this section on the factors in life that need to be accepted with responsibility will be taken from the prison experience of Oscar Wilde. Richard Aldington, ed. The Portable Oscar Wilde (New York: Viking Press, 1946), pp. 500-530.

[31]Ibid., p. 516

[32]Ibid., p. 528.

[33]Ibid., pp. 529-530.

[34]Adrian van Kaam, _Religion and Personality_ (Garden City, New York: Doubleday and Co., Inc., 1968), pp. 34-36.

[35]Wilde, op. cit., pp. 527-528.

[36]Ibid., p. 516.

[37]Ibid., p. 517.

[38]Rollo May, _Man's Search for Himself_ (New York: New American Library, 1953), pp. 191-202.

[39]Ibid., p. 196 (Italics in the original).

[40]Oscar Wilde, op. cit., p. 518.

[41]Adrian van Kaam, _In Search of Spiritual Identity_ (Denville, New Jersey: Dimension Books, 1975), pp. 177-187.

[42]Ibid., pp. 183-196.

[43]Ibid.

CHAPTER III

WORKING THROUGH TO THE CENTER OF MY LIFE

INTRODUCTION

If we reflect upon the original definition of
simplicity given by Rapoport[1]--that our quest for
simplicity stems from a conviction that beneath wide
dissimilarities there are underlying regularities to
be discovered--we find further direction in our search
for simplicity. In the foregoing chapter the dissimilarities that tend to complicate an individual's
response to the everyday world were presented. It now
seems necessary to explicate underlying regularities
that may, in a sense, make possible the living of
simplicity in the everyday.

In the center of my being there is a unique core
called spirit.[2] My unique response to my vital and
personal self dimensions and my participation in world
and life situations is influenced by this spirit. This
unique spiritual identity that colors my way of being
in the world is the center of my life. To be in touch
with that center, to "let be" after "letting go" will
constitute this chapter. Developing possible means
of discovering my unique spiritual identity, which is
never fully achieved, will allow me to be in touch with
the fuller reality of the world as I respond to its
demands in interaction with others, and hence, make
my response more simple.

Adrian van Kaam[3]
Spirit as Core Motivating Force

To be human is to be spirit in the flesh.[4] Because
no other being has a spirit, a human being is the only
one capable of transcending beyond vital reactivity
that binds other creatures. The power of spirit,
which is the core motivating force in humanity, allows
for the discovery and unfolding of each person's
unique identity. It lets emerge a personal life
beyond the vital life, while at the same time fostering
participative interaction between the personal and
vital levels of the person. The power of spirit also

65

fosters participation with relevant people, events and
things as they appear within the civilization, culture,
sub-culture and life situations of the person concerned.

The spirit calls the emergent self into being by
inwardly prodding and evoking the person to growth
through fuller participation in one's humanness. However, it is important to remember that people as spirit
can only grow, can only develop, by means of the
limitations of one's body and the limitations of the
culture in which one is concretely embedded. Without
denying or destroying the vital drives and strivings,
the spirit calls the emergent self to a gradual unfolding to meet the changing life situations as they are
revealed through successive life events.

Spirit as Unique Identity

Spirit is a human being's power of becoming one's
own unique self, participating in and open to all that
is. The discovery of one's unique self is a lifetime
process. Through participative interaction between
the vital and personal aspects of my limited being,
within ever changing life situations, a slender thread
can be seen to weave one's life together uniquely.

The only test I have, to find out whether I am
living my unique identity is a consistent style of
living that is in harmony with all aspects of my life.
In effect, I cannot build or discover my identity in
isolation from what has happened historically, what is
still happening now, or what may happen in the future
in my vital and personal life.

Spirit as Evoking Emergent Selfhood

Emergent selfhood depends for its very existence
on the spirit. Because of the spirit core, the emergent self becomes able to take responsibility for itself.
It acts instead of reacts. The vital life is no longer
the totality of life. Enlightened by the life of the
spirit, the vital life becomes elevated to a true self
dimension as it freely participates in personal human
life.

The emergent transcendent self exists only to the
extent it is grounded in the spirit's inexhaustible

66

range of possible life responses. By incessantly
prodding, pushing and evoking, the spirit calls the
emergent self to transcend the automatic drive-stimulus-
reaction cycle that so readily may become a patterned
way of life. By creating room for another horizon, the
spirit presents more possibilities for living and acting.
When these new possibilities are opened up, the personal
dimension of the emergent self takes cognizance of the
new possibilities and remains receptive to still further
possibilities within the concrete dailiness of life.

REFLECTION

Spirit as Core Motivating Force

Because my spirit is not tangible and perceivable
in the same manner as my body, I often do not sense
the messages sent to me by it. When there is something
"not right" with my body, I sense it concretely, e.g.
pain, swelling or fatigue. I remedy the situation by
taking the needed rest and/or medication. In personal
relationships, I may again find that there is something
amiss. I question and perceive why I am angry or why
I am depressed. I work through the situation as best
I can, being open to the possibilities for growth in
the happening. Spirit, on the other hand, makes itself
known through restlessness. Spirit persistently calls
me to continuous emergence beyond the drive-stimulus-
reaction cycle. It calls me to own my unique free
responses and invites me to be more myself, drawing
together into an integrated whole the vital drives,
sensations, and reactions with personal responses which
I have accepted as belonging to me. This unique
spiritual identity can never be fully perceived or
understood. It seems to reveal itself ever more fully
in successive, concrete life events.

The experience of helplessness and meaninglessness
during my retreat I can now accept as the probing of
the spirit itself, calling me to respond. In response,
I tried to simplify my life, to make my responses more
genuinely my own. I can only simplify my life by being
keenly aware of the limitations I find there.

Henry Bugbee indirectly speaks of the power of
spirit drawing each person to simplicity:

67

What but simplicity renders us whole
and heals us of our anguish, our anxiety,
our grief and our perplexity? Yet when
we come upon simplicity in men, would it
not be foreign to think of it as something
toward which they have bent efforts, as
something in the nature of a difficult
accomplishment with which we must credit
them. Is it not more accurate to think of
simplicity as: something which comes to
us, which we are infused, as a precise
mode of being contained and sustained in
reality?[5]

Spirit as Unique Identity

The "something" that Henry Bugbee refers to seems
to be the unique spirit that each person is imbued
with at birth, but which only becomes revealed over a
lifetime. My life may become one of simplicity as I
remain open to the workings of the spirit in my life.
Without striving, without setting goals as to how my
life may become simplified, my spirit keeps emerging.
Its message of how that may consistently happen, takes
place in the everyday situations of life. Bugbee
further describes the openness of simple persons:

They were men alert, sensitive, poised
in themselves, yet utterly receptive. They
were independent, yet set no barrier around
themselves. Also, they were not trying to
prove anything, in the colloquial sense.
They seemed to be taking an even strain,
yet patiently, on the burden of the world's
work. They did not seem to be laying claim
to the enabling power that was in them, nor
effecting themselves, either, before the
world.[6]

In other words, a truly simple person remains open
to the unique possibilities of life. That person does
not try to be anyone else, but has a keen sense of one's
own potentialities and limitations. A simple person
has responded to the unique spirit's call within.
Although to make a similar response in my own life may
take a life time, and although I may never fully understand how and why the spirit calls, I need to respond
with the whole self that I am. This basically means

accepting the whole comet's tail of past experiences,
my personal and vital limitations, and the limitations
placed upon me by the culture and the changing situations in which I live. At times I may sense a wholeness
and integrity. At other times I may again find my life
too complicated, too scattered. If I remain open to
the suffering and joy involved in the unfolding of my
life I will become more and more in touch with my
spiritual identity.

Spirit as Evoking Emergent Selfhood

Each new situation in my present life draws me to
a still greater awareness of who I am called to be.
The retreat experience was for me one of sheer agony.
It had the power to draw me to become more myself.
Through reflection and consideration of all the circumstances surrounding my relations with friends, family,
working situations, and time alone, I will not become
caught in static existence but will be ready for the
unfolding of the untapped resources of my life. I will
also be far more ready to allow the unfolding of circumstances and the lives of others.

Centering in the emergent self I am discovering
myself to be, I will not hold false expectations for
myself; and will be more able to meet other persons as
also emerging into their uniqueness and far more ready
to become a part of the unfolding of daily circumstances
of life:

> The spirit of simplicity is a great
> magician. It softens asperities, bridges
> chasms, draws together hands and heart.
> The forms which it takes in the world are
> infinite in number but never does it seem
> to us more admirable than when it shows
> itself across the fatal barriers of position,
> interest and prejudice, overcoming the great
> obstacles, permitting those to whom everything
> seems to separate, to understand one another,
> esteem one another, love one another. This
> is the true social cement, that goes into
> the building of people.[7]

Mary Caroline Richards[8]
Centering

Using her experience on the potter's wheel, Mary Caroline Richards finds that centering is the act that precedes and determines all others. Drawing the wobbly chunk of clay into center allows the clay to be shaped and formed into a vessel of artistic beauty. Through life experience she had discovered that by an act of centering, oppositions are resolved into a single experience and an individual comes in touch with the life-power of the universe. As one becomes drawn into center again and again, everything seems to strengthen everything else:

> It becomes unnecessary to choose which person to be as we open and close the same ball of clay...The activity seems to spring out of the same source: poem or pot, loaf of bread, letter to a friend, a morning's meditation, a walk in the woods, turning the compost pile, knitting a pair of shoes, weeping with pain, fainting with discouragement, burning with shame, trembling with indecision: what's the difference.[9]

Transformation takes place, not by adopting certain attitudes toward ourselves but by bringing into center all sensation, thinking, emotions, and will. Centering is not a leaving out of any of these elements but bringing them together into a unity. When we act out of an inner unity, when all of self is present in what is done, then we can be said to be "on center." Reality can thus be experienced in depth, rather than in partition.

> If we can stay "on center" and look with clear eyes and compassionate hearts at what we have done, we may advance in self knowledge and in knowledge of our materials and of the world in its larger concerns.[10]

Centering is the wonderful moment when one feels pliable, feeling a part of the world, taking a shape that only one's freedom can create.

REFLECTION

In describing the inward qualities of woman, F. J. Buytendijk speaks of symmetry and interiority. Using the image of the flower he fleshes out these qualities. He says: "A flower has a heart, an inwardness, and this is its mystery: the call of its perfume, the promise of its fruit."[11] The heart of the flower can be compared to the spiritual identity that makes me uniquely me. Out of this inwardness, this center, each new person, event, and thing met in the day-to-day world, can be approached as mystery. Out of this inwardness the daily tasks no longer need to be approached as a problem, but as the unfolding of life as it has been destined to be for all time. The requests of others, the plans that fail, the foul weather that dampens the picnic plans for the day, all seem to find some meaning. Opening and closing the "same ball of clay," without pretense, without front, opens one to the mystery to be revealed in even the disagreeable happenings. The functions that become necessary in my role in life take on a new importance, and drudgery and meaninglessness again becomes meaningful.

The unfolding of the petals of the flower speak of an openness and a risk; openness to receive the sun's rays as well as the nourishing rain. The petals always unfold, strongly anchored and rooted in the center. In life, unfolding takes place in receptivity and creativity, rooted in the unique potentialities that are personal. Receptivity has many dimensions. It means to be open, hospitable toward persons whose ideologies are similar to mine, and to those whose ideologies are dissimilar. But even more, it means to be receptive to those whose receptivity differs in outlook and style of life, and even to those who may be entirely repulsive. With creativity I may face the failures in simplifying my life as stepping stones to a greater purification and simplification. Just as the sunflower faces the sun and follows it from sunrise to sunset, so, too, might my life be an endless turning toward the source of light, the whole of reality.

And finally, the fruit of the flower is the outcome of the total unfolding of the petals. In human life, too, the fruit of unfolding, of simplifying, is not in the task of unfolding, but in becoming the ripe fruit of the self I have been uniquely destined to be. In

comparison to the rather rapid unfolding of the flower
and its maturing to ripe fruit, our life of unfolding
occurs in slow motion, never really coming to fruition
until the day of death. This, however, should not be
discouraging. The unfolding of a flower is beautiful
for a time, then fades out of memory. The unfolding
of a life into simplicity is a far greater beauty.

Although centering life on the unique destiny
each person is called to is essential, there are other
means by which one's life may continuously become more
simple. Some of these means will be presented in the
following section.

MEANS BY WHICH MY LIFE MAY BE CONTINUOUSLY SIMPLIFIED

Adrian van Kaam[12]
Hierarchy of Modes of Presence

Life is not lived on an even plane with each
aspect of life holding the same importance. Family
life, professional life, personal life and recreational
life seem to hold more or less importance. According
to van Kaam, some modes of existence seem more central
while others become more peripheral and subordinate.
Somewhat automatically the modes of presence fall into
a hierarchical arrangement. One mode usually becomes
more central. If living my spiritual identity becomes
most central, family, profession, personal and recreational life become subordinate and cluster around it.

In the beginning the mutual interpenetration of the
more peripheral modes of profession, family and recreation may be weak. I may devote an excess of time to my
profession and neglect family life. I may also become
so involved in each performing facet of my life that
the central core of my unique spiritual identity could
be ignored. To the degree that all aspects of life
become more integrated, the more fully will they
permeate one another. van Kaam expresses this interpenetration as "interwovenness: with the people whom
I love, with the tasks which I fulfill, with the dreams
and hopes I cherish. They are all me, and I am all of
them."[13]

It takes a lifetime to grow to this existential
unity where all aspects of life can become centered in
the person I am called to be. The interplay of modes,

those most central as well as those that are fleeting
and changeable, evolve into a unique and central mode.
Even when living out of one's spiritual identity becomes
most central, this mode does not become static, unchanging or closed in upon itself. It remains open and
receptive to the new influxes that may alter one's way
of being in the world. One must not forget that to
unfold one's unique identity all action and advancement
must be done in the concrete dailiness of life. One
cannot move faster or slower than the callings of the
spirit, or life will become an illusion, a fantasy that
is no longer in touch with real life situations. If we
are being led by nervous tension, loss of peace and
indecision, most likely we are not moving along the
right path in life.

REFLECTION[14]

My life may become simplified as all aspects of it
come into proper perspective within the whole setting
of my life in the present. Once the retreat experience
was over, I could not immediately "turn over a new
leaf." Gently and slowly, through reflection and
drawing together the whole of my life, I needed to see
my professional life as teacher in proper perspective
along with my family and personal life. I became aware
of the sporadic direction my life had taken and yet
could not suddenly change it and make it neat and easy.
To bring the whole of my life into an integrative unity,
I needed to keep the past in mind, realize what had
become central and then slowly allow the thread running
through my life to be woven into a new fabric, a new
way of being involved in that life.

In reflection on her life up to the time of the
tragic loss of her son, Anne Morrow Lindbergh recalls
other tragedies that made this loss even more unbearable:

> Finally, I must admit that in rereading
> the letters of the last months of 1931, I
> was aware of hurrying through them (or was
> life itself hurrying?). They seem unreal.
> It is as if, in looking at my life, I were
> watching a swift-flowing stream, satin smooth
> on the surface, rushing headlong to the
> sheer drop of tragedy.[15]

Without reflection, without expressing true feelings
because of the ever present public eye, she soon found

her life to be superficially smooth, but tragically
without meaning. Being in the public eye as the wife
of the pioneer flyer Charles A. Lindberg, in a sense
forced her to be purely concerned about public image.
She found the rest of her life suffered. Her personal
life, the expression of her real emotions had to be
safely guarded and hidden. She soon found her life
becoming lopsided, restless and without meaning as the
public clamored to know still more. Inwardly she knew
she needed to write more, to reflect upon her true
feelings and the life she shared with her husband. Once
she realized in tragedy that her life need not be
directed by public desires, she again became free and
could find an integrated unity in her life.

> In replying, I let myself write from
> the depths of feeling. The hand of grief
> released me from the hand of the censor.
> There were other values, I was beginning
> to learn, more important than discretion or
> even privacy. As I discovered the follow-
> ing spring in the abyss of tragedy, I
> needed to return to a deeper resource. I
> had to write honestly.[16]

The lopsidedness of her life came into focus in
tragedy. As for me, I became aware of the tragic
complication and meaninglessness of my life during my
retreat. Through reflection and consideration we both
came to the realization of the lack of a center in life.

Even though the task of unfolding began in the
midst of tragedy and confusion, it was a starting point
for both of us to draw all aspects of life together
into a centering hub. Life was then based upon potential destinies in life and not the centripetal forces
that tended to pull us off center. The past could be
accepted; the present became a fresh unfolding of our
unique possibilities based on the past; and the future
was viewed as a continuous movement toward a more
simplified presentation of self in life. As life
became more simplified, images became far less necessary.
The risk of being one's unique self could be taken.

Adrian van Kaam[17]
The Rhythm of Mindfulness and Forgetfulness

Working through to the center of my life, to find
it successively more simplified, requires a rhythm of
mindfulness and forgetfulness. At times I need to be
more mindful of the ways in which I complicate life by
my responses to it. When I become cognizant of the
relations I have with people, events, and things, my
life becomes firmly rooted in the everyday real existence. People can sense that I am really "in" my words,
gestures, and actions. They sense that I am not just
responding as "they" think I should. Mindfulness not
only implies an acute awareness of the day-to-day
interaction but it also includes a more transcendent
presence to the deeper meanings of the whole of life.

Forgetfulness is just as necessary as mindfulness
to live a well balanced, integrated life. We need
periods of quiet reflection, but we also need to be
forgetful of our reflections and live in a spontaneous
way. At times we need to become one with the natural
flow of daily life. Without forgetfulness that heals
us of the pain of our shortcomings, we may become
alienated from the everydayness of life and the powers
it had to draw a unique response from each person.

REFLECTION[18]

The ebb and flow of different periods of the day
and seasons of the year, also indicate the rhythmic
mindfulness and forgetfulness in human life activities.
Anne Morrow Lindbergh relates her need to find this
rhythm in her life:

> I think I shall be very happy, though, as
> soon as I digest some of the experiences of
> the last weeks and months. Of course one
> is happy doing things, but there is a
> different kind of happiness that comes
> from fully realizing afterwards the things
> done: the "recollection-in-tranquility"
> feeling that comes when you are alone and
> quiet and see your experiences as a whole.[19]

At another time, while on tour of the Appalachian
hill country, she experienced the need for a sudden
stopping. Something about the destitute family, clothed

75

in rags, made her more mindful of something deeper, even though she could not express exactly what this was:

> They really moved me quite a little--
> at least the sensation of <u>stopping</u> in your
> mind, a kind of still island in the stream
> of thoughts and emotions. You have to stop
> and pay attention to it and you are not
> quite sure what it means to you but you go
> on thinking about it.[20]

She also discovered that the same need to stop and step aside announced itself in the everydayness of life. At times we are too mindful of the broad generalities of life, such as what to do, what profession to be engaged in, how to care for the family, that we cannot grasp the spontaneous and the small:

> I sometimes think that perhaps our
> minds are too weak to grasp joy or sorrow
> except in small things. Joy in fresh
> fragrance of flowers, or warmth of a fire,
> or a handshake. Sorrow in faint flowers,
> a lost dog, a fretful child's cry. In
> the big things joy and sorrow are alike--
> overwhelming. At least we only get them
> bit by bit in tiny flashes--in <u>waves</u>--
> that our minds can't stand for <u>very</u> long.[21]

Mindfulness usually occurs in the world one normally inhabits: the office, home, neighborhood, one's car. Forgetfulness may imply getting away from the familiar. Sometimes it may demand distancing oneself in order to be more in touch with spontaneous responses to life:

> I think one's feelings and thoughts,
> the real true deep ones, are better focused
> when you get away because they are detached
> from their stale associations: one's desk
> and room and bed and mirror. They become
> clear and just themselves, the way colors
> of a sunset or birch grove seen upside down
> become clearer, because the colors are
> disassociated from their familiar forms.[22]

It is much easier to get in touch with one's true self, as the ebb and flow of mindfulness and forgetfulness becomes the tenor, directing the unfolding of one's responses to the ever-emerging and changing situations of life.

Provisional Life Projects and Ideals

Closely associated with the rhythm of mindfulness and forgetfulness is the unfolding of provisional, successive life projects and ideals. Very slowly and gradually projects and ideals evolve in tune with the vital, personal, spiritual and situational aspects of the person as he concretely is here and now. When van Kaam says that the projects and ideals are provisional, he means that they are set only for a time; they do not become absolutized as the only project or ideal of a person's life. Life projects are met in the daily changing situations of life, in tune with the capacities of the person involved. Within limited insight, each person has to try quietly and relaxedly to incarnate and own the ideal. It is in this way that one makes it a part of one's personality. Because we are called to be emergent by our very nature as enspirited bodies, we need to be open to the joys and sorrows of the possibilities of growth placed before us.

REFLECTION

One of our natural tendencies is to become embedded in already achieved ideals or to aim for ideals that are beyond the limited capacities of the individual. Today, I may set as an ideal: I will become simple.

To become simple involves taking into account present attitudes, life history and individual defenses. Without these awarenesses the project becomes grandiose and unattainable. Attitudes of centering must develop; life history in totality must be accepted; defenses need to be acknowledged and dropped. Striving for an ideal beyond my capacities can be compared to a paralytic who today decides: I am going to walk tomorrow. The capacities are not presently there; the ideals remain unattainable and frustrating.

To make possible simplification of life, small steps need to be taken each day. Today, it may be to catch myself responding to another as I think they want me to respond, instead of how I need to respond. Tomorrow, I may have to accept my lack of artistic ability. Simplification of life is a life long process. The key to the gradual unfolding of my life in its uniqueness is to listen to the call of situations, people, and things, and then respond in a way that progressively becomes more my way.

Anne Morrow Lindberg realized the need for
provisional ideals in her life. At the time of the
death of her son, courage seemed to be the ideal to
bear the burden of the loss. She soon realized that
other ideals had to take its place:

> Courage is a first step, but simply
> to bear the blow bravely is not enough.
> Stoicism is courageous, but it is only a
> halfway house on the long road. It is a
> shield, permissible for a short time only.
> In the end one has to discard shields and
> remain open and vulnerable. Otherwise,
> scar tissue will seal off the wound and no
> growth will follow. To grow, to be reborn,
> one must remain vulnerable--open to love
> but also hideously open to the possibility
> of more suffering.[23]

Remaining open and vulnerable, to be reborn through
the possibility of suffering, continues to call for the
rebirth of new ideals and new life projects. In the
following section I shall consider further ways of
becoming in touch with the center of the uniqueness of
my life through a creative response to the new unfold-
ings of that life.

RESPONDING CREATIVELY TO THE NEWNESS OF LIFE

Erich Fromm[24]

Living the Creative Attitude

To be creative may have two meanings. In the
most familiar meaning it means to be gifted with a
special talent, to be able to produce something special,
e.g. in art, music or drama. Creativity in the sense
it will be used here, is rather the ability to see, to
be aware, and to respond to that awareness. In full
awareness there are no abstractions. An object is
perceived in its uniqueness and remains fully concrete.
To live the creative attitude, to wake up fully to
reality inside and outside of oneself, one has to reach
a degree of inner maturity so that objects and people
alike can be seen without distortion or projection.

Fromm lists five conditions for living a creative
attitude in the midst of daily life. A first prerequisite is the capacity to be puzzled: to wonder about
and be amazed about the ordinary things of life, such

78

as, why peas grow in pods or how a child is formed.
Secondly, a creative person must possess the ability to
concentrate, to be fully present to the new moment.
This is difficult because most people live either in
the past or in the future. A person must also experience his own uniqueness, to find onself to be the
center of one's world, the true originator of one's own
actions. As a fourth condition, one must be able to
accept conflict and tension in life; to be aware of
them, to experience them deeply with one's whole self,
not just one's intellect. The most essential condition
seems to be the last: the willingness to be born every
day. Every act of birth requires a letting go, the
courage to eventually let go of all certainty. "To be
creative means to consider the whole process of life as
a process of birth, and not to take any stage of life
as a final stage. Most people die before they are
fully born. Creativeness means to be born before one
dies."[25]

REFLECTION

Most people would not describe themselves as
creative because they have not found in themselves a
special "doing" talent. Many feel like a "bull in a
china closet" when it comes to producing in the familiar
sense of creativity.

In speaking of creativeness in the sense described
by Fromm, I find the same five conditions for someone's
growth in simplicity. To be puzzled, to be amazed
about the ordinary things of life, also sets someone
on the road to simplicity in a stance of expecting the
unexpected. It is a readiness to respect and stand in
wonder before the mysteriousness of life. The unfolding of the pale green leaves in the spring...the buds
pregnant with life ready to burst forth in rainbowed
colors...people who pass through the world unfolding
as they themselves unfold in their uniqueness...all hold
a mystery usually not questioned. One who is simple
often expresses what seems most obvious, unaware of
one's special gift of wisdom and insight. The simple
person seems marked by a naivete--not that of a child,
but a mature sense of seeing without guile. The now
moment holds more attention for that person than the
past or the future. There is so much of life exploding
all over, that to miss this present, would be to make

the "future past" less meaningful, and the time to come
without real expectancy.

To be the center of one's world for a creatively
simple person, does not mean that that person is self-
centered, but that this individual owns the uniqueness
of the self slowly being discovered in each phase of
life. A truly simple person fully appreciates and
experiences deeply that uniqueness is a life time task,
a way of life for one who truly desires to live one's
life and not the life of another. Without a doubt, to
live in this manner entails conflict and tension, mis-
understandings and failures. For one who desires to
simplify one's life these conflicts and tensions will
not be viewed as blocks to full unfolding, but will be
the birth pangs of further growth, stepping stones to
a fuller understanding of oneself, one's world and the
aspects of life that seem to be most in conflict with
one's goals and provisional ideals.

Each of the preceding conditions can be summed up
in the last: the willingness to be born anew each day.
Today the birth pangs may come about through a misunderstanding with another; or, it may mean accepting one's
inability to help another through personal difficulties.
It may also be an awareness of how little self-knowledge
one possesses or one's blindness to the needs of others.

Abraham Maslow[26]
Creativity as Childlikeness

Further unfolding the concept of creativity, Maslow
especially refers to the aspect of "childlikeness." The
nonrubricized openness to experience, and the spontaneous
expressiveness so characteristic of children, is also
witnessed in a self-actualized creative person. Persons
evidencing childlikeness either retain or regain the
naive expressiveness of a child. One could be said to
have attained a "second naivete", which is even more
striking than the innocence of a child because of the
experiences and knowledge that could have made one
sophisticated. After observing those whom he would call
self-actualizing creative persons, Maslow conjectures
that his subjects were far more natural, less controlled
and inhibited. Their behavior seemed to flow more freely
with less hindrance, complication and self-criticism.
Creativeness seemed to spring from an inner core and
showed itself widely in the ordinary affairs of life with

a certain aliveness and sense of humor. Maslow finally
concludes that the creative person lives far more in the
real world of nature, emotions, and feelings in regard
to persons, events and things, than he does in the
verbalized, conceptualized world many people confuse
with the real world.

REFLECTION

In an effort to draw together the means by which
one's life may be continually simplified, and how the
concept of creativeness can be seen in the everydayness
of life, let us dwell for a moment on a description of
one such life.[27]

My mother is a small woman with short, feathery
brown hair, held in disarray with bobby pins. Brown
eyes sparkle behind glasses that have finger prints of
earth pressed on them when she is gardening; flour
smudges from bread and cookie dough when she is baking.
A faded cotton apron is tied around her waist, its
pockets bulging with all sorts of things, ranging from
the treasures retrieved from laundry to pieces of candy
ready for probing little hands. They are the hands of
a farm woman: rough, gentle and strong.

Mom shares dad's work and plans, his hopes and
dreams, his joys and pains. Not always understanding or
finding farm life easy, she still remains ready to
listen, to help and understand. Mom has a special way
of doing everything she does, from patching torn jeans,
baking the weekly batch of bread, to experiencing the
growing pains of each child. She enjoys being with us
in our make-believe child world of "playing house",
and "going to school." The demands of harvesting seldom
seemed to cut her off from us.

I have watched mom tired from a day's labors bend
over a prized flower bed in the front of the house. I
often heard her gently humming, expressing tired joy
at the end of another busy day. I have watched her
weed a little patch of earth with a simple and generous
delight known only to those who love to help things grow.

Mom works hard, sharing in the disappointments of
life. Fun and good times are strongly tied in her
philosophy of life. She makes the normalness and everydayness of caring for home and family, bright and alive
with a gladness that spread to all in the family. She

simply is herself, drawing us to be the persons we are called to be.

The creative childlikeness portrayed by this mother may be lived differently by me. I need to be aware of my call in life, and what situations that call invites me to live with the whole of my being. The response of childlikeness is not static. It remains dynamic insofar as it remains in touch with succeeding life events and the capacities I possess to meet them.

Inevitably, waiting for the unexpected, and allowing for the unfolding of life, leads to a sense of mystery and awe. When life is lived as a mystery, as something to be pondered and entertained, instead of as a problem or a set of complications to be analyzed, solved or organized, one's response is more simple. In the following section, we shall explore the meaning of living life as a mystery and how it applies to the simplification of life.

LIVING LIFE AS A MYSTERY

Gabriel Marcel[28]
Life as an Ever Revealed Mystery

Our experience of the world involves us in such a way that it remains intelligible only as mystery. The more things are experienced in depth, the more fully can one participate in the mystery surrounding the whole of existence. The mysteries of life can only be recognized insofar as one participates in that life and does not remain a mere spectator on the drama of life. To participate fully in that mystery, one must respond in humility to the inseparable bond one has with the world of people, events, and things. As participant, each person helps to create the other.

To be involved in mystery, one needs to be involved as a total person in an intrinsic set of relationships that cannot be grasped apart from the full experience of one's life. Thus, the knowledge of mystery becomes something new for each person. Each must discover for onself:

> ...the reality of his own freedom, the
> value of fidelity and love in interpersonal
> relationships, the way to a deepening partic-
> ipation in the mystery of being.[29]

In the realm of mystery there are no blanket
solutions. Only through the gradual unfolding of the
mystery of one's life, in the wilderness of everyday
existence, may the meaning of one's life be clarified.
Its mystery only will be revealed to me as I turn
inward in recollected presence to myself. Though my
being constantly eludes my grasp, each day's participation draws me to a closer understanding of that
mystery. If I were to ever fully comprehend its mystery,
it would no longer be real living, but a stagnation of
a life once lived. Marcel says this search for meaningfulness is an ongoing search in which I accept
humbly each new situation, each new encounter with
other beings, each glimpse of being as a gifted moment
and as a taste of what the future has in store for me.

REFLECTION

Being in touch with the mystery of life and allowing that mystery to take hold of us is an act of
supreme trust. Paradoxically, accepting and participating in the mystery of life is the only solution to
our unquenchable thirst for certainty. Living life as
a mystery and not as a problem places experience on a
plane that is uncommon to most people in their sifting
for answers amidst the uncertainties of life. Each
person must become a wayfarer, a traveler along the
road of life, daring to have faith that the mystery of
being intends fulfillment and not frustration as the
ultimate destiny for us.[30]

As there are many routes that lead to any one city,
there are infinitely more roads one may travel to come
to the destiny of life--fullness of being. Allowing
for the mysterious unfolding of one's life presents the
possibility of continuing on the yet untraversed paths
that life may take.

Loren Eisely speaks of this concept of mysteriousness of life by referring to it as the "hidden teacher."[31] He says that no matter the circumstances of
life, there is a hidden teacher, revealing some mystery
to us, if we were only able to see, to hear and understand the message. All of nature, each circumstance
of life, has some hidden aspects that can be perceived
only as mystery.

Eisely at one point compares our limited awareness
of the world to the limited awareness of a spider caught

in a spider's world. The strands of the web set the
boundary for that world. A spider can only act as
spider, patiently waiting in the center of its web for
the tugging of its prey. Its world consists only in
this--its means of survival. When we, in turn, exist
as mere spectators of life, we become involved only in
a small portion of our world. We only respond to needs
and limited desires without awareness of the deeper
meanings that appear in that immediacy. An individual,
as spectator, cannot respond in humility to the hidden
teacher as it is presented in others, in the situations
of life and in things. In other words, to discover
the hidden teacher, to fully experience the mysteriousness of life, I must participate as fully as I can with
an awareness of who I am, the freedom I possess, and
the limitations I experience. I cannot become embedded
in the web of my past. Nor can I forget that past
and become totally absorbed in the present. I must
remain open to the mystery of the yet unbuilt future.

Glimpsing this mysteriousness in the beauty of a
rose-colored sunset, or in the free responsiveness of
a child opens me to be receptive to the hidden teachers
that are constantly calling me to a fuller awareness
of the whole of reality in the everyday situations of
life. Strongly convinced that my life has meaning and
will unfold in still greater meaning, allows me the
freedom and the responsibility to be open to the
unfolding mysteriousness of life. I will not become
shocked by what the hidden teachers lead me to, but
will be receptive of whatever may or may not happen
in my life.

Conclusion

The process of "working through" to a further
simplification of life is a life-time one. The whole
of life unfolds in its mysteriousness in the everyday.
Enumerated here were several means by which the
"working through" itself could be an unfolding process.

The primary premise on which this section proceeded
was that people are enspirited flesh. Spirit, which is
the centering core of each one's being, continuously
calls for further unfolding in uniqueness. Developing
a modulating hierarchy of values allows one to be more
open to the fluctuations of life situations, personal
needs and accidental happenings.

"Working through" to a fuller awareness of life calls for creative attentiveness, and sometimes a fresh naivete strongly childlike in a wise sort of way.

And finally, the "working through" summons one to experience the fullness of life in its mystery. Mysteriousness lies in the unfolding newness of each life. More importantly, unfolding draws one to a greater relationship with the all encompassing mystery of life.

Summary and Transition to Part Two

In a sense, we have come full circle. We began with slowing down to see by jumping off the merry-go-round of life. We concluded with an even deeper involvement in the mystery of life, that is, in its deeper realities. In the initial section, the main intent was to show the necessity of slowing down and taking a deeper look at life, in order to see its direction and meaning when lived with an attentive awareness. Seeing leads one to discover ways to live in order to meet the demands of our contemporary world. Some of these ways make life less directed, less trans- lucent, less integrated. Becoming aware of those aspects in life is needed so that one can let go in order to live more freely and hence more simply.

The deepening, spiraling movement of unfolding life is never ending. But because I realize this identity is never fully understood, always emerging, I can work through the everyday, little by little, discovering it for myself, while being fully in touch with my limited life situation in its mysteriousness. I am drawn to discover more deeply the mysteries of life, especially the Great Mystery who is already present in my life. In the following division, I will explore the ways in which the Great Mystery, the Holy, is made known through the everyday happenings of life. My life may then be lived in deepening simplicity, expectant of what may be revealed to me by the Holy.

ENDNOTES

[1] Refer to footnote in the Introduction, page

[2] The use of the term "spirit" in the sense it is used here, presupposes the personality theory of Adrain van Kaam. I will expand on his theory of a whole person and the place of spirit in that theory throughout this chapter.

[3] Adrian van Kaam, In Search of Spiritual Identity (Denville, New Jersey: Dimension Books, 1975), pp. 110-140.

[4] Spirit, as it is used in this context, refers only to that aspect of a person which makes one human. In Part Two of this study I will further expand the notion of spirit as pre-presence to the Holy. For the moment this concept will be bracketed. Spirit as it is used here refers only to that power which enables individuals to be open to the whole of reality as it is.

[5] Henry Bugbee, Inward Morning (State College, Pennsylvania: Bald Eagle Press, 1958), p. 70.

[6] Ibid., p. 171.

[7] Charles Wagner, The Simple Life trans. Mary Louise Hendee (New YorkL McClure, Phillips, and Co., 1901), p. 193.

[8] Mary Caroline Richards, Centering in Pottery, Poetry and the Person (Middletown, Connectivut: Wesleyan University Press, 1964), pp. 9-54.

[9] Ibid., p. 23.

[10] Ibid., p. 12

[11] F. J. J. Buytendijk, Woman: A Contemporary View trans. Dennis J. Barrett (New York: Newman Press, 1968), p. 257.

[12] Adrian van Kaam, Religion and Personality (Garden City, New York: Doubleday and Co., 1964), pp. 41-45.

[13] Ibid., pp. 42-43.

[14] Reflections in this section are based on the diary of Anne Morrow Lindbergh, Hour of Gold, Hour of Lead: Diaries and Letters of Anne Morrow Lindberg, 1929-1932 (New York: Harcourt, Brace, Jovanovich, 1973), pp. 11-316.

[15] Ibid., p. 11.

[16] Ibid.

[17] Adrian van Kaam, In Search of Spiritual Identity (Denville, New Jersey: Dimension Books, 1975), pp. 194-195.

[18] Anne Morrow Lindberg, Hour of Gold, Hour of Lead, op. ci., pp. 25-237.

[19] Ibid. p. 25. Italics in the original.

[20] Ibid., p. 69.

[21] Ibid., pp. 237-238. Italics in the original.

[22] Ibid., p. 38.

[23] Anne Morrow Lindberg, Hour of Gold, Hour of Lead op. cit., p. 215

[24] Erich Fromm, Creativity and Its Cultivation, ed. H. H. Anderson (New York: Harper and Row, 1959), pp. 44-54.

[25] Ibid., p. 53.

[26] Abraham Maslow, Toward a Psychology of Being (New York: Van Nostrand Co., 1968), pp. 135-145.

[27] The following description of a creatively simple woman is given by a daughter who has loved her mother's simplicity and has grown to a unique simplicity in her own life.

[28] Gabriel Marcel, Being and Having trans. Katherine Farrar (Oondon: The University Press, 1949), op. 47-56, 86; The Philosophy of Existentialism trans Manya Harari (New York: Citadel Press, 1956), p. 8; H. J. Blackham, Six Existential Thinkers (New York: Harper and Row, 1959), pp. 70-75; and Samuel Keen, Gabriel

Marcel (Richmond, Virginia: John Knox Press, 1967),
pp. 19-22.

[29]Samuel Keen, op. cit., p. 21.

[30]Ibid., p. 17.

[31]Loren Eiseley, The Unexpected Universe (New York:
Harcourt, Brace, Jovanovich, Inc., 1969), pp. 48-66.

PART TWO

THE RELIGIOUS PERSON'S MOVEMENT TOWARD SIMPLICITY

INTRODUCTION

Through my retreat experience I began the process
of self-simplification which was necessary to more
closely approach the whole of all that is, and my
limited place in that whole. I began the process by
stepping aside, by "going into my own woods" to see where
my life was going and to discover the meaning it held
for me. Through slowing down to see I discovered the
aspects of my life that were un-simple. And through
the gradual "unfolding of the cloth" of my life, I
came in touch with the self I have been called to be.
In the ongoing "working through" to the center of my
life, my spiritual identity, I discovered ways in
which the process of simplification may become a lifetime task of unfolding. I then concluded Part One by
reflecting how one's life may be lived in greater
simplicity when it is lived as a mystery rather than
as a problem.

Being open to mystery in life allows a person to
be in touch with a greater, more encompassing horizon
than the whole, namely, the Holy. Therefore, in this
Second Part of this study I will explore our human
pre-presence and openness to the Holy. By becoming
centered within this more encompassing horizon of the
Holy, I would like to show how a religious person's
response to life's complications may become more
simplified if life is lived in awareness of and as a
response to the Holy. For the most part I will be
following the same structure as was used in the first
part. Corresponding to the first chapter "Slowing
Down to See," I will consider the slowing down that is
necessary for a religious person to become aware of the
Holy in one's life; how the Holy implicity is the all-
encompassing ground of one's being; and how explicitly
the Holy is apprehended in two religious traditions,
namely, Zen and Judaism.

Secondly, I will consider "An Awareness of a Need
to Let Go," in the context of the religious person's
world by questioning what is un-simple about my response
to the Holy. Here I will explore how a refusal of my
dependence on this Holy and the refusal to live my own
spiritual identity forces me to adhere to false images

89

of the Holy and a false response of dependence. By
discussing childish and childlike responses I hope to
differentiate between true and false responses to the
Holy. Eventually I will conclude this Part by presenting means by which one may work toward a recovery of
simplicity in response to the Holy. In looking at the
spiritual "way" of Lao Tzu and true childlikeness I
will show that a return to simplicity implies a return
to one's true center in the Holy.

CHAPTER IV

SLOWING DOWN TO SEE THE HOLY

INTRODUCTION

With the drawing of this Love and the voice of
this Calling

> We shall not cease from exploration
> At the end of all our exploring
> Will be to arrive where we started
> And know the place for the first time.
> Through the unknown remembered gate
> When the last of earth left to discover
> Is that which was the beginning;
> At the source of the longest river
> The voice of the hidden waterfall
> And the children in the apple-tree
> But heard, half-heard, in the stillness
> Between two waves of the sea.
> Quick now, here, now, always--
> A condition of complete simplicity
> (Costing not less than everything)
> And all shall be well and
> All manner of thing shall be well
> When the tongues of flame are in-folded
> Into the crowned knot of fire
> And the fire and the rose are one.[1]

Again and again we come face to face with the
mystery of life. The pristine beauty of a rose
colored sunset that seems to warm and blanket the city,
the experience of innocent wonder expressed by a small
child, the sharing in the illness or death experience
of a close friend--each of these experiences leaves
something that can be sensed but not put into words,
appreciated but not fully understood. Eliot speaks of
these ordinary happenings of everyday life as having
the power of drawing us to explore more deeply the
mystery of life. Through all the exploring, searching
and getting in touch with life, we keep returning to
the same things. Our exploration never ceases until
it has come full circle, finding at the beginning what
we have searched for all along. What is that searched
for place, beginning, or someone? We find a clue in
the opening lines of this selection: "With the drawing
of this Love and the voice of this Calling." Somewhere

91

beneath the mystery of life an invitation emanates from the Holy who is our ground and our center. Slowing down to see the Holy in the dailiness of life holds even a far greater treasure than the slowing down to see that we discovered as being necessary in every person's search for simplicity.

In beginning our exploration of how a religious person moves toward simplicity, we shall first present Paul Tillich's thoughts on faith as a centering act. He sees faith as the centered movement of the whole personality toward "something" of ultimate meaning and significance.

Paul Tillich[2]
Faith as a Centering Act

Tillich speaks of faith on the natural level as the state of being ultimately concerned. An ultimate concern gives unity, depth and direction to all secondary concerns. It especially gives meaning to the whole personality that, in an act of faith, is engaged in a centered movement toward something of ultimate meaning and significance. All the elements of a person--bodily, conscious, unconscious aspects, every nerve of one's body and each striving of one's soul--participate in the centering act of faith that demands a total surrender· of the person if it is truly an ultimate concern.

While our experiences, feelings and thoughts are conditioned and finite, we are able to transcend the relative and transitory experiences of life. This is shown by one's ability to transcend limitedness and have concerns that go beyond what appears concretely in the ordinary flux of life. This ability to transcend the concrete in life presupposes in us the element of infinity. Thus, through faith, we are able to understand in an immediate, personal and central act, the meaning of the ultimate, the unconditional, the absolute and the infinite. We will find further insight into our perception and experience of the ultimate in the work of Frederick Streng, who speaks of the experience of the Holy as related to the nature of humanity.

Frederick Streng[3]
Apprehension of the Holy

When the awareness of the Holy becomes the center
of personal life, all of our functions, abilities and
decisions are ideally oriented by the special impact
of this experience. Through this experience we
discover who we are and what we are, not only in our
limitations, but, more importantly, as being related
to the Holy. We are aware that the Holy is something
radically different from us and our everyday existence
while, at the same time, we discover that everyday
existence is dependent upon this "wholly other." For,
to be "human" requires that we have a relationship of
dependence on the Holy because of our very being. To
avoid an encounter with the Holy is to forego the
possibility of becoming fully real, and to forestall
the potentiality of acknowledging the way things really
are. By living in relationship to this source of all
reality, we can hope to find meaning for life.

REFLECTION[4]

The child's one concern as she circled around on
the merrry-go-round was to find her parents who had
"blurred" in the fast movement. All of her energies
strained as she tried to find them in the crowd so
that she could again feel safe in their presence. The
child's limited faith centered on a concern that seemed
ultimate at the moment.

As I tried to jump off the merry-go-round of life's
activities, as I ventured into the retreat experience,
my one concern was to find the meaning my life held
for me. I discovered that by being embedded in the
natural attitude,[5] it was difficult to be in touch
with the experiences of my life. These experiences, so
to speak, "blurred" for me. My ultimate concern became
centered upon my own interests and needs.

The religious person also finds life rooted in everyday experiences. For the religious person, though, concern should be founded in the mysterious elements of those
everyday experiences because that person has discovered
a grounding and rooting in a horizon that is deeper and
more encompassing than the "seen" world of the child
concerned about safety, or the "meaning" world centered

93

on self. The religious person discovers that one's ultimate concern and total personality is oriented toward
the Holy who has been revealed as "totally other" and
as the ground of all that is. For the one who acknow-
ledges a dependence on this deeper ground, that is on
the Holy, one is constantly in search of finding all
aspects of one's immediate and personal world centered
in this apprehension of that which lies outside of oneself. Eliot describes this search:

> We shall not cease from exploration
> And the end of all our exploring
> Will be to arrive where we started
> And know the place for the first time.
> Through the unknown remembered gate
> When the last of earth left to discover
> Is that which was the beginning;
> At the source of the longest river
> The voice of the hidden waterfall
> And the children in the apple-tree
> But heard, half-heard, in the stillness
> Between two waves of the sea.[6]

Through the everyday experiences of life, through the
exploration centered upon the mystery that the religious
person has perceived with the whole of one's personality
one "hears" and "sees" the "drawing of this Love and the
voice of this Calling." One's ultimate concern is somewhat "blurred" as it is "hidden and half-heard." But,
the religious person finds life centered and simplified
as one tries to discover and uncover the extent of a
personal relationship to one's ultimate concern, the
Holy.

    van Kaam explains the relationship that the reli-
gious person has with the Holy as stemming from one's
human nature as enspirited flesh. He describes this
relationship as one of prepresence to the Holy.

Adrian van Kamm[7]
Pre-presence to the Holy

    To be able to be beyond all things and yet in the
midst of them is to be spirit. Because of one's spirit
dimension, a person is endowed with an implicit presence
to the Holy. This implicit presence is revealed both
negatively and positively. Negatively, one tries to
deny or resist the Holy's appearance in the world.
Positively, one develops attitudes of reverence, respect

awe and wonder. Both denial and reverence point to the
fundamental hidden presence that the Holy is in and to
human beings. If this were not true, says van Kaam, we
could not even ask about the Holy or experience the
religious desire that seems to emerge steadily in us.

> It is the life of the spirit that opens my
> life to the mystery that can fulfill my most
> intimate aspirations; that can endow my per-
> sonality with assurance, graciousness, peace-
> fulness and wholeness which are given only to
> those who have discovered the infinite in the
> finite and who have accepted the Holy as an
> invitation to union with their own deepest
> ground.[8]

Seeing the Holy

The person who lives in presence of the Holy not
only fosters a renewed attention to growing in intimacy
with this mystery, but that person also is able, in
light of the Holy, to perceive, appreciate and understand the potentialities in people, events and things to
which others are often blinded.

> Living religious presence he attains the poverty
> of spirit which makes him see the Holy beyond
> the complexities of human passion, weakness and
> failure. This simplicity of perception is in-
> deed a blessed poverty or purity of vision,
> making me free as a bird taking off into the
> sky, merging with the rays of the sun, singing
> out in joy, and returning to the earth renewed
> and beautiful.[9]

The person who lives in the presence of the Holy
no longer finds one's perceptions guided by jealousy or
envious self-centeredness. The person no longer sees
out of a merely categorical stance, but leaves room in
one's perception for the free unfolding of the mystery
that lies hidden in the fine nuances of everyday circumstances.

Centering in the Holy

A person who freely accepts a religious presence is
able to transcend self-preoccupation and center all other
experiences within the experience of the Holy. Becoming

centered in the unifying, ever widening horizon of the
Holy as seen in the universe, in history and daily
events, keeps one from feeling spiritually dismembered
and fragmented by the separate meanings of daily engagements; it allows one to be at home with oneself and be
spontaneous   Freely choosing to acknowledge my religious presence modifies my personality and gradually
transforms all my life situations into religious
situations.

REFLECTION

Through interpersonal relationships a child's
world slowly unfurls. It loses some of its mystery and
yet deepens in meaning for the child. Through daily
experiences the world of the religious person unfurls
as a world that is permeated by the mysterious presence
of the Holy. Each person met, each event experienced
and each object perceived is surrounded by an attitude
of reverence and awe. It is the mystery of the Holy
held hidden in the core of every person that calls for
respect and reverence. It doesn't matter whether the
person is a member of one's immediate family or a total
stranger; the degree of respect merely changes as the
mystery of the Holy working within the person becomes
more evident through shared everyday experiences. Each
person, event or thing is able to point to the infinite,
to be an invitation to relate to the Holy.

For the religious person who searches to simplify
one's life, everything finds a meaning centered in the
all-encompassing ground of the Holy. To deny or resist
the invitation of the Holy is to create unnecessary
complications, to keep the fullness of the reality of
the world from finding a grounding and centering point.
A person who denies the Holy can be likened to a child
who is unwilling to explore one's surroundings. The
child is contented to sit perfectly still in the midst
of toys, having nothing to do with them, not attempting to pick up the shiny or colorful toy. Such a
reaction seems almost unnatural. So too, it is unnatural for us to remain caught behind the categorical
"walls" of thought and perception by denying any relation to the Holy. It is like seeing the beauty of
nature, but seeing it only as meeting our needs, not
sensing the one who created the beauties to enhance our
world; like meeting people, but only seeing what they
can "do" and not who they really "are", not perceiving
the Mysterious One who is the source of their very

existence.

As was seen earlier, the deer leaping out in front
of the car reminded me of my pact with the world. The
taken-for-granted world I was driving through captured
my attention as all my energies reacted in an effort to
keep me from a "could be" fatal accident. For the
religious person, thought does not end here. I am reminded of the presence of a deeper ground. I sense a
protecting, caring presence. I can only respond to
this mysteriously vague presence in an attitude of
grateful respect. My many cares, concerns, disappointments, failures, anger and envy momentarily seem to
melt away as I realize the full impact of the moment.
I had sensed the source and ground of my being, the
Holy.

The almost desperate moment in my retreat experience, when I came face to face with the fragmentation
and non-direction of my life, also brought me to an
awareness of the deeper ground of my life. It seemed I
needed to come to that moment to be able to let go of
my control of life and let it be directed by another.
Saying yes to the Holy, centering in that unifying
presence, gave direction and meaning to the scattered,
non-related engagements of daily life. By being open
to the Holy making itself know, my self-centeredness
had a chance to melt away. I became more in touch with
the fullness of life experiences. From seeing people
as they are without my pre-conceived notions or needs,
to respecting the unfolding events and things of life,
my whole way of being became transformed, if only
mementarily, by living in an awareness of a ground
deeper than myself.

How may I make a more concerted effort to see the
Holy in my everyday experiences of life? As was pointed
out in Part One, I may come in touch with the fullness
of life through developing the art of distancing self
through reflection and the meditative way of life. Here
I will point out how through natural meditation the
ground of the Holy may continue to emerge for me. I
will also show that wide-awakeness in the spiritual
horizon is evidenced by an openness to spiritual
insight.

MEDITATION AS A MEANS OF SEEING THE HOLY IN EVERYDAY LIFE

Phillipp Dessauer[10]
Natural Meditation

Dessauer says that the purpose of natural meditation is to keep open the sources of life and draw
continually more deeply from them. Natural meditation
is the active welcoming, awakened preparedness to
conceive, to let grow within oneself the gift the
everyday gives, and to become more in touch with the
source of this gift. Dessauer uses the "Parable of
the Guiding Thread," as told by the Indian Yogi Swami
Vivekananda to clarify for us what is necessary for
meditation and the gifts it brings to us.

A high official once fell out of favor with his
king. The king had him imprisoned in the top room of a
tower. One moonlit night, the prisoner went up to the
pinnacle of the tower and stood looking down. He saw
his wife standing below. She made signs to him and
touched the wall of the tower. The man stared down
intently to see what she was doing. But he could not
understand it, so he waited patiently to see what
would happen next.

The woman at the foot of the tower caught a honey-
loving insect and smeared its antennae with honey.
Then she fastened the end of a silken thread to the
beetle's body and put the little animal on the wall of
the tower with its head upward, pointing exactly toward
where she could see her husband standing far above. The
beetle crept slowly toward the smell of the honey, moving ever upward till at last it reached the place where
the man stood.

The prisoner was alert. He was straining his ears
in the darkness and gazing downward. He saw the little
creature climbing over the ramparts and, taking it
carefully, loosed the silken thread, freed the insect,
and drew the thread slowly and carefully up toward him.

But the thread grew heavier and heavier. Something
seemed to be hanging onto it. And when he had drawn it
all up, he saw that a length of sewing cotton had been
secured to the end of the tower-long length of thread.
The man drew this cotton to him, too, and it also grew
heavier and heavier, and at its end he found a strong
string. Slowly and carefully he drew up the string,
and its weight also increased continually, and when he

98

came to the end he found a strong rope tied to it. He
secured the rope to the pinnacle of the tower.

What happened after that was simple and obvious.
The prisoner slid down the rope to freedom. He went
away with his wife through the silent night and left
the country of the unjust king.

Dessauer then takes each part of the parable to
explain the art of meditation. Who is the person in
the locked tower room? The prisoner is the symbol of
anyone who responds quietly, waiting in stillness for
his innermost depths to be revealed to one through
meditation. The tower room in which one is locked is
likened to a world built by us, a world that captures
and cuts us off from the meaningfulness of everyday
life because of the facades and regulations, the pretenses and fronts.

Who is the wife? She is anyone who, through
meditation, has been able to give up, look above ego-
centric notions and has awakened her yearning for what
could exist in her innermost being and in the world
around her. She comes in the night, the symbol of an
absence of covetousness. She is ready to endure the
threat of emptiness and meaninglessness she may be led
into in non-striving. She is not afraid. For in meditation a light from above, coming from the ultimate
object of all meditation, and a light from within unite
to become the inner light. The meditator becomes all
"inner eye" and "inner ear" when all her forces become
centered around the foundation of life.

Whatever is meditated on becomes alive in us,
becomes accessible to our touch. The beetle can become
for the wife, not just a scary creature that needs to
be exterminated. It becomes the symbol of the small
everyday things we need to be awakened to, those things
that will lead us to a realizaton of who we are, what
our place is in all creation and who it is that created
us.

The honey symbolizes the gift each person has been
given to fulfill the expectations of one's innermost
being, the gift of freedom, the gift of freely choosing
a response to what we have been given. A response such
as this is a response of gratitude that comes near to
praising God.

The long arduous path of meditation slowly leads to the top of the tower, to the foundation of life. The first gifts of meditation are very small but repeated over and over again these gifts can eventually bear the full weight of a person. The meditator is not afraid of the problems of the meaning of life and everything it involves, both its glories and its gravity.

The reward? For the man in the tower, his freedom. For the meditator the reward is a clear view of oneself, of one's center in which do peacefully lie and in which do find one's origin. In a sense, one leaves the "tower" behind and yet dwells more fully within the world, in touch with deeper meanings vaguely experienced. Henry Bugbee speaks of being in touch with the deeper meanings, the absoluteness of situations through meditation:

> . . . as far as we are sensitive to the absoluteness of our situation, we live in a dimension of meaning which is the depth of our experience--we live in eternity. Certainty involves that simplicity which is true to being in a situation that is absolute and registered as such in depth. It seems to me that I have known men to live with such simplicity for the most part "without knowing it."

> . . . .

> It has seemed to me that meditation can be continuous with experience in depth. It can be an activity consonant with the absoluteness of our situation, somehow opening and answering to the demands of our situation as absolute.[12]

While Dessauer is careful not to get caught into saying that natural meditation (that which is fundamentally proper to humanity) leads directly to a perception of the Holy, he points out that meditation rightly cannot come to any other center, any other ultimate meaning. In the following section we will see how the gift of meditation--spiritual insight--is an awareness of all reality as coming from and eventually leading toward the Holy. Spiritual insight will be spoken of here as corresponding to the "shocks" into wide-awakeness as presented in Part One.

Frederick Streng[13]
Spiritual Insight

Meditation has the power to eventually draw a person to sense with one's whole being the all-encompassing Being, the Holy. Spiritual illumination or insight is a potency that removes the blinders that have prevented us from seeing ourselves and seeing the world as they truly are. In the moment of insight, a person awakens, "comes to" as if out of unconsciousness. The light dawns and one sees where one is. It seems as if some obstacle has been removed between the seer and what is seen. The moment of insight changes one's perception of what it means to exist, and releases a power for ultimate transformation of the individual as truth is experienced spontaneously and naturally.

In apprehending the Holy in spiritual insight, a person senses that here is reality that cannot be known in any other way. Though the blinders are lifted, there is something that by its very nature cannot be reduced to an identifiable object, but is regarded by a religious person as the source of one's very existence.

REFLECTION

The few words of the retarded man brought me face to face with myself. I needed to question what he said and why he said it. I could not come to an explanation of what he meant by: A smile on your face and in your heart. His words, though simple, evoked in me a profound realization and a faint grasp of a reality that I had been asleep to previously. The "epiphanous moment"[14] brought me face to face with myself, with this man, with the world of my shopping day. But most especially, it awakened me to a greater awareness of a Presence that transformed my partial preoccupation with shopping into an experience of centeredness. Though this Presence could not be described concretely, the joy I experienced, the transformation that took place in my perception of other shoppers, changed the tone of the day. Everything seemed to become freed of the blinders that had previously hidden meaningfulness from me.

In the painful moment of insight in my retreat experience I sensed a lack of direction and meaningfulness. I experienced the dreadful moment of non-centeredness. This experience, too, had the power to draw me, to almost surrender my control and find my life centered in the Holy. I experienced my smallness, my finiteness, my inability to control my life. I was somehow led to sense that there was a Greater Presence who could and

did control my life. I sensed that I needed to become
awakened to that Presence, to surrender my efforts to
control the complications of my life. I became aware
of a need to let go.

These two experiences are but two moments in which
I became awakened to an awareness of the Transcendent
Holy. Bugbee speaks of others--the simple ground, the
still desert and the silence. "There is a constant
fluency of meaning in the instant in which we live.
One may learn it from rivers, in the constancy of their
utterance, if one listens and is still.15 As was seen
in Part One, these experiences of wide-awakeness convince me I need to see more clearly the fuller meaning
of my life, to experience more fully the Transcendent
Being who surrounds and encompasses that life. Therefore, in the following section we will present spiritual
discipline as a means of opening one's self to a possible perception of the Holy. Discipline, in this sense,
will allow me to sense the Holy in the everydayness of
life. Up to this point we have been speaking about the
implicit presence of the Holy to us. In the following
section we will point out several ways in which we may
become aware of this presence explicitly, that is,
through spiritual discipline in general, and more specifically, through two religious disciplines--Zen and
Judaism.

SPIRITUAL DISCIPLINE AS A MEANS OF SENSING
THE HOLY EXPLICITLY IN LIFE

Frederick Streng16
Spiritual Discipline

Streng says that spiritual discipline is a process
human beings employ to overcome human limitations. As
such, it is a method for releasing spiritual potential.
Discipline that leads to spiritual insight, to see
things as they really are, is not an attempt to
construct a perfect image, nor to copy an eternal order.
Instead, it is a dissolution of religiosity and philosophical knowledge about religion through a direct,
personal realization of what lies buried beneath mere
information about one's relation to the Holy.

The purpose of spiritual discipline is to obtain
spiritual insight, of getting a new image of life
through an ecstatic moment of transcendent consciousness.
According to Streng, some meditative schools of the East

set as their goal a new way of life. They hold that
spiritual discipline is a guide to maturity. It is a
guide that does more than make us aware of a Transcendent Being. Spiritual discipline also allows the person to realize the nature of truth and to seek who one
is. "New sensitivities and new relationships with one's
environment well up when a person applies the new knowledge of one's self to his everyday experience. Living
becomes an art rather than a task."[17] In this sense,
if we are to know our true nature, we must avoid attachment to things that may seem important--fame, money,
status and bodily pleasures. Each individual will only
be able to make use of one's potentialities if one is
freed from attachment to anxieties, if freed from the
superficial bindings of goals, values and images one
has of oneself. Only then will a person be free to live
spontaneously in an open relationship with all existing
things.

REFLECTION

I know from experience the tremendous task it is to
slow down, to quiet my mind and body to reflect upon my
life. It is even a greater task to allow the Holy to
become my central concern. I realize that I can never
force this fullness of presence to the Holy. But as
van Kaam says,

> I can prepare myself for this gift by liv-
> ing life in such a way that the Holy does
> not find me closed or wandering about
> when it silently appeals to me, but finds
> me ready to fill my field of consciousness
> to overflowing.[18]

I may prepare myself for the emergence of the
Sacred by distancing myself from the surface appearances
of people, events and things. I may slowly and gently
begin to detach myself from involvements that have the
tendency to fragment and dissipate my energies. By
developing a new way of sensing and a new way of life,
I might prepare the "seedbed" for the emergence of the
Holy in all aspects of life. My preparations however,
must be based on personal conviction and personal action.
Knowledge about religious discipline, and knowing about
how to ready myself for the emergence of the Holy will
remain only information and "dead" discipline unless I
daily put forth the effort in a personal way, to gently

103

allow the whispered appeals of the Holy to be heard.

What else does spiritual discipline entail? Besides shaping my religious presence in tune with my concrete life situations, I also need to be aware that my religious presence must be founded on a concrete project of spiritual life. This project needs to be based on a lived tradition of openness to the Holy, and also must be in tune with my present life situation. In the following section I will briefly present two such religious traditions in an effort to show how these disciplines may prepare a person for living life more simply and in tune with who that person has been called to be. First, we will look at Eastern tradition as portrayed in the "art of archery" and in the "tea ceremony." Although neither of these two are strictly religious in the sense of being an aspect of a particular religion, they do prepare an individual for emergence of full religious presence, the emergence of the Sacred in life.

Conrad Hyers and Thomas Merton[19]
Zen Response to Mystery in Everyday Life—Seeing

The Chinese and Japanese have shown a profound appreciation of and a keen sensitivity to ultimate mystery as is shown in their development of the arts, especially poetry and painting. For them, religion and art seem to meet as the fundamental experience of the mysterium manifests itself in the most ordinary and commonplace. These ordinary everyday things are seen perfectly, clearly, beyond categorical slots and in an unusually fresh and lucid light. As things are viewed in their "suchness", they are also perceived in their inexhaustible mystery.

Following the teaching and experience of Buddha, people seek to comprehend the real nature of existence and rediscover real roots in the true ground of all being. Merton says that the Zen experience is a "direct grasp of the unity of the invisible and the visible, the noumenal and the phenomenal . . ."[20] An experience of Nirvana, of perfect wisdom, awareness and compassion, heals a person of one's brokenness, and truth is found in wholeness and simplicity. The pith of brokenness is viewed for the first time as

> an illusion, but a persistent and invis-
> ible illusion of the isolated ego-self,
> setting itself up in opposition to love,

demanding that its one desire be
accepted as the law of the universe,
and hence suffering from the fact that
by its desire it is fractured in itself
and cut off from the loving wisdom in
which it should be grounded.[21]

Zen uses everyday human existence as material to
mend our brokenness by a radical transformation of
individual person's consciousness. Merton quotes D.T.
Suzuki saying: tasting, seeing, experiencing and
living all demonstrate something common to enlighten-
ment-experience and sense-experience--one takes place
in our innermost being, the other happens on the periphery of our consciousness.[22] Zen is an awareness of
the ontological ground of our own being here and now in
the midst of the world. Zen explains nothing; it does
not teach. It merely enables us to wake up and become
aware. It just sees--not an Absolute Object, but
Absolute Seeing.

Thomas Merton[23]
Experiencing "Self"

Merton explains that to attain the experience of
the transcendent "Self" is to:

penetrate the reality of all that is, to
grasp the meaning of one's own existence, to
find one's true place in the scheme of things,
to relate perfectly to all that is in a relation of identity and love.[24]

The human personality is the force which effects the
fusion of self with the highest reality, the True Self.
It is the total union in which the hopes and fears of
the individual are forgotten and done away with. Because the individual self is no longer centered on its
own affirmation but on union with the True Self, its
small pre-occupations and ego-strivings seem also to
fade into non-existence.[25] The end of Zen training is
then to become "absolutely naked", to be without striving, without image or preconceived notions. Merton
again quotes Suzuki who says that the value of human
life thus lies in suffering. For where there is no
suffering, no letting go, there can be no consciousness
of karmic bondage (link between this world and the next),
and no power for attaining spiritual union. Unless one
agrees to suffer one cannot be free from suffering.

Herrigel shares with us his personal experience of
learning the art of archery. Here we will experience
with him the suffering he went through as he slowly let
go, as he slowly was able to face himself in trying to
become master of this art.

Eugen Herrigel[26]
Zen and the Art of Archery

Archery, in the sense it is experienced in the Zen
tradition, is not the skill of hitting the bull's eye.
Rather, it is a contest with the archer oneself. It
becomes an "artless art" because nothing is accomplished
outwardly with bow and arrow that is not first mastered
inwardly. The bow and arrow are merely accidentals, a
pretext for something that could just as well have
happened without them. When the archer becomes, inspite
of oneself, an inward center,

> art becomes "artless", shooting becomes not
> shooting, a shooting without bow and arrow,
> the teacher becomes pupil again, the Master
> a beginner, the end a beginning, and the
> beginning perfection.[27]

Herrigel describes the slow subtle battle one
carries on with oneself. The student tries to find the
"secret" that one thinks the Master is withholding.
Through the trial of many months one discovers little
"tricks" really don't permit one to master the art although the student learns to shoot the arrow straight
and sure. Where did the difficulty lie? In the striving. The student could not wait for the right, ripe
moment for the release of the shot. He could not let
go of himself to allow the shot to happen independent
of him. The following dialogue with his teacher describes what must be done.

> "The right art," cried the Master, "is
> purposeless, aimless! The more obstinately
> you try to learn how to shoot the arrow for
> the sake of hitting the goal, the less you
> will succeed in the one and the further will
> the other recede. What stands in your way is
> that you have a much too willful will. You
> think that what you do not do yourself does
> not happen."

> "But you yourself have told me often
> enough that archery is not a pastime, not a

purposeless game, but a matter of life and death!"

. . . .
        "What must I do, then?" I asked
thoughtfully.
        "You must learn to wait properly."
        "And how does one learn that?"
        "By letting go of yourself, leaving
yourself and everything yours behind you so
decisively that nothing more is left of you
but a purposeless tension."
        "So I must become purposeless--on pur-
pose?" I heard myself say.
        "No pupil has ever asked me that, so
I don't know the right answer."
"And when do we begin these new exercises?" ·
        "Wait until it is time."28

If the shot is to be loosened in the right way,
mental and spiritual loosening must go hand in hand
with the physical letting go to make the action free
and agile. While breath-control aids in physical re-
laxedness, it does little to attain spiritual freedom.
To become spiritually free, the archer must become
utterly egoless and detached so that the soul sunk
within itself stands in the plenitude of its nameless
origin.29

A state of egoless detachment is truly spiritual
as it is charged with spiritual awareness and "right
presence of mind." In this state the spirit is present
everywhere because it is nowhere attached to any particular place and remains present because it does not
cling to any place by reflection. The right presence
of mind and meditative repose become necessary preparations for loosening all one's powers for creative work.
When no trace of egohood is present, awareness is so
deep that distance and depth are pierced by "eyes that
hear and with ears that see."30

Toward the end of his training, Herrigel realizes
the apparent paradoxes the artless art of archery is
founded upon. Another dialogue between Master and
student gives us an idea of some of these paradoxical
movements.

        "Do you now understand," the Master asked
me one day after a particularly good shot, "what

107

I mean by 'It shoots,' 'It hits'?"

"I'm afraid I don't understand anything
more at all," I answered, "even the simplest
things have got in a muddle. Is it 'I' who
draw the bow, or is it the bow that draws me
into the state of highest tension? Do 'I'
hit the goal, or does the goal hit me? Is 'It'
spiritual when seen by the eyes of the body,
and corporeal when seen by the eyes of the
spirit--or both or neither? Bow, arrow, goal
and ego, all melt into one another, so that I
can no longer separate them. And even the
need to separate has gone. For as soon as I
take the bow and shoot, everything becomes so
clear and straightforward and so ridiculously
simple . . ."31

In the following section we shall also see that
the Japanese "Tea Ceremony" requires a similar response
of the person to come to full oneness with the "Self."
To fully take part in the ceremony the hostess and her
guest must become egoless. Even the smallest movement
in the ceremony is fraught with meaning, drawing the
participants into simplicity.

Frederick Franck and Thomas Merton 32
Japanese "Tea Ceremony"

The "art of tea" depicts a style of life in which
art, spiritual experience, communal and personal relationships combine with one another to form an expression of God in his world. It is a deeply spiritual,
almost liturgical expression of art and faith. While
the tea ceremony follows a traditional set of rules,
there is also room for originality, spontaneity and
spiritual freedom.

The spirit of the ceremony is founded on the four
basic elements: Harmony, Respect, Purity of Heart, and
Stillness. The untranslatable Japanese term, Wabi,
describes this spirit as an inward joy in poverty and
simplicity. Merton quotes Hasumi who also describes
the spirit of the ceremony as

an inwardly echoing of aesthetic poverty. The
"Stillness" and the "Listening" in which we
reverence the poverty of man, the harmony of
the world, and the "incompleteness of nature"
opens into a deep awareness of the eternal

108

present in which all ideals flow together
in the "Nothing."[33]

In the ceremony the guest and the host surrender
their personal selves and become united with each other.
Franck describes his experience of a tea ceremony in
which he witnessed the host coming to inwardness and
practicing the "art of tea."

As Michiko-san, who is in her third year of
study prepares for her turn, a shadow moves on
the paper screen of the sliding door. A third
girl kneels in the door opening, bows from her
kneeling position until her head touches the
floor, silently slides to an empty cushion.
Michiko's face is closed in inwardness. Her
every movement becomes an infinitely tender
precision. The placing of the sizzling kettle
back on the brazier, the contemplation of the
wooden ladle that will scoop the boiling
water into the bowl, have become acts of tender
devotion, absolute precision. She had brought
her own tea caddy, a red and gold lacquered
heirloom, protected by an embroidered glove.
Michiko-san is no longer a librarian. She is
no longer Michiko-san, she is the priestess
clothed in wabi, in solitariness, in tranquility,
poverty and gentleness of spirit. She has
become who she is. The deep obeisance, the
reverence with which she offers me the teabowl
is no longer either personal nor an impersonal,
but a transpersonal homage. Michiko's ego-
mask has evaporated, she has become intensified,
mysteriously centered; she has become her Self.[34]

REFLECTION

Quick now, here, now, always--
A condition of complete simplicity
(Costing not less than everything)
And all shall be well
All manner of thing shall be well
When the tongues of flame are in-folded
Into the Crowned knot of fire
And the fire and the rose are one.[35]

Through the teaching and experience of Zen, we try
to comprehend our true nature and in that true nature to
come to full union with the "Self." Through serious

search we discover that we have been substituting our
own desires for the law of the universe. We realize
that we need to mend and heal our brokenness in order to
find our true place in the scheme of things and to become totally absorbed in Being. We have to give up
illusions about ourselves, others, and even the Holy
and become "absolutely naked." As Eliot says, we have
to attain "a condition of complete simplicity--costing
not less than everything."

Each person travels one's own way in life so each
person has to discover what simplicity will cost personally. We may have to give up our search for the
"withheld secrets" as Herrigel had to give them up to
come to be master of the art of archery. The cost will
be far less if one slows down to experience the ripe
moment, to allow it to happen when the time is right.
It means to wait without hope, without goals in mind,
to wait in egoless repose so that the Holy may be made
known explicity. At times the Holy will not withhold
and is experienced in either grateful awe and respect
or extreme dread. One seems to either sense the profound harmony in all of creation, in all persons,
events and things or experience his powerlessness, lostness and aloneness within all of creation. When the
experience is one of awe, everything receives respect
for what it is, not for my own self-centered notions of
whan it could do for me. In a state of egoless repose
I may attain a purity of ·heart and come to a sense of
stillness in which I may sense that "all shall be well."
To ponder these things is to allow them to remain a
gentle guiding light for the remainder of my life's
actions.

The "costing not less than everything" also shows
itself in the profound everydayness of the tea ceremony.
The tea caddy, brazier, pot, ladle, napkins and tea
bowl--all are the everyday utensils that hold within
them the makings for a spiritual experience.36 The
ceremony only appears as a stilted ritual, one that is
without meaning, for those who cannot let go and allow
the meaning to emanate from each movement and gesture.
Western people, unfamilar with the ceremony are notor-
ious for reacting this way to the ceremony. We are not
moved by the gentle precision, the warm respectful
caress that is given to each object, the calm and stillness that pervades the atmosphere. We see the ceremony
as making a "great deal over nothing."

When I was able to partake in a tea ceremony, conducted by some Japanese visitors, I was elated because I had heard and read so much about it. I was shocked by the remarks and seeming disrespect of some of the other observers. Why were our reactions so different? I would be slow to say that I was more in touch with the full meaning of the ceremony, for I know that I was partially motivated by curiosity. The others were not aware of the religious significance, nor were they aware of the deep meaning the ceremony held for this cultural tradition. Again, I became aware that we find meaning only where there is at least some small degree of knowledge and openness to the experience. One who is open to the possibilities of true experience (that this ceremony which is based on the everyday may have) approaches the ceremony with reverence and awe, for the celebration holds the possibility of revealing the ground that exists in and around the everyday. One who sees it only as an elaborate way of honoring a guest does not allow the deeper meaning to flow forth from it.

Though the tea ceremony is not a part of my cultural heritage, I may learn important values from it. Namely, that the everyday happenings of life may at times reveal the Holy to me, the Holy who surrounds, strengthens and cares for me. Secondly, the ceremony teaches me the slowed down manner in which I need to live to experience in a non-selfcentered way the respect that should be given to each person, place or thing, because they also find their roots in Divine creation. And lastly, through the example of the tea ceremony, I might experience the wholeness and immense simplicity of things. As Eliot concludes in his poem, referring to the intense union of fire and rose, so too my life experiences may find me in-folded in an intense union with the Holy.

In the section we just concluded we presented the Zen tradition as one way of relating to the Holy that makes itself known explicitly in life. We spoke of this way as a way of in-being with the Holy. We would now like to look at the Judaic tradition and its view of the Holy. We will present those aspects that apply to our relation to the Holy as being "wholly Other"[37] and will again present means by which the Judaic way of life may lead to a life of childlike simplicity in response to the Holy.

Huston Smith[38]
Jewish View of the Holy as "Wholly Other"

Whatever a person's basic philosophy, that person is somehow aware of an "other" who created everything that exists. One also soon becomes aware of one's own limited powers. None of us is able to control the forces of nature, not demand that nature respond to us. When we experience limitedness we sense that there is a Being of tremendous power and majest. This Being formed all of nature, is without limit, of inexhaustible worth, controls one's own life as well as that of all other life, and is so magnificent in greatness that it can never be fully comprended.

The Jews reached for the most exalted concept that would encompass this sublime Being of infinite power and majesty. Since they found a greater depth and mystery in persons than in any other wonder at hand (this was in contrast to all other religions who venerated some object of nature) this Being was viewed as a person, a "Wholly Other." This view is not prosaic, for their God is not limited as we are but is viewed as a Being of unutterable greatness and holiness. Their belief is centered in the One God, Yahweh; therefore their God is not chaotic, nor is he a God of vengeance. Their religious beliefs centered on a God of righteousness and love.

It follows from the Jewish concept of God as a God of love that people are beloved children and as such would do all He could to achieve an answering goodness from us. The prophet Hosea beautifully illustrates our relationship to God like that of a toddling infant to one's father. The metaphor he uses also shows that even though God is good, we run from God to fulfill our own desires.

> When Israel was a child I loved him, and I called my son out of Egypt. But the more I called to them, the further they went from me; they have offered sacrifice to the Baals and set their offerings smoking before the idols. I myself taught Ephraim to walk, I took them in my arms, yet they have not understood that I was the one looking after them. I led them with reins of kindness, with leading-strings of love. I was like someone who lifts an infant close against his cheek; stooping down to him I have given him his food. (Hosea 11:1-4) [39]

Even though God loves and cares for us, we often
fail. God treated us as infants in his home; we react
by offering sacrifice to idols. The Jewish concept of
a God of love is shown in the following section. Even
though God could rightly be vengeful, his love proves
the stronger.

> They will have to go back to Egypt, Assyria
> must be their king, because they have refused
> to return to me. The sword will rage through
> their towns, wiping out their children, glutting
> itself inside their fortresses. My people are
> diseased but he does not cure them. Ephraim how
> could I part with you? Israel, how could I give
> you up? How could I treat you like Admah, or deal
> with you like Zeboiim? My heart recoils from
> it, my whole being trembles at the thought. I
> will not give rein to my fierce anger, I will
> not destroy Ephraim again, for I am God, not man:
> I am the Holy One in your midst and have no wish
> to destroy. (Hosea 11:5-9)

As can be seen by this and many other readings on Jewish
history, the main goal of the texts was to show that
there is an order of reality unaffected by our flighti-
ness, that God purposely is found within the limitations
of the world of change and struggle, and that He reveals
himself in events which are unique, particular and un-
repeatable. The chosen people experienced God directly
intervening in their affairs. Nothing does more to
explain the extraordinary response the Jews have made to
the severe and sometimes grotesque challenges that have
befallen them than the conviction that God loves them
uniquely and was counting on them to make his will known
to all the nations.

Maybe because of their smallness and insignificance
as a nation they had to believe in a provident God who
would intervene in their everyday affairs. They saw
human frailty and greatness, "missing the mark" through
sin, and freedom to choose, as signs of the love and
greatness of a God on whom they were dependent for
everything. Theirs is a God who had a very definite
part to play in everyday existence. He was seen as a
wholly Other Being who used the everyday as a stage in
which to make his will known to us and to show his love
for them. All of life becomes hallowed for the Jews as
the smallest, most insignificant event reflects the

infinite source of holiness which is God himself.
From rising in the morning, to eating a simple meal,
to plodding along a rushing stream, to watching the
sun slowly slide beyond the distant mountain--each
small thing glows with the love of God. "To religious
man," says Abraham Heschel, "it is as if things stood
with their backs to him, their faces turned to God."40

In the following reflection we shall take a brief
look at a woman of the Old Testament Judaic tradition
who experienced deeply the love and goodness of her God.
This woman is also noted for her strong faith which was
lived out in simplicity. We will also take a brief
look at how the modern day Jew still finds God to be
provident, even after the horrendous experiences of the
last century. The Jewish faith is simple, at times
ritualistic, but always aware of God intervening directly in their day to day lives.

REFLECTION

When we look at the beliefs of the Jews and their
relationship to Being as "wholly Other," we perceive an
entirely different tonality from what we saw in the Zen
tradition. While Zen's goal and emphasis is total in-
being, becoming absorbed in some vague sense of Being
expressed as "Self," the Judaic tradition roots its belief in a provident God whom one can never fully comprehend because of His majesty and greatness. He far sur-
passes our humanness and is so great that He remains
"wholly Other" while continuing to use the everyday
circumstances of life to show his love and goodness. In
Zen, people strive through non-striving to become egoless,to rest in meditative repose. In contrast we see
the Jews actively engaged in showing gratitude for the
many gifts God has given them. An Orthodox Jew sees
each small action as being a way of answering God's
goodness. We also see that while absorbed in the "artless arts," Zen masters are totally involved in in-being,
a vague, non-descript sense of being afloat in a nameless
void. For a Jew the opposite is true. The Jewish
people have an exact record of every historical event,
both good and bad, in which God's direct intervention is
shown.41

In speaking specifically about the Judaic relationship to God, let us take a brief look at the life of
Judith who exemplifies the Judaic life style by her

114

prayer, patience, penance and utter simplicity, even in
the face of difficulty. (Judith 8-12) Judith is a young
widow who has just lost her husband, Manasseh, who died
of a sunstroke during the barley harvest. As his widow
she stays inside her room for a little over three years,
only joining her people for festival gatherings. The
remainder of her time is spent in prayer and fasting.
She wears the traditional widow's weeds and sackcloth
around her waist. Though her husband left her great
wealth, she did not flaunt these treasures carelessly.
She was a woman of great beauty and simplicity because
of her devout fear and love of God.

Her people were greatly troubled because of the
water shortage that was caused by the armies of Holofernes. She hears that the elders propose a plan to
turn the city over to the enemy in a few days time.
Greatly troubled by their lack of confidence in the God
they have never before abandoned, she says to them:

> Who are you, to put God to the test today, you,
> out of all mankind, to set yourselves above him?
> You of all people to put the Lord Almighty to
> the test! You do not understand anything, and
> never will. If you cannot sound the depths of
> the heart of man or unravel the arguments of his
> mind, how can you fathom the God who made all
> things, or sound his mind or unravel his pur-
> poses? No, brothers, do not provoke the anger
> of the Lord our God. Although it may not be
> his will to help us for as many days as he pleases,
> just as he has the power to destroy us before
> our enemies. But you have no right to demand
> guarantees where the designs of the Lord our
> God are concerned. For God is not be be coerced
> as man is, nor is he, like mere man, to be
> cajoled. Rather, as we wait patiently for him
> to save, let us plead with him to help us. He
> will hear our voice if such is his good pleasure.
> (Judith 8:12-17)

She goes on to recount all the wonderous deeds that God
has done for them through Abraham, Isaac, Jacob and all
others who were near to His heart.

After the elders left her with the assurance that
she would do something, she fell on her knees and prayed
that her God would use her as a fit instrument to bring

about the safety of her people as he had done for her people through all of history. Finding her confidence in God, she goes out to perform the task that would save her people--the beheading of Holofernes. Because she found her courage in God nothing seemed to be too horrendous. She did what she had to do to save her people. When she returned with the head of Holofernes her people exclaimed loudly: "Blessings on you, O our God, for confounding your people's enemies today." (Judith 13:18)

Judith's ancestors today strongly believe in the same saving power of their God. Even though many Jews in America today have been forced from their homelands by the terror of Hitler Germany and the persecutions of Russia, they still have a strong faith in a loving and provident God, a God who tries them to test their faith in Him. Recently a reporter visited an Hasidic Jewish settlement in Brooklyn, New York. There he discovered that the lives of these people still revolve around their strong faith. They observe the mitzvahs, their many commandments, as though they were newly issued today. Their whole life revolved around their religious beliefs. For them, every aspect of life is a joyful act of worship in ecstatic love of God and joyful communion with Him. They continue to be poor and for the most part unlearned because of their religious obligations. But they believe what "matters was not as much the loftiness of one's intellect as the purity of one's soul, however humble."[42] Each act they perform is a conscientious fulfillment of God's command, bringing about the santification of even the smallest act of everyday life. Very touchingly the author describes the concrete way in which a three-year-old lad is initiated into the lifetime of "toiling with the Torah." A bit of honey is placed on the aleph, the first letter of the Hebrew alphabet. The child's finger is placed in the honey and then to his lips. This simple act is to teach him that the study of God's law is sweet, that the study of his Jewish tradition's formulation of man's yearning for God is an alive, reverence-filled worship of God in the everydayness of life.

Summary and Transition

Throughout this chapter we have considered the necessity of slowing down to see the Holy concretely in our everyday lives. First we spoke of faith as being a

centering act, one in which the whole of one's personality is focused on an ultimate concern. For a religious person, that ultimate concern is focused on the
Being of the Holy. When the explicit awareness of the
Holy becomes the center of life, we realize that our
dependence upon this "wholly Other" denotes a relationship with the Holy. van Kaam refers to this relationship as a pre-presence to the Holy, meaning that because
we spirit in the flesh we already have a relationship
with the Holy before we become aware of it. A religious
person who consciously lives in the presence of the Holy
also sees persons, events and things in relation to the
Holy and therefore can no longer live out of purely selfish motives.

As a means of deepening my perception of the Holy
in everyday life, I discover the necessity of meditation
which allows me to be open to the deep sources of life.
Through a stilled waiting for these deeper meanings to
be made known, my ego striving may also become stilled
and quieted. I will be far more ready to receive the
gift of meditation--spiritual insight. How do I further
ready myself for the possible emergence of the Holy?
Through discipline. Discipline in the true sense helps
me to personalize religious knowledge and beliefs. It
does not conjure up a perfect image of who I want the
Holy to be for me, but allows the Holy to be for his
own sake. It is a means of developing the art of seeing
the Holy in everyday relationships. Religious discipline
aids in my personal development of a concrete project of
religious presence.

We concluded this chapter by taking a brief look at
two explicit religious disciplines that stress the necessity of seeing clearly through the eyes of faith and
thereby simplifying my response to the Holy in life.
Through the art of archery and the tea ceremony we saw
the Zen way of in-being with the Holy. Through our
presentation of Judaic tradition we looked at the opposite pole, that of counter-being with the Holy, a tradition in which the Holy is viewed as being "wholly
Other." We discovered that a significant component of
both religious traditions is the meaningfulness of the
concrete dailiness of life. To know the Holy in either
tradition demands a surrender of my ego-striving tendencies, to see the plan of the Holy fulfilled. To
really live in either tradition calls for a simplification of life. In the following chapter we will discuss

the return to simplicity that is necessary to fully respond to the Holy. In this chapter we will first consider what in my response to the Holy is un-simple and then we will propose a recovery of simplicity through childlikeness as a means of purifying my response to the Holy.

ENDNOTES

[1]T. S. Eliot, Four Quartets (New York: Harvest Books, 1971), p. 59.

[2]Paul Tillich, Dynamics of Faith (New York: Harper Torchbooks, 1957), pp. 1-9.

[3]Frederick Streng, Understanding Religious Man (Belmont, California: Dickenson Publishing Co., 1969), pp. 47-80.

[4]For the content of these reflections I will be referring to the experiences of Part One, pages 2-3.

[5]See pages 4-5 of this book for an explanation of the term "natural attitude."

[6]Eliot, op. cit. Italics mine.

[7]Adrian van Kaam, Personality Fulfillment in the Spiritual Life (Denville, New Jersey: Dimension Books, 1966), pp. 13-44.

[8]Ibid., p. 14.

[9]Ibid., p. 55.

[10]Philipp Dessauer, Natural Meditation, trans. J. Holland Smith (New York: J.P. Kennedy, 1965), pp. 17-33, 51-111.

[11]Ibid., pp. 123-124.

[12]Henry Bugbee, Inward Morning (State College, Pennsylvania: Bald Eagle Press, 1958), p. 37.

[13]Streng, op. cit., pp. 77-79.

[14]Adrian van Kaam speaks of the possibility of an epiphanous experience taking place only when the person is totally, undividedly centered with his whole being in the present moment. He says, in principle, any concrete experience can become an epiphany--a sign of a Transcendent. An experience of nature, an aesthetical experience, an experience of a meaningful human situation, or an ethical experience may lead to an experience of the Holy.

[15]Bugbee, op. cit., p. 83

[16]Streng, op. cit., pp. 64-80.

[17]Ibid., p. 79

[18]Adrian van Kaam, Personality Fulfillment in the Spiritual Life (Denville, New Jersey: Dimension Books, 1966), p. 21. See also Adrian van Kaam, In Search of Spiritual Identity (Denville, New Jersey: Dimension Books, 1975), pp. 108-137 in which van Kaam presents the psychodynamics of spiritual presence. Here he explicitates the five dimensions of presence: naturally and divinely illuminated supraconscious, the infraconscious and conscious. Each of these dimensions directly affects each other, coloring what response a person gives to present experience.

[19]Conrad Hyers, Zen and the Comic Spirit (Philadelphia: Westminster Press, 1973), pp. 80-99; and Thomas Merton, Zen and the Birds of Appetite (New York: New Directions, 1968), pp. 37-53.

[20]Merton, Ibid., p. 37. Italics in the original.

[21]Ibid., p. 84.

[22]Ibid.

[23]Ibid., pp. 72-118.

[24]Ibid., p. 72.

[25]Adrian van Kaam speaks of the experience of fusion with the True Self, with the Divine as being one of the essential dimensions of the Experience of God. The dimension that has been described here he calls in-being. He says that in the experience of in-being, the self is so totally at one with, so totally identified with the Holy, that the person can no longer distinguish what is the Holy and what is "I." One becomes totally lost in Being. In Search of Spiritual Identity op. cit., pp. 310-312.

[26]Eugen Herrigel, Zen and the Art of Archery (New York: Vintage Books, 1953), pp. 9-109.

[27]Ibid., p. 20.

[28]Ibid., pp. 51-52.

[29]Ibid., p. 56.

[30]Ibid., p. 67.

[31]Ibid., p. 88.

[32]Frederick Franck, Pilgrimage to Now/Here (Mary-knoll, New York: Orbis Books, 1974), pp. 106, 133; and Thomas Merton, op. cit., pp. 90-91.

[33]Ibid.

[34]Franck, op. cit. pp. 106-107.

[35]Eliot, op. cit., p. 59.

[36]For a further explanation of how the everyday may become a way of transformation see Karlfried, Graf von Durchkeim, Daily Life as Spiritual Exercise trans. Ruth Lewinnek and P.L. Travers (New York: Perennial Library, 1971).

[37]van Kaam refers to the experience of the "wholly other" as a counter-being experience. Adrian van Kaam, In Search of Spiritual Identity op. cit., pp. 310-312.

[38]Huston Smith, The Religions of Man (New York: Perennial Library, 1965), pp. 254-300.

[39]Scriptural quotes throughout are taken from The Jerusalem Bible, Reader's Edition (Garden City, New York: Doubleday and Co., 1971).

[40]Heschel as quoted by Smith, Ibid., p. 284.

[41]In this portion of my reflection I draw together the two poles of an experience of God, namely, in-being and counter-being. I do not wish to negate the good that can be derived from either, though as we shall see in the Third Part, these dimensions by themselves are only part of the total picture. We will later describe the full human experience of God as presented by van Kaam as an experience of intimacy with the Divine. Adrian van Kaam, In Search of Spiritual Identity op. cit., pp. 310-312. The significance of both of these traditions as explicit formulations of our relationship to the Holy is that they both stress the necessity of

seeing the Holy as being present in the everyday; and they both call each believer to simplify a response to life to become more fully in touch with that Holy.

[42]Harvey Arden, "The Pious Ones," National Geographic CXLVIII:2 (August, 1975), 288.

CHAPTER V

A RETURN TO SIMPLICITY AS A RESPONSE TO THE HOLY

INTRODUCTION

The thrust of this chapter will be similar to
Chapter II of Part One. I will again concentrate the
major portion of this chapter on the etymology of
simplicity--without fold. The guiding question for this
section will thus be: what is un-simple about my response to the Holy? By considering the personal, social
and cultural factors of my life, I hope to show that
what is "folded up" keeps my response from being simple
and keeps me from living out my true identity centered
in the Holy.

In Part One we used the experience of a small child
on the merry-go-round. In the experience we find the
child terribly frightened because she could not find
her parents in the fast circling motion of the horses.
van Kaam's theory of the defensive uncongenial life
style suggests that perhaps the child was frightened
when she experienced her own powerlessness and vulnerability. Later we saw that the reason she found this
experience so frightening was because of the awakening
of her spirit. Throughout Chapter IV we presented our
innate openness to the Holy because of our spirit core.
We shall see that on the personal level one often re-
verts to defenses that keep one safe, that keep one
from admitting this relationship thereby making a response to the Holy almost impossible unless this
defensiveness is surrendered. Let us look at ways in
which I may try to deny my relation to the Holy by
"covering up" my experience of lostness, aloneness and
vulnerability.

Adrian van Kaam[1]

Uncongenial Life Style--Cover-up for My Dread of the Holy

Through the emergence of a unique spirit early in
life, a person soon discovers a lack of omnipotence.
This spirit makes one feel inserted in a vastness that
either allows the person to be aware of an utter helplessness or calls one to emerge uniquely. A child experiences this polarity and tension. At times we reach

out and accept our limitedness; at others, we build
defenses to cope with the tension. In reaction we
develop defensive styles of life to cope with the anxiety we experience. When we are young, we may be able
to cope with fears by objectifying them in fairy tales
and ghost stories. These objects, we have learned
from others, make the mysterious unknown less frightening.

In effect, the child falsifies reality in order to
cover-up the extreme dread that is felt. Reactions become uncongenial--not in tune with a real self--as the
child tries to negate feelings of limitedness and cope
with dread of the mysterious Holy. Without knowing why
or exactly how, the child refuses to be dependent upon
the Holy, to answer the appeals of the Holy, or to
emerge uniquely by surrendering to the Holy. The remainder of life seems to be an endless striving to heal
the break, to regain union with the Holy. We may try
to move out of the encapsulating shell of a defensive
life style in order to cope with deficiencies, limitedness and vulnerability. At times, one may go far toward
healing the break, but most often some concern other
than the Holy becomes ultimate and central. The Holy
becomes displaced by other lesser concerns. William
Kraft presents several such displacements that are often
approved of by society.

William Kraft[2]

Displacement of the Holy

Theoretically, displacement refers to a distortion
or a replacement of a true but inaccessible goal with a
substitute, lesser, but achievable goal. A person tries
to make sense out of life, to satisfy desires and thereby gain a sense of fulfillment even if it is not a true
sense of fulfillment. If the Holy, is rejected, the
ground for existence is lost. One fails to recognize
that one can only be wholly oneself by giving oneself
wholly to others and to the Holy.

In effect, by rejecting the Holy, we reject ourselves. We feel fragmented, find life meaningless, and
sense that there is a part missing. A lack of ultimate
concern makes life sterile and helpless. Full pleasure,
fulfillment and maturity are never reached as the person
tries to escape from a sense of meaninglessness by dis-
placing the Holy by these lesser goals. The Holy does
not remain a motivating force or ultimate concern for

most people so relationship to the Holy becomes a mere
formality, a peripheral aspect of life. We live an
anxious existence as we try to repress a desire for the
Holy but we fight a losing battle as our defense mech-
anisms only seem to increase our desires instead of
lessen them. We live in a state of unawareness and out-
of-touchness with ourselves. Because the normal person's repression of the Holy is unconscious, that person
differs from the person of bad faith who willfully re-
jects the Holy and actively promotes his own benefits.
Following will be several particular displacements one
may use to "cover up" a desire for the Holy.

   Theorism. In this displacement Kraft says the
person takes a system of thought or particular theory
as one's ultimate concern. One lives theoretically
instead of experientially. In a sense we live "out of
our heads" instead of through the whole of our person.
At times psychology or group therapy substitutes for
the yearning, giving the person a "partial" sense of
fulfillment and being in touch with life.

   Workism. For this person life centers around a
profession instead of around a commitment to the Holy.
A hierarchy of modes of presence become distorted as
work becomes the all consuming concern. For this functional person, life is doomed to dissipation as work
becomes an end instead of a means. Work substitutes
for a person's yearning for the Holy.

   Powerism. In this displacement a person becomes
one's own central concern. The person strives to
attain independence and control over all aspects of
life. One tries to be a god and redeem oneself as an
overcompensation for feeling of helplessness in the face
of the Holy. After a time life becomes meaningless
because nothing is clearcut; the person is no longer in
control. By letting go and returning to childlikeness
a person may become free enough to direct one's yearning
for the Holy to the Holy.

   Sexualism. Sex is used as a very subtle displacement for the Holy as the person gains a sense of satisfaction and grounding in the sexual experience. The
person loses a sense of aloneness and lostness as the
other becomes an ultimate concern. Sex here becomes a
"cover up" for narcissistic self-centeredness as displacement for the person's yearning for union with the

Holy. In sexualism the other is exploited for selfish
reasons.

   Religionism. The most subtle form of displacement
is inauthentic religion. Here the person lives merely
the external rules of religion, not a life of faith.
The person seems to know all the right answers and uses
ego functional skills to dispel ambiguity and mystery.
Religious values are rooted in rules instead of actual
lived experience. The advocate of religionism blindly
submits to external rules in a childish sort of way as
actions are guided merely by external "shoulds" and
"should nots."

   Each of the above displacements substitutes lesser
concerns for the ultimate concern for the Holy. The
role of "thinker," "worker," "pious one" and "church
goer" meets the approval of society as appropriate goals
in life. Only when these roles are seen in the light
of ultimate concern do we realize how they fall short
of the highest goal--union with the Holy. In the following section we will also see that the profane orientation of culture seems to displace the Holy by lesser
concerns.

Adrian van Kaam[3]
Cultural Orientation as Displacement of the Holy

   van Kaam presents the aspect of cultural orientation
toward the profane in life as another obstacle to religious presence. He says that by burying myself in the
world of functionalism and pure ego striving I refuse to
admit that there is a transcendent aspect to my life.
What I produce, how well I function, and what meaning
I discover in life substitutes a partial, profane presence for a religious one. My preoccupation with the
surface meaning of things affects my presence to people,
nature and daily situations. Nature is not sensed as
mystery and beauty but as a supply of useful ingredients
for my use or misuse. Others are approached as fulfill-
ers of my needs. Daily situations are seen only in
relation to functional efficiency. A person with a
profane orientation either is, the isolated, absolute
creator and ruler of one's own life and that of the
universe, or one adheres to the opposite notion of extreme alienation from any meaning in life. Through
scattered activity persons who live in a profane orientation try to cover up the secret yearning for the Holy

who dwells within each person's very being.

REFLECTION

Every person is caught in the tension of remaining dependent and striving for independence. Each tries to "walk" one's own way and yet desperately hangs on to the guiding hand of a mother. In trying to become "one's own child", defenses are built that allow one to continue to feel omnipotent and in control. When one's spirit awakens the child denies the powerlessness and vulnerability experienced. Limitedness is denied. The call of the Holy is refused. Instead of surrendering and trying to emerge uniquely within life limitations, the person begins a private idolatry in trying to redeem and save oneself. The more defensive the person becomes, the less in control one feels, the more threatened one grows. Life becomes complicated, closed in upon itself as the unique call of the Holy is denied.

When I ventured into the retreat experience I had no idea what it held in store for me. My ultimate concern and motivating force was being a good teacher and being respected by both my students and other teachers. When I stopped to re-evaluate my life, I was struck by its meaninglessness, its lack of direction. Why did I feel so fragmented and not in touch with life? In facing myself I realized I had found my worth in what I produced, how my students progressed, the image the other teachers saw. Although these appeared to be good motives for me, I knew that they were only partial and not really as important as I had allowed them to seem. My life was missing something. I felt caught behind the images I had tried to live. In living these images I felt even less myself, more dissipated, less centered. I now realize that I too had refused to hear the Call of the Holy as He was making it known in my life. I had little notion of what was being asked of me.

Besides living out of the images I had built for myself, I also discovered that I had relegated the Holy to certain images that seemed to meet my needs. I did not allow God to be God for God's own sake. I resisted the "face" that was shown, substituting instead my image of a God who would be the "filler" of my needs. Prayer was only something I performed; it really did not touch my life on a day to day level. Periods of silence were filled with my plans and requests. I could not listen

to His Will out of fear of what would or would not be
asked of me. I became aware of a need to let go of my
defenses--knowing that the Holy would not ask more of
me than I could endure with His help. I needed to let
go of the images I had of myself--gently trying to uncover and discover my true spiritual identity. I needed
to let go of the images I had of God--allowing Him to be
my ultimate concern instead of just a peripheral aspect
of my life.

"A condition of complete simplicity--costing not
less than everything . . ." is the only route I can go
to allow the Holy to be my ultimate concern. To allow
the Holy to touch my life I need to follow the path of
simplification by acknowledging the way things really
are, by living with them as best I can. Eliot outlines
this way as a way of dispossession:

> You must go by a way wherein there is no ecstasy.
> In order to arrive at what you do not know
> You must go by a way which is the way of ignorance.
> In order to possess what you do not possess
> You must go by the way of dispossession.
> In order to arrive at what you are not
> You must go through the way in which you are not.
> And what you do not know is the only thing you know
> And what you own is what you do not own
> And where you are is where you are not.[4]

For the beginner who does not know the way of simplification, whose footing is at best precarious and
"wobbly", there is no other way than to wait, to wait
in quietness for the first moment of faith, for the way
to be made clear. Eliot as wayfarer says:

> I said to my soul, be still, and wait with-
> out hope
> For hope would be hope for the wrong thing; wait
> without love
> For love would be love of the wrong thing; there
> is yet faith
> But the faith and the love and the hope are all in
> the waiting.
> Wait without thought, for you are not ready
> for thought:
> So the darkness shall be the light, and the still-
> ness the dancing.
> Whisper of running streams, and winter ligtning.

The wild thyme unseen and the wild strawberry,
The laughter in the garden, echoed ecstacy
Not lost, but requiring, pointing to the agony
Of death and birth.[5]

Summary of What is Un-simple in my responses to the Holy

In summary, we can see that my personal reactions
to the powerlessness, aloneness and vulnerability experienced in the awakening of my spirit is defensive as
I try to remain omnipotent, covering up for my limitations. My inability to acknowledge the Holy as ultimate
concern in my life causes me to displace the Holy by
lesser values in my interaction with others in society.
And lastly, the profane orientation of my culture makes
it difficult and almost impossible for me to find my
life rooted in the Holy. We have lost our simplicity
of life. How can the religious person recover this
lost simplicity? How can we "unfold" and "uncover" an
original orientation to life so as to allow the Holy to
be our ultimate concern and motivating force? In the
following section we will present the "way" of Lao Tzu
as a return to simplicity. We will also show that a
return to true childlikeness is a return to our roots
in the Holy.

RETURN TO CHILDLIKENESS AS A RETURN TO SIMPLICITY

Lawrence Sullivan[6]

The "Way" of Lao Tzu--A Way of Simplicity

The classical Chinese word for way, "Tao," expresses the supreme mystery of the universe as well as the
spiritual direction for human life. Lao Tzu records a
"way" as a way of entire simplicity and childlikeness.
Replying to a disciple's request, he gives basic advice
about this Way of Life:

> Can you hold the One thing fast in your em-
> brace? Can you keep from losing it? . . .
> Can you rest where you ought to rest? Can
> you stop when you have enough? Can you give
> over thinking of other men and seek what you
> want in yourself alone? Can you flee from the
> allurements of desire? Can you maintain an

129

entire simplicity? Can you become a little child?[7]

The disciple further inquires whether <u>pursuing</u>
entire simplicity constitutes perfection. Lao Tzu
responds in the negative, for he says a child moves
about unconscious of what is being done or where one
is going. So, too, the one who seeks to return to
simplicity seeks without pursuing or striving after it:

Those who would by learning attain to this
seek for what they cannot learn. Those who would
by effort attain to this, attempt what effort
can never affect. Those who aim by reasoning
to reach it, reason where reasoning has no place.
To know when to stop is the highest attainment.[8]

A distinctive element of Lao Tzu's thinking is the
return to the simplicity of a child who does not become
anxious over complicating difficulties met along the
way. For Lao Tzu, this is the key to spiritual growth.
To advance along the spiritual way one must first
rectify one's inner world and its conflicting tendencies
and only then can the outer complications be approached.
Great priority is given to establishing inner peace and
avoiding the danger of over extending oneself. The
way is easy and yet most people prefer to take by-paths
that lead them far from their goal. He says, "without
stirring abroad, one can know the whole world; without
looking out of the window, one can see the way to heaven."[9] The way to heaven hides its power in stillness,
its strength in weakness. Paradoxically, the way that
leads forward, seems to lead backward, the way of perfection seems to be a return to the beginning. "You
must" says Lao Tzu, "return to being a babe."[10] The
state of infancy most perfectly mirrors complete perfection.

REFLECTION

Like a curious child, the religious person who
desires to simplify a response to life, will find it
simplified by simply being present. One wonders what
life is all about, yet does not want to be overly possessive or pursuing. One wants to have "no fold";
wants to make no claims to what is not one's own, or
stake new territories where one does not belong. To
return to simplicity is to "look again" at who I am
and try to re-discover what God wants of me in this

journey of life. In returning to simplicity, one does not strive after it. Rather, in quieted stillness, one listens, waits and watches for the movement of the Sacred in life.

The difference between "striving for" and "returning to" simplicity can be compared to a similar difference found between a child clinging to its mother's knee or being held in her arms. A child tires more quickly from clinging than from being held. Resting peacefully in the hand of God is far simpler than hanging on to the images I may have of Him. In clinging to these images I cannot see clearly whether it is really God or not. I cannot see others in his sight, nor can I appreciate the beauty of nature all around; nor can I allow God to change for me.

The basic anxieties each person experiences in the presence of the overwhelming mystery of the Holy never really leaves because the Holy is never fully comprehended. The journey of life is never fully walked until it is finished and then one discovers that it is only the beginning. The journey of life, the way to heavenly perfection, should be far less frightening when one puts faith in a loving God. Thus, one way of walking the mysterious road of life is through childlikeness, characterized by establishing inner peace, inner stillness, and by finding one's strength in weakness. In the following section we shall speak a little more concretely about what the characteristic ways of childlikeness demand from the religious person.

Conrad Myers and Thomas Merton[11]
Childlikeness--A Way of Simplicity

The great Zen master Nishida has said: "If my heart can be pure and simple like that of a child, I think that there can be no greater happiness than this."[12] To develop this childlikeness is to grow in the art of self-forgetfulness, to return to the spontaneity of childhood and recover as far as possible, the lost freedom and naturalness of "innocent glee." Becoming once again a little child does not imply returning to a second childhood or becoming childish. Rather, it implies recovering the lost characteristics of childhood in a deeper way: purity, simplicity, unity, innocence, immediacy, spontaneity, naturalness and freedom. A sage is one who has recovered these characteristics and has attained the spiritual maturity that rises

above the artificiality of do's and don'ts. A return
to true childlikeness is not only an unfolding, a
recovery of what was once there, it is a genuine transcendence, a spiraling deeper, finding new meaning and
attaining new freedom--seeing with the eyes of a child
while being fully mature. Having this childlike simplicity is being true to the self one has been destined
to be from the beginning of time.

REFLECTION

The recovery of childlike simplicity must take
place within the realm of everyday life. The moments
in which we stand more deeply in the everyday also call
us to reaffirm and reappreciate the simplicity of the
experience itself. These moments also allow us to perceive the Holy that surrounds and permeates each of
these happenings, calling for a still greater response
of simplicity.

While a child exists before the distinctions between the Holy and the world are made, the sage exists
beyond artificial distinctions, and is able to spiral
more deeply into the mystery of everyday life and is
present there in purity, simplicity and spontaneity.
The sage treads the way of seeing the Holy and the
world as interpenetrating each other. A deep reverence
and respect for the everyday because of the awe-filled
mystery, becomes present within. The spontaneity of a
child that was once there is rediscovered.

Whether I am a mother in a home providing for the
needs of my family, a career woman engaged in the world
of business, or a teacher intent upon leading the students to a fuller, more personal knowledge--my response
may become one of greater simplicity if I live out my
life commitments by being true to the self I have been
called to be. In other words, living simplicity does
not depend upon what I do as much as it depends upon
how I do it. For example, as a mother in the home I
may provide for the minimal needs of husband and children. Or, I may express my full concern and reverence
for them by attempting to draw them out of themselves
to be the best person each of them can be. The reverence and respect I show towards them, the permeating
presence of the Holy I sense in all events, and the
respect with which I use things to beautify the home all
point to a deep reverence for all of creation because of

the horizon of the Holy that surrounds the whole of my
life.

I may be a "sage" only in the arena of my own home,
office or classroom. Unlike other sages, the extent of
my following is unimportant as long as I continue to
unfold in simplicity as I allow and aid others to unfold in theirs in relation to the sacred dimension of
life. When the Sacred becomes my ultimate concern, with
all other concerns rightly subordinate to that concern,
my response to all persons, events and things can be
none other than simple.

In the journey of a return to simplicity lies the
renewal of wonder and the sanctity of everyday experience, the rediscovery of the mystery within the common-
placeness in all persons, events and things. The inward
journey is a recovery of the self I am in relation to
all that is. It is an ongoing unfolding of my own unique spiritual identity within the situations of my life
and in relationship with the Holy who continues to make
itself known in the everydayness of life. In essence,
I will be most a sage when I am most myself. My responses will be most simple when they are in tune with
my deepest self.

Summary and Transition

In the chapter we have just concluded we have
stressed the necessity of discovering what is un-simple
about my response to the Holy. From very early in life
each person yearns for the Holy and yet fearfully tries
to deny its Call. Life soon loses its simplicity as a
defensive system is built to keep the person protected
from the experience of total aloneness, lostness and
vulnerability.

Life becomes further "folded up" by my inability
to acknowledge the Holy as the ultimate concern of my
life. God becomes displaced by excessive involvement
in theory, work, power, sex, or inauthentic religion.
And because of the profane orientation of my culture,
the transcendent realm of the everyday is not acknowledged and some times even denied.

How do we recover this lost simplicity of life?
By striving and not striving; by returning to simplicity
but not pursuing it; by simply being present to the Holy

as he shows himself in light or darkness in the persons, events and things of everyday life. By being present in inner stillness and peace amidst the complexities of life, I will be far freer to return to an ever deepening simplicity.

Through reflection and meditation on who I am called to be, I may be led to simplify my responses. And I may come to know the God of love who calls me uniquely to be myself in relation to Him. Though I will never fully comprehend his ways or my relationship to Him, through the search for simplicity I may come to find my life more centered in the Divine and more in tune with who I am called to be in Him.

In this division we have spoken of the partial encounters with the Holy in either in-being (as in Zen) or in counter-being (as in Judaism). As we shall see in the Third Part, "in-being, counter-being and personal intimacy form a three dimensional unity of the fully unfolded spiritual encounter with the Divine."[13] Personal intimacy with the Divine is only possible because of the personal love of the Divine made incarnate in Jesus Christ. When this intimacy becomes the ultimate concern of my life, my life may become an imitation of the life of Christ. Through the everydayness of Christ's life, through his relationship with his disciples, his followers, his mother and even the Pharisees and rulers, he lived simply in response to the Father's will. He calls each of us to live our lives in simplicity too.

ENDNOTES

[1] Adrian van Kaam, op. cit. pp. 161-162.

[2] William Kraft, The Search for the Holy (Philadelphia: Westminster Press, 1971), pp. 124-166.

[3] Adrian van Kaam, Personality Fulfillment in the Spiritual Life (Denville, New Jersey: Dimension Books, 1966), pp. 70-122.

[4] Eliot, op. cit., p. 29.

[5] Ibid., p. 28.

[6] Lawrence Sullivan, "Therese of Lisieux and the Wisdom of China," Spiritual Life, XIX:3 (Fall, 1973), 179-203; and Lao Tsze, The Simple Way of Lao Tsze (Surrey, England: The Shrine of Wisdom, 1951), pp. 10-52.

[7] Ibid., pp. 183-184. Here Sullivan quotes from Book 23 of Chuang Tzu: Genius of the Absurd, Clae Waltham, editor, (New York: Ace Books, 1971).

[8] Ibid., p. 184.

[9] Ibid.

[10] Ibid., p. 188.

[11] Conrad Hyers, Zen and the Comic Spirit (Philadelphia: Westminster Press, 1973), pp. 170-180; and Thomas Merton, Zen and the Birds of Appetite (New York: New Directions, 1968), pp. 54-70.

[12] Merton, Ibid., p. 70.

[13] Adrian van Kaam, In Search of Spiritual Identity (Denville, New Jersey: Dimension Books, 1975), p. 314.

PART THREE

THE CHRISTIAN CALL TO SIMPLICITY

INTRODUCTION

Jesus came as a tiny babe when the world had hoped for a powerful leader who would free them from their centuries of bondage. He was born and grew in grace, wisdom and age in the small country villages of Bethlehem and Nazareth, not as we might have expected, in the prophetic city of Jerusalem. He spoke of his Father and the kingdom of heaven in parables using the symbols of bread and water, life and death when the people had anticipated a ruler who would liberate the oppressed by wielding his unsurpassable power.

He came quietly and unobtrusively so that those who could see and hear his message could respond to Him in freedom, with a loving heart intent upon doing His will. He did not coerce any one to follow him, yet he was followed by the multitudes who could sense his new and exciting message. He came to call. They had the option to respond.

Christ beckons his followers today in the same manner. But like the people of his time, Christians today are allowed the freedom tc respond or not. Many today, like the people in Christ's own time, tend to look for the great and mighty, the glorious tidings of his message, instead of following his call in simple day to day faithfulness. Therefore, in the Christian part of this study, we will again look at the slowing down that is necessary to return again to that state of childlike responsiveness and dependence that has somehow been left behind. Through the grace of Baptism I have the possibility of responding in an ever greater simplicity because of the relationship of intimacy that God has established through Christ. But before that is possible, I have to let go of the grand ideas and expectations I have of Christ and listen to his word in the stillness of my heart. Only then will Christ become the ultimate concern of my life. My life may grow in simplicity as daily my relationship with Christ becomes more personal, more truly my own.

137

CHAPTER VI

SLOWING DOWN TO DISCOVER MY RELATIONSHIP WITH CHRIST

INTRODUCTION

There was one of the Pharisees called Nicodemus,
a leading Jew, who came to Jesus by night and
said, "Rabbi, we know that you are a teacher who
comes from God; for no one could perform the
signs that you do unless God were with him."
Jesus answered:
  "I tell you most solemnly,
  unless a man is born from above,
  he cannot see the kingdom of God."
Nicodemus said, "How can a grown man be born?
Can he go back into his mother's womb and be
born again?" Jesus replied:
  "I tell you most solemnly,
  unless a man is born through water and the
  Spirit,
  he cannot enter the kingdom of God:
  what is born of the flesh is flesh,
  what is born of the Spirit is spirit.
          (John 3:1-6) [1]

Nicodemus is a person of our times, as well as his
own, one who is trying to understand the hidden meaning
of things with intellect alone. Christ says to him
you must be born again; you must, in other words, develop the trusting ways of a child. See what is really
there. Allow the Spirit to move you where it wills.
Allow the grace of Baptism to cleanse your eyes and
ears to see and hear things with your inner senses
attuned to the hidden meaning of the message of Christ.

The process of slowing down, of being born again
to allow the spirit full play in my life, is not an
easy task. As I discovered in my retreat experience,
it is far easier to be involved in the hectic pace of
life, unthinkingly performing tasks in the name of
Christ instead of slowing down to discover the deeper
meanings, the hidden message of Christ calling me to a
personal relationship with Him. In this chapter I
shall discuss this return to childlikeness, this being
born again to which Christ calls each of us through the
grace of Baptism.

Tying in with the previous two parts, I shall follow the same general format throughout this chapter.
To research the Christian call to simplicity, I shall
first distinguish the Christian faith experience from
the natural faith experience I spoke of previously.
Since the Christian faith experience is a gift from God
calling a person into a deeper relationship, a Christian
can only respond in grateful love to God who is revealed
in nearness.

Adrian van Kaam
Christian Faith Experience

     For the Christian, the faith dimension of religious
experience is dominant. The faith experience permeates
and transforms religious experience with a new awareness,
with a new insight. Rather than experience the Divine
as a vague, somewhat illusory ground of being, the Holy
Spirit enables a Christian in faith experience to see
the Divine ground as being very intimate, as being very
near. This is the most essential distinguishing characteristic of Christian faith. The essence of Christianity is the announcement that the great mystery that
permeates, encompasses, and surrounds the universe is a
personal God of nearness, who calls me to an intimate
relationship with Him.

     This calling God I cannot see. Neither can I know
what I am being called to be. The call that I receive
comes as a whisper, leaving me free to hear the call or
to deny its existence in the everyday situations of
life. I can only reach out to my call step by step as
I grow through successive transcendent life ideals as
they appear in the concrete situations of life. In
other words, van Kaam notes:

          full religious spiritual experience is the
          situated intimate encounter with a personal
          saving mystery that carries, encompasses and
          permeates me totally and calls me to a free
          unique destiny in its eternal project.[2]

The faith encounter with God is not a lofty or vague
experience; it is the concrete, personal presence of
God in my life. It is concretized, first of all, in
God becoming man in the person of Jesus Christ. Secondly,
the faith encounter becomes personal for me as I wait in
readiness to hear the subtle calls of God in the situa-

139

tions of my life. Christian faith experience is the
openness to accept the gift of grace that God may be-
stow upon anyone who remains open to that call.

REFLECTION

To describe this faith experience more concretely,
let us take a brief look at Christ's encounter with
Nicodemus. Nicodemus stands at the balancing point between natural religious experience and the Christian
faith experience. Being a master in Israel he knew
well the rituals and laws, the history of his people and
their response to the goodness of God. Christ's message
--unless a man is born from above, he cannot see the
kingdom of God--jolted him. How was he, a grown man to
be born again? Was he to forget all that he knew and
experienced, give up all the prized concepts he held
about God? This was asking too much of one who dearly
loved his God.

Nicodemus was in a dilemma. On the one hand, there
was something about Christ that captivated his attention.
He sensed that God was with Christ, that he experienced
a deep relationship with God. Christ spoke profoundly
about the Father's love. Nicodemus sensed that Christ
was not just talking about this relationship but that
he truly lived it-- " . . . no one would perform the
signs that you do unless God were with him." And yet,
on the other hand, Christ's words confused and troubled
him. His God has been a gracious and generous God.
Christ no longer spoke of a God of justice, but of a
God of love who draws himself into nearness to those
who would come to Him in faith and fidelity. For Christ,
God is no longer personified in the image of a judge who
controls His life from a distance. Christ now speaks
about God as his Father, a God who directly intervenes
in all of life's happenings. God has made himself known
in a new way in the everyday situations of life. God
was a person for Christ, a person more exalted than any
other and yet more near and intimate than any other. He
could be called by no other name than Father.

Christ explains to Nicodemus how a man is to be reborn. The waters of Baptism cleanse and simplify. These
waters clarify and wash away subtle distinctions and
systematized concepts that are too rigorous and to some
extent paralyzing. The grace of the Holy Spirit blows
where it will. When a person is ready to be reborn that
person may be able to respond to the power of the Spirit

working within a unique spirit. When anyone, like
Nicodemus, lends too attentive an ear to human reasoning
alone, the kingdom cannot be entered. Rather, a person
remains wandering through all the outer precincts of
truth, knocking on all the doors of human reasoning,
peering curiously through the windows of insight, but
never fully entering the kingdom within unless that
person is willing to be reborn, willing to allow the
Spirit to move where He wills.

Christ's message to his followers today is the same.
Unless I am willing to be cleansed, to be born anew
through the grace of Baptism, I never come to the fullness of experience with Christ who continues to show
himself through the everyday situations of life. Christ
calls me to a relationship with His Father that is comparable to His relationship with Him. Thus, Christian
faith seems to be founded on the unifying principle of
love. Only out of love for the Father will I let go of
my own concepts of Him to allow Him to share his love
with me. Pure love presupposes a childlike faith in the
fatherly goodness of God and a boundless trust in His
mercy. Pure love presupposes that, urged and invited by
this immense goodness, the human heart will set itself
determinately to render love for love. When love of God
becomes the ultimate concern of my life as a Christian,
I may discover His goodness both in the trials He sends
to purify and simplify my love for Him; and in the joys
and the love He sends to confirm His love for me by
drawing me to the fullness of stature he has destined
for me in calling me to be a follower of His.

Kevin O'Shea speaks of the necessity of "resensing"
the grace of Baptism through the everyday encounter with
the person of Jesus Christ. In the following section
O'Shea gives us insight into the unexplainable mystery
that each person is, and how in response to grace one's
life may become simplified through the tenderness and
intimate love of Christ.

Kevin O'Shea[3]
Encounter with the Person of Christ

O'Shea says that the classic word <u>koinonia</u> (which
means communion) gives a key to the meaning of grace.
We have been made companions of the divine nature
through grace. God has opened up to us, giving himself
in communion with us. We are made whole, are healed of
our brokenness by the bond of tenderness extended to us

by Christ through the gift of living grace which is the experience of being at one with oneself and with the living God. In the da'ath (which means intimacy experience) of God's love, each person may sense that through the healing of grace, the non-direction and complicated motivations of life are cleansed.

In the total experience of the healing power of grace viewed with a new understanding of grace as communion, our focus naturally shifts to the relationship each person may have with Jesus. Because Christ is like us in all things save sin, he experienced deeply the healing and whole-making presence in the total and unconditional acceptance he experienced from His Father. Because His experience of the Divine presence was so intimate, he could no longer refer to this presence as "God" or "Yahweh." Instead, he coined a new word that expressed his deeper relationship. O'Shea refers to this happening as an Abba experience, an experience in which he expressed the human discovery that God, Israel, the unnamable One was a Person--a Person in a unique and new sense. He also experienced himself in a new way. He experienced himself as someone so intimately and utterly related to and accepted by Abba that He was Abba's exact co-relative, His very Son, His well-beloved.

Through the healing power of grace we also sense a like relationship. We know an identification with Jesus that allows us to also experience the Abba. We too, with Christ, can say "Abba." We can locate God as the source of the tremendous gift of grace and know God as a personal One. In this sense we experience the profound awareness that everything that has been done in and through Christ through grace, is also done in us because of a very great love for us.

This special gift of grace is only possible because of the gifting of the Holy Spirit. "The Spirit is the bond of love between Abba and Jesus, and the Spirit is the bond set by the creative love of Abba with us, for the sake of Jesus, and in union with Jesus."[4] The experience is of the deepest Spirit of God. It is the discovery of the meaning of being human. Thus, as O'Shea remarks, humanness is the condition of a graced person.

The healing of grace provides a unified focus for many mysteries, human and divine. It implies a way of life that is exceedingly simple, not only because it is centered on a single experience, it is even more simple because that experience of being graced is knowing the healing presence that is given. Living in the healing presence of grace suggests living in the total simplicity of the present moment in the wisdom of the accepted grace. An attitude of simplicity allows God to be present in life in a very real way, not as a distant, independent, unrelated aspect of life. It simply lets God live in the trust, transparency and compassion that characterizes the One God. By resensing this graced presense and responding to the continual gift of grace, one receives the quiet assurance that the grace for the next step of authentic development is already there, waiting to be received. It is a response of continuing and deepening dependence upon the gift of grace in a relationship of intimacy with God.

REFLECTION

Through the experience of God as a God of nearness, as one calling me to a personal intimacy, I can only respond out of the deepest self that I am. Because of the gift of grace that I have experienced, I have been given a "taste" of God, I have been identified and have been touched by God. As Thomas Merton says, "ultimately the only way that I can be myself is to become identified with Him in Whom is hidden the reason and fulfillment of my existence."[5] All distinctions, all divisions seem to disappear as I find myself identified and related to Him. In this intimate relationship I can be most myself because I do not have to hide anything from One who already knows all there is to know about me. Because of the gift of grace I will be able to find God in discovering my own deepest spiritual identity, my own deepest self, because it is firmly rooted in God, related to in love, and ready to respond to all affairs of daily life. Through the personal encounter with Christ I may come to discover the unfolding will of God in my life.

In the following section I shall search a bit more deeply into the intimacy relationship I am called to through the grace of Baptism. I will also explore how this relationship may be lived out in the concrete daily situations of life. In the previous section I have presented only one aspect of this relationship, that is, the gift of grace that God bestows. In this section another aspect, that of the Christian response, will be explored.

Adrian van Kaam[6]
Christian Experience of Intimacy

For the Christian, faith is the total response to
the invitation of intimacy extended by God through
Christ. Because faith is a total response to God who
has become our ultimate concern, it cannot be merely an
act of the mind, but calls for a response from the total
person. Faith as the source of the fundamental attitude
of the Christian spiritual life, is our presence to a
God who is revealed as the One who wants to be our intimate lover. As van Kaam remarks, with my intelligence
I acknowledge God as the one who wants to be for me a
redeeming and uniting love; and with my will I assent
and surrender to this love.

Since faith implies a surrender to Christ who is
the visible personification of the Divine initiative in
my life, it also suggests a gradual metamorphosis of
the human way of the spirit already lived implicitly by
all Christians in some measure. Surrender to Christ
involves a surrender to the gift of God who offers self
to each person as the object of a faith, hope and love
that transcends human nature. This gift of God to us is
grace. In response to this gift of grace, a person
surrenders oneself, is willing to be reborn, and for the
first time, becomes one's own true and deepest self.

Faith is the revelation of God in the hidden core
of my being. God is the One who calls me to a unique
relationship of intimacy of life and love. Grace gives
rise to my recognition of God as my destiny and fulfillment, as my intimate and lasting friend, though I may
never fully understand what this relationship implies.
Therefore, living in grace is a prayerful search for
the hidden God. It is an attempt to come to know God
in the quiet whispers of everyday life.

At times I feel the need to emphasize this hidden
presence of God in my life. Through worshipful concentration in prayer, my attention is focused on the Presense itself that pervades my graced and spiritual
identity and on its many incarnations in persons, events
and things in the day to day world. Through successive
life events God is made known as my intimate lover,
friend and Father/Mother. As I Become more attuned to
hearing the whisperings of God, our relationship becomes
a relationship of intimacy.

144

Differing from the relationships of in-being and counter-being spoken of earlier, the experience of intimacy combines the relationships of being alike and being different into an experience of freely chosen togetherness that transcends and integrates the two components of sameness and uniqueness.[7] All three aspects, that is, in-being, counter-being and transcending intimacy, are, according to van Kaam, essential constituents of a full grown, loving encounter. In Christianity we find the fullness of all three dimensions of spiritual experience. God is proclaimed in Christianity as a loving Being--so loving that we in Christ become one with God, for in Christ we are adopted sons and daughters.

REFLECTION

> I shall not call you servants any more,
> because a servant does not know his
> master's business;
> I call you friends,
> because I have made known to you
> everything I have learnt from my Father.
> (John 15:15)

In the Judaic tradition the Jews experienced themselves as servants, even though they were servants to a loving master. A servant does not know his master's business--the master would only give to the servant what was needed to carry out the tasks for which he was hired. Because he was servant, he was, in a sense, held in bondage. He was neither free to respond to nor ignore the requests of his master. As servant he had to obey or find himself without a master. Christ tells his disciples that their relationship to him is no longer the relationship of servant to master but one of friend or child to father, as Christ is child of the Father. But even in this relationship, the Father does not reveal everything to a child at one time--it would be too much for the child to remember or to respond to. Rather, a father, out of concern for the welfare of his child, reveals only that which can he understand.

In instructing the disciples, Christ speaks of his relationship to God, the Father. Everything that Christ has learned from the Father he willingly shares with us because God has called us to a like relationship through Christ. The foremost message that Christ communicates

145

with us is the message of love. This message of love is shared with us through the Holy Spirit who graces us with a likeness of God in our spirit. A relationship of intimacy does not imply that we come to know God fully. That is as impossible as anyone knowing my inner self fully except my own spirit. This relationship of intimacy can only be shared with those who also accept the aspect of not-knowing, of God remaining hidden though at the same time holding himself in nearness.

Christ allows us to be so utterly free that we have the option to respond or not to God in nearness. Because he has called us to be friends or sons in intimacy, he asks us to listen to him in the stillness of a loving heart. Christ has made known to us everything that the Father has revealed to Him. In my life I have the option to listen and respond. Through my retreat experience I realize that the only message I have been listening to was the message that came forth from my own reasoning, from my own concerns. God was a distant God. I did not take the time to allow myself to listen to whispered words to me. I could not discover what was being asked of me in my life because my interests were centered on my own concerns, my students, the image I wanted to give to my students and other teachers. The only time that I was even vaguely aware of my intimate relationship with Christ was in the few brief moments when I found myself hemmed in by the non-direction of my life. I had become a slave to the work I was performing. I also became a slave to the calls I thought I was receiving from God. Now, by slowly waiting for God's love for me to unfold in the daily happenings of life, I am not thrown by the seeming non-direction much of daily life often leads to. I can wait for the revelations of the whisperings of God is made known in the students I meet day by day, in events--both joyful and filled with pain--and in things that remind me of a caring presence for me. I realize that unless God is the ultimate concern of my life, there is no meaning, or not much less that scattered meaning. Therefore, I need to constantly, gently, re-evaluate my life motivations and ideals.

Christ lives, not only in the historical time of two millenia ago; he also lives in a very real sense today. Though I do not experience Him at all times, there are key situations that "turn the trend" of the day and prove to be stepping stones to a yet greater intimacy with Christ. In the following section we will look briefly at both historical and personal key situations that may clarify my relationship with Christ.

Adrian van Kaam[8]
Key Situations

It is important that we become aware of the situations in which we may experience the self-communication of God in concrete daily life. van Kaam has differentiated these into historical and personal key situations. Historical key situations are those that we receive through our Christian heritage recorded in Old Testament, New Testament writings and in the writings of spiritual masters who experienced the self-communication of God in the concrete dailiness of their everyday lives.[9] Personal key situations are as important and not in opposition to historical situations. They are situations of early life in which God allows for the modification of natural affinities. For example--a child may be baptized at birth because of the Christian atmosphere that will surround the child in his home. God may use the situation of the home to modify the child's inner spiritual affinity and to lead the child to a possible intimate experience of Christ because of the surroundings of that home. Although at times the atmosphere of the home may not be the most conducive for spiritual growth, it does set the child on a pathway that if looked at in the proper light, allows for the unfolding of the plan of God for the unique emergence of the child's spiritual identity.

The importance of these key situations lies in the fact that they "hook" into each other. That is, the historical key situations, those experienced in doing spiritual reading and participating in word and sacrament of the Church, must find meaning in the daily situations of life. Through both historical and personal key situations, it is important that the person remain open to the possible self-communication of God. In drawing together the occasions of both historical and personal situations a person may unfold and discover one's own spiritual identity in the step by step revelation of God's love and care in the immediate situations of life. In the following reflection we shall pause briefly at three situations that may call for a simplification of my life.

147

REFLECTION

In the course of their journey he came to a
village, and a woman named Martha welcomed
him into her house. She had a sister called
Mary, who sat down at the Lord's feet and
listened to him speaking. Now Martha who
was distracted with all the serving said,
"Lord, do you not care that my sister is
leaving me to do the serving all by myself?
Please tell her to help me." But the Lord
answered: "Martha, Martha," he said, "you
worry and fret about so many things, and yet
few are needed, indeed only one. It is Mary
who has chosen the better part; it shall not
be taken from her. (Luke 10:38-42)

Christ's meeting with Mary and Martha took place
centuries ago but it is pregnant with meaning for my
life today. Martha invited Christ into her home and
became busy about serving his needs. She anxiously
tried to serve him. Mary, on the other hand, found
solace in his presence and quietly sat at his feet waiting and listening to what he had to say. In other words,
Martha is concerned about may things, but all of them
are finite, preliminary, and transitory. Mary is concerned about one thing which is infinite, ultimate and
lasting.

As I reflect upon this meeting between Christ and
his two friends I wonder what meaning this passage from
scripture has for me. It can remain just a story, an
incident in the life of Christ. Or, it may become for
me a key situation, one in which I begin to question my
relationship with Christ.

Am I more like a Martha concerned about serving
what I perceive to be the immediate needs of Christ? Am
I filled with anxiety and worry about doing the right
things, giving a good impression, serving the needs of
others? Am I more concerned about what I do than about
what Christ is asking of me? Christ may be saying to
me: you worry and fret over so many things, yet one
thing is necessary. If I am like Martha every preliminary, superficial concern becomes ultiamte, demanding
my whole heart, mind and strength. Being caught up with
less than ultimate concerns saps my energy. I haven't
the time nor the insight to discover the one, ultimate
concern--Christ--underneath the pretext of busyness.

Even though the Mary-like stance is more true to the calling of Christ, the Martha concern is necessary and good. The difficulty with her multi-faceted concerns is that lesser concerns do have the tendency to substitute for greater concerns, for the one concern--love of God.

If my stance in life is to become more like Mary's, I need to listen in the way that Mary listened. I cannot be busy at all times about the business of the Lord. At times I need to sit quietly at his feet so that he can reveal to me how I am loved. My life will become immensely simplified if Christ becomes my ultimate concern and if doing his will becomes the guiding and motivating force in my life.

As Christ said of Mary--she has chosen the better part and it shall not be taken from her--so too, one who chooses to simplify her response to the many calls of life will find that even in the scattered activities that call for one's attention there is a peaceful calm, a feeling of centeredness and serenity that shall not be taken away.

Another historical key situation that may hook into my life experience can be found in the lives of the early Christians. They seem to be liberated by the message of Christ. They lived a life of simplicity that was free from legalistic preoccupation about the right and wrong ways of eating, the right and wrong ways of living. Thomas Merton quotes the words of the first Christians: "to praise God and to take one's food in simplicity of heart."[10] For them, receiving the word of Christ was accepting the dynamic gift of grace and living in the fullness of love given to them through Christ. Legalism and mere concern with external ritual detracted from the message that Christ delivered to them.

In light of the response of the early Christians, I may question my response to the fullness of the message of Christ. Do I live my personal conviction that Christ is the ultimate concern of my life? Do my actions bespeak a simplicity of heart? Or, am I more concerned about the image I portray, the doing of the "right thing" whether my heart is in the action or not? If I reflect upon the way in which I approached the retreat experience, I discover that my actions speak more about

149

appearance than about actual performance in the name of
Christ. I discovered through this experience that the
only true response I could give to the scattered non-
direction of my life was to let go of the multiple concerns and find my life centered--like Mary and the early
Christians--on fulfilling the will of the Father in my
life. To discover what that will is for me and to be
able to say "yes" to that will calls for a deep, personal relationship with Christ in the dailiness of my life.
It demands a transformation of my way of being through
a personal intimate relationship with Christ. van Kaam
gives insight into this needed transformation, and how
this transformation brings about a simplification of
life.

Adrian van Kaam[11]
Personal Relationship with Christ

        Through a relationship of intimacy with Christ, I
may become transformed into the unique design that God
has intended for me from the beginning of time. This
transformation may take place through the present moment which is the sacrament of the Divine Will here and
now in my unique life situation. In response to God's
grace, the defects that keep me from fully loving God
or others, are spiritualized. God demands that I cooperate with a saving help. St. Augustine, in one of
his sermons, has said that "He that created you without your knowledge, will not save you without your consent."[12] As my life begins to unfold in response to
the ever present grace of the moment, I will be able to
meet the challenges of God's Will for me as it slowly
unfolds through the situations and persons of my life.

        At times, however, I may find that I do not grow
spiritually in spite of the time and energy I spend in
prayer, spiritual reading, mortification and charitable
activities. It may be that I care too much about developing my relationship with Christ. I, in a sense, care
too much, am too preoccupied, too busy about making a
success of my spiritual and personal growth. By my very
actions I say that I am unwilling to remain present in
the simplicity of my heart to the unfolding path of my
life in the present moment.

        On the other hand, I must not be hindered by my
past by worrying needlessly about past failures and
shortcomings. By placing myself as my ultimate concern
or by mourning over the past, I am unable to experience

the joy and equanimity that makes me available for the
relaxed and creative fulfillment of God's will in the
here and now. The more willing I am to listen to the
unique eternal calling to me, the more light will be
shed on who the Lord is for me and what meaning the relationship with Christ holds for me.

van Kaam notes that what is demanded of the true
follower of Christ is a prayerful immersion in the
attitudes of Christ. It requires a sincere self-apprais-
al on the vital, familial, cultural, spiritual and actual
levels of his life through a careful evaluation of his
own unique time and place.[13] In effect, as reasoning
and performing becomes less and less involved, because
of this prayerful immersion in a relationship with Christ
my whole following becomes more and more simplified.

REFLECTION

Francis smiled at the complexity of this own
thoughts. Brother Elias would surely frown at
such complicated thinking from someone so
simple as Francis. But Brother Leo, who had
copied down his words and listened to his
thoughts, would not frown, nor would he smile.
Brother Leo always understood the difference
between a simple man and a simpleton. One is
not born simple; one becomes simple by walking
the maze-like journey out of the cavern of self
into the light. Man is complex and God is
simple and the closer one approaches God, the
simpler one becomes in Faith, Hope and Love.
To be completely simple is to be God, and Francis knew how far he was from being God. His
constant prayer was, "Who are You, O God, and
what am I?"[14]

Francis by his very life lived in an intensely intimate
relationship with Christ. But it was not always so for
Francis. As a young man he found his life scattered,
without meaning and purpose. He sought for pleasure in
song and dance, wine and merry-making. To change his
life and find meaning there, he had to do an "about face."
His transformation was so radical that he appeared to
have gone mad. His joy was so complete in the Lord
that he appeared to be delirious. His transformation
was not something that took place merely in times alone
in prayer. His being "stung by the dart of love for

God" affected the whole of his life. He lived Christ so intensely that he saw Christ in each poor beggar, he experienced God's love in each creature. His life of poverty and utter simplicity spoke more about his relationship with Christ than words could ever tell. He had scaled the walls of the cavern of self-preoccupation and grew in the warmth and light of Christ's love.

His life became filled with a deeper joy than he could express. His only sadness was that he was not completely transformed into the person God had intended him to be. He counted the blessings he did receive and prayed constantly to know God still more intimately and to know his place in that relationship.

For me to discover the will of God in my life also takes a radical transformation. Through my retreat experience I saw the light ever so briefly. I still have to continue to scale the walls of my own self-preoccupation to find my ultimate concern in Christ alone. At times the will of God for my life seems crystal clear. Then it is easy for me to accept the burdens of the day. I don't feel lost and alone. But at times when I become caught up with myself, God seems to be hidden. I find my life complicated and uncentered. Every little burden that crosses my path appears as another mountain to be scaled. When I am so self-centered I cannot accept the differences of others, nor can I accept the message of God they might be whispering to me in their call for my love and care for them. With Francis I need to pray: Who are You, O God, and what am I? It is only in discovering and unfolding my relationship with God through the everyday meeting of persons, events and things that speak of that presence, can I grow in intimacy with my God. Though the process of growth seems difficult, I know that with the continued gift of grace and love I may find my life centered. I may find my life then simplified and filled with a tranquillity and peace. But before that may begin to happen I realize that I need to step aside, to go into solitude in prayer and meditation to be able to find love present in the active involvements of the day. In the following section we shall consider meditation and prayer as means of communicating with Christ in every day life and as a means of simplifying life.

MEDITATION AND PRAYER AS MEANS OF COMMUNICATING
WITH CHRIST IN EVERYDAY LIFE

In parts One and Two we spoke of each person's
possibility of distancing oneself from immediate involvements by reflecting on the meaning these involvements
may have for life and the possibility of becoming more
in touch with the Holy in the everydayness of life
through the practice of meditation. In this Part, meditation and prayer will be presented as ongoing means of
deepening one's relationship with Christ As in the
previous Parts I hope to show that, among other things,
meditation and prayer are necessary to come to a simplification of life in response to the call of Christ.
First of all, we will consider aspects of van Zeller's
thought that relate prayer and meditation to the simplification of life in response to God who is more simple.

Hubert van Zeller[15]
Prayer and Meditation as a Response of Simplicity

van Zeller says that the grace of simplicity is
present in every person's life to a degree because each
person has been given a unique identity from which to
reflect the simplicity of God. At times our lives become scattered and complicated because we forget our
relationship with Christ. It is then in Christ that we
fallen creatures are "re-deemed worthy" to stand before
God and reflect simplicity. By looking at the oneness
of God we try to integrate ourselves, to be made whole
by stretching out to the simplicity of God in prayer and
silence.

Through prayer and the practice of silence we become more transparent as we move away from the selfishness which has enveloped us in a fog of confusion.
When we stop making evaluations on our progress we become more open, more artless, less concerned about the
reactions of others. When all that matters to us is the
life of God to which we have become heirs through Baptism, we will become dispossessed of ourselves and truly
become adopted children.

We find recorded in the Book of Proverbs: "God's
communication is to people of simple heart." (Proverbs
7:1-3). In order to answer this call and receive the
gifts prepared for us we have only to unlearn worldly
wisdom and prepare ourselves for the communication of
grace from grace itself. A person of prayer and meditation, one who places all hope, joy and love on the dom-

153

inant theme of Christ as the cornerstone, Christ as the
head of the body, Christ whose resurrection is the
ground of all our faith and the surity of all our hope,
finds life centered and simplified. Christ then becomes
for a person of prayer the way to God, the embodiment of
truth, the perfection and source of life. Thus centered
on Christ, the person of prayer acquires a certain over-
all grasp of who he is in Christ which relieves that
person from searching too closely into the ways of God
and of trying to work out God's mysteries. It is this
kind of person whom St. Paul has in mind when he prays
that:

> Out of his infinite glory, may he give you the
> power through his Spirit for your hidden self
> to grow strong, so that Christ may live in your
> hearts through faith, and then, planted in love
> and built on love, you will with all the saints
> have strength to grasp the breadth and the length,
> the height and the depth; until, knowing the
> love of Christ which is beyond all knowledge,
> you are filled with the utter fullness of God.
> (Eph. 3:16-19)

Holding all things in readiness in silence and recollection, a person of prayer prepares for the revelation of Christ to take place. Our likeness to Christ
is developed mostly in the waiting, in the darkness of
unknowing. Here it is also most possible that a person
will grow in the simplicity that is a reflection of the
light of Christ. When a person is wholly bent upon God
in prayer, the thousand fretting cares and vexing problems which tear the lives of others into pieces, simply
cease to exist.

To speak more concretely about one who has centered
her life in Christ, we will present Mary as an example
of a person who found her life exceedingly simple because of her ability to wait peacefully for whatever the
Word had to tell her.

Sister Miriam Louise[16]
She Pondered the Word in Her Heart

Mary is the supreme model of the Christian who
strives to receive the Word of God, respond to it, and
witness to it before the world. In the little that is
directly recorded about Mary in the New Testament we

become aware of her unique mission to ponder the Word in her heart. When greeted by the angel with the message that she was to be the mother of God, she did not make any false protestations. Rather, in utter simplicity, she asks: how can this come about since I am a virgin? When the angel tells her that the spirit will overshadow her, she rejoices because God has deemed her worthy to be the mother of His Son. Her Magnificat of praise confirmed that she was ready to do His will in all things.

Mary's response to the message of the angel was but a beginning. Throughout her life and the trials that she suffered because she was so greatly blessed, she continued to be the one "who ponders the Word of God in her heart." (Luke 2:19) With the special connotation that the word "heart" had for the Hebrews, she pondered the Word in her deepest core, in the center of her being. It was the dwelling place of the "immortal spark--God's own life within the soul.[17] Though she could not always understand the message, she could ponder and wait. She was a woman of prayer, of silence and stillness. From the wedding feast at Cana where she asks the servants to "do whatever He tells you," until she stood at the foot of the cross, each action she performed was done in simplicity because she had first pondered the Word. She was able to trust in her Son because of her intimate relationship with Him.

Finally, we read about Mary and her role in the Church today in Chapter 8 of Lumen Gentium: "Embracing God's saving will with a full heart and impeded by no sin, she devoted herself totally as a handmaid of the Lord to the person and work of her Son."[18] Because of this, Mary can be for us a model of full Christian maturity that is characterized by a simplicity that is centered on Christ alone.

REFLECTION

Reflecting on the life of Mary, one cannot help but be drawn through her to Christ. Her every action ("do whatever He tells you"), her peaceful serenity, ("she pondered the Word of God in her heart"), her peaceful serenity, ("she pondered the Word of God in her heart"), and her very great love and centeredness in Him speak of a deep faith in Christ who has become the sole reason for her existence.

155

Though she was specially blessed, her life was not easy. She suffered the humiliation of conceiving a child out of wedlock. She suffered through the loss of Jesus in the temple. She endured through the ridicule she witnessed being heaped upon her son as he was misunderstood by the teachers of Israel. She agonized through her son's painful and disgraceful death on the cross. The whole of her life was so centered on Christ that even in the midst of these hardships she continued to ponder the Word in her heart. Her life became immensely simplified because of her centeredness and rootedness in Him. Everything seemed to have a reason though she herself could not always voice the why.

I too mean to live a life of simplicity,

> . . . a life that is so unified and single-hearted that it truly can be, in all respects, simple. I mean a simplicity that is so clear and pure that it stands as a silent but unmistakable witness against a world of complexity, ambiguity, and comfortableness; a simplicity that is so utterly possessionless that it is free to discover the preciousness of every creature. I mean a simplicity that is so patient and gentle that it can wait for the inevitable onrush of God's presence and listen to the full message of His whispering within all of nature.[19]

Listening to the Word, peacefully pondering His message in the disharmony and disunity of life can draw my life into simplicity. The pain-filled flash of insight I received during my retreat experience was an experience in which I was drawn to the desire for simplicity through Christ. It was a moment of grace in which I could pause for a few brief moments and allow Him to direct and take over my life. My defenses were down as I realized I had no other option but to turn to Him, to let go with Him. The experience was for me a gifted moment of insight when I could see for the first time that Christ had to become the ultimate concern of my life or I would continue to wander about in helter-skelter fashion for the rest of my life.

That moment has deeply affected my life since then. But I cannot continue to recall that moment alone. I need to remain open, to listen to the new messages that are being whispered to me today by the people I meet, the events in which I participate, and the things of nature that are constantly echoing the message of Christ's love for me. I need to be drawn at times during the day into a prayerful presence to the Lord. In the following section we will see what prayer may mean for today's Christian, and how a right understanding of prayer may lead to a further simplification of life.

Jacques Ellul[20]
Prayer as a Means of Simplification

In order to better understand the meaning of prayer today, we will first present Ellul's thinking on prayer as a response to the invitation of the Word. Secondly, prayer will be presented as obedience to the invitation of the Word as being of the essence of prayer. And lastly, we will consider prayer as a listening to the Will of God.

Prayer as a Response to the Word

Prayer, however spontaneous, fervent, or holy, is never other than a consequence, a sequel to the word of invitation first made known to us through Scripture. Only through faith is the word discerned as coming from God and received from the hands of God alone. Prayer is not the work of faith. It is the <u>possibility</u> of the work of faith if a person is willing to pray without ceasing.

According to Ellul, if we cannot pray, it is ultimately that we cannot believe that God acts, that He is a creator, that He takes a hand in all of reality. On the other hand, we may not believe that prayer will do anything to change His will to suit our prayer, so that our will and His will may perhaps be more in agreement. Both of these notions speak of a misconception of prayer, a lack of real faith in a God who already knows our greatest needs.

Prayer is, instead, a mirror in which we are called to contemplate our spiritual life. Since prayer is a real encounter with God, we can, through it, see ourselves as God sees us. Prayer in the fullest sense of encounter with God appears to spring to the lips directly from the heart. As Ellul notes:

It (prayer) seems to be something more profound, more simple, more direct, more spontaneous in

157

the reality of man, for he is speaking to the
Unknown as to the commander in chief of his
powers and at the same time as to the one who can
hear and understand.[21]

Since prayer is to the Unknown who is distant and
yet very near, we often do not know what the context of
our prayer should be. That is why St. Paul has said
that the Holy Spirit himself "intercedes with sighs too
deep for words." (Romans 8:26-27) Only when the Spirit
intercedes in a way that cannot be expressed, which transcends all verbalizing, then is the prayer, prayer. It
is a relationship with God, "who searched the hearts of
all," (Romans 8:27) and knows our deepest needs. We can
only conclude then that prayer is a gift from God, and
its reality depends upon God.

However, it is not possible to pray without some
kind of risk on our part. Prayer never escapes the risk
of faith or dispenses us from doing what God gives us to
do. Prayer is not a onesided "gifting" from God. Instead, it is a dialogue. God acts and requires us to
act. We must work along with the gift that God gives.
Then is prayer fully answered.

Essence of Prayer: Obedience to the Word

Even though God may be felt to be mute, blind and
deaf to the cry of creatures, the person who prays is
never engaged in a monologue. Even when everything
seems to have gone wrong, (as it did for Elijah in the
Old Testament and for Christ in the Garden of Gethsemane)
one can still pray, "My, God." The relationship is there,
it cannot be taken away or broken by God. We often forget that the fullness of response to God's message may
require a dying, if not to our very life, then to our
desires. Ellul quotes a section from the journals of
Søren Kierkegaard in this regard:

The immediate person thinks and imagines that when
he prays, the important thing, the thing he must
concentrate upon, is that God should hear what HE
is praying for. And yet in the true, eternal
sense, it is just the reverse: the true relation
in prayer is not when God hears what is prayed
for, but when the person praying continues to
pray until he is the one who hears, who hears
what God wills.[22]

158

In prayer God demands a free subject who gives self
in obedience through prayer. But, we for our part,
would rather bring objects which we offer in order to
make God more amiable and understanding. Ellul surmises
that when we come with our hands laden with gifts, they
are really empty. God doesn't want the gifts; he merely
wants our openness to listen.

While most relationships and situations in the
world lead to the breakup of each person into a series
of irreconcilable patterns, scattered activities and
the splintering of personalities, prayer leads to a reunification of life energies. It involves the discovery
of God in the midst of scattered activities that often
speak of his apparent abandonment of us. In other words,
prayer is not just an affair of the moment in which I
speak to God who asks the impossible of me. Prayer instead is the "woof on which is woven the warp of my
occupations, my sentiments, my actions."23 The "warp"
without the "woof" would never weave the tissue of life.
Without prayer we are like children who are carried away
by every solicitation, by every wind of doctrine.

As Christians we are called to be children, not in
the sense of bondage and obedience to the Father, but
in the sense of maturity. The Christian response of
relationship is not like that of an adolescent rebelling
against a parent. It is instead, a response of an adult
who enters into responsible liberty as a child and heir
to the kingdom of God. In calling God, by whatever name
I give, I give up being god to myself. When I pray,
"Our Father" I also pray "Thy will be done." The message
is as simple as that. And because of its simplicity it
is extremely difficult to live what is prayed. The
prayer that Christ taught is centered on God's needs, not
ours. It requires that we realize that God's name needs
to be hallowed by the entire creation and that his will
must be freely obeyed, loved and carried out by each person. How is His will discovered and carried out?
Through genuine prayer.

Listening to the Will of God Through Prayer

Obedience to Christ is the opposite of duty or obli-
gation. There is only the hearing of the word which I
receive and which commands me because of my responsibility in communion and dialogue with Christ. Therefore,
there can be no vigilance, no waiting in prayer without

159

a prior relationship with God. Because of this relationship, Christ could say to the apostles, "Watch with me."
(Mark 14:35) It is also because of this relationship
that prayer eventually becomes joyful, full of power
and hope, even if the occasion be that of Gethsemane.

Prayer of this nature presupposes a ·discipline because prayer is to be intentional and thoughtful, not
haphazard and sporadic. If prayer is to be genuine, it
requires a struggle against the promptings of the world,
which "denature" the relationship with God. Through the
daily, disciplined going aside to pray, life becomes
more inner directed, not guided by consumer satisfaction,
but by an effort to come to a deeper relationship with
Christ through the situations of life.

REFLECTION

Sing God a simple song: Lauda, Laude . . .
Make it up as you go along: Lauda, Laude . . .
Sing like you like to sing.
God loves all simple things.
For God is the simplest of all.[24]

No matter what words one utters in prayer, no
matter where or how one tries to draw together life's
meaning around a central theme, one reoccuring thought
keeps emerging: God, simply God. He is the one who
has called me into being, "has knit me in my mother's
womb" (Ps. 139), has formed a relationship with me that
is like no other. My only true response can be a song
of praise: Lauda, Laude.

As the days slowly unfold into years, my song of
praise can deepen. Through situations of shared joy
and love as well as through the painful moments of dying
and death, the song of praise I sing crescendoes into a
full melody of praise. The more I become like Him, because of a deepening relationship with Him, the simpler
my song will be: praise, only praise.

Because of His lack of double-meaning and duplicity,
His message of love for me should echo loudly and clearly even though at times He may keep Himself in hiding to
keep me from becoming too dependent upon the "good feelings" I may experience when everything seems to be going
my way. Through the reading of scripture and the journals of spiritual masters of the past, I become deeply

convinced that He desires that I "sing my own melody,"
that I don't rely on His consolation but on His love.
Often Christ went apart from the crowds not knowing for
sure if He was about the work of His father or not;
often times too, spiritual writers like Teresa of Avila
and Therese of Lisieux needed to communicate with Him
alone to reassure themselves that all their actions were
guided by love alone.

> I will sing the Lord a new song
> To praise Him, to bless Him, to bless the Lord.
> I will sing His praises while I live
> All my days.
>
> Blessed is the man who loves the Lord,
> Blessed is the man who praises Him.
> Lauda, Lauda, Laude . . .
> And walks in His ways.
>
> I will lift up my eyes
> To the hills from whence comes my help.
> I will lift up my voice to the Lord
> Singing Lauda, Laude.
>
> For the Lord is my shade,
> Is the shade upon my right hand,
> And the sun shall not smite me by day
> Nor the moon by night.
> Blessed is the man who loves the Lord,
> Lauda, Lauda, Laude,
> And walks in His ways.

The words of this song ring praises over and over
again. It seems to re-echo the words of Mary as she
said "yes" to the Will of the Father that she be the
Mother of His Son. She believed with the whole of her
being that He would guide her, strengthen her, help
her to walk in His ways. There was little fear in her
because she loved the Lord and mirrored all that he had
destined her to be.

In order to draw my life into simplicity, I too
must sing the praises of God as only I can. Mine has to
be a "new song of praise" that is in tune with my vital,
personal and spiritual rootings. The melody I sing with
my life must be heard not only in the times that I reflect upon its meaning in a special way in prayer, but
through my everyday actions, through the manner in which

my actions speak of the love of others, even those that try me the most. The disharmony of situations that at times cause me to be defensive and self-righteous also produce a movement in my life's melody.

"Sing God a simple song . . ." Sing a song that is ever more in tune with the fullness of life experience. Let life emerge in simplicity because of a prayer-filled immersion in the life of Christ. Let each action speak of a centeredness in Him, a belief in His saving help, a hope through the darkness of disharmony, and a love that He alone gives to those who love Him in return. With St. Paul we pray: "Glory be to Him whose power, working in us, can do infinitely more than we can ask or imageine . . ." (Eph. 3:20). Trusting in His power and His love I can continue to emerge into the fullness of my destiny even though at times that emergence takes place in darkness and unknowing.

If we reflect upon the words of St. Matthew: "Where your treasure is, there will your heart be also," (Matt. 6:21) we can only conclude that the life of intimacy with Christ can only be maintained as long as <u>nothing</u> is allowed to come between Christ and ourselves. Only by following Christ alone can we preserve a single eye and heart. It is only in resting on the light that comes from Christ, the light that has no darkness or ambiguity about it, that we will be able to discover where our true treasure lies. Working toward a centeredness in Christ, the whole of our lives must be bent upon the "simple intention" of doing the will of God. In the following section Thomas Merton explains the discipline of living in such a manner.

<u>Thomas Merton</u>[25]
<u>Simple Intention</u>

When we have a simple intention we are less occupied with the thing to be done, we are more aware of Him who works in us than we are of ourselves. Merton remarks that it may happen that one who works with this "simple" intention is more perfectly aligned to the exigencies of one's work and does the work far better than the worker of "right" intentions who has no such perspective.

The person of simple intention works always in an atmosphere of prayer, for all that one does is done not only for God but <u>in</u> Him. That person works out of a

recollectedness. Spiritual reserves are not all poured
out in one's work but are stored in the depths of being.
This person is detached from work and leaves the results
of the job to God alone. The end of a simple intention
is to work in God and with Him--"to sink deep roots into
the soul of His will and to grow there in whatever weather He may bring."[26]

Our intention cannot be completely simple unless it
is completely poor, and that is a rare gift of God. It
seeks and desires nothing but God which, in actuality,
is everything. But between the desire for God and the
actualization of that desire in our lives there lies a
huge chasm, a desert that must be traveled in order to
find Him. This waiting in emptiness without intent is
a life of perpetual death in Christ. This simple intention seeks its treasure in heaven. "It prefers what
cannot be touched, counted, weighed, tasted or seen."[27]

In the following section we will see that the goal
of "spiritual childhood" is to live Christian simplicity,
so that the soul through simple intention may abandon
itself wholly to God through the help of grace.

William McNamara, Susan Muto and Lawrence Sullivan[28]
The Way of Christian Spiritual Childhood

Essentially the Christian way of childhood is a
way of entry into the Trinitarian mystery of fatherhood,
filiation and that eternal breathing of love (bestowing
of grace) which is the Holy Spirit. It requires no
strong act, no glittering achievements, no spectacular
successes. What it does require is a total love that
lasts forever. The way of spiritual childhood is a
continual effort to uncover what the Godhead is saying
to me in the here and now moment of my life, my prayer
and my situation. It is an experience of listening to
the Lord who teaches in an aura of childlike simplicity
all that we need to know to enter into union with Him.
"Unless you become as little children you cannot enter
into the kingdom of God." (Matt. 18:3).

The way of spiritual childhood is also characterized by an uncovering, a strengthening of the bond of
love between God and the soul. The result of this bond
is an incredible simplification of life, a being at one
with God in all thought, action and will. Then I may
see as the Little Flower did, that "My task was simpli-

fied as soon as I realized I could do nothing by myself.
Spiritually I bothered about nothing except uniting myself more and more closely to God. My trust has never
been let down."[29]

McNamara points out that the way of spiritual childhood was not discovered by Therese of Lisieux. It is
the Gospel way discerned by the Little Flower as she
struggled with every fiber of her being to surrender unconditionally to the "overtures of God's love."[30] Her
autobiography is simply an account of the entire undeserved grace she experienced as she abandoned herself
completely in a relationship of intimacy with Christ.
Therese found it difficult to speak of her relationship
to Christ. One day Sister Febronie spoke to her about
her difficulties:

> "My child, it seems to me you don't have very
> much to tell your Superiors." "Why do you say
> that, Mother?" "Because your soul is extremely
> simple, but when you will be perfect, you will
> be even more simple; the closer one approaches
> to God, the simpler one becomes."[31]

Jesus had instructed her that the only path to God's
love, the source of sanctity, is the "abandonment of
a little child sleeping without fear in its father's
arms."[32]

As confirmed by the way of spiritual childhood, the
general paradox of Christian discipleship is that maturity and childhood are somehow identical. It was Christ
himself who made the recovery of childhood the condition
of discleship and of human maturity. McNamara notes
that it is in the child that the beauty of the flower of
simplicity becomes a living reality, a practiced ideal,
a life of abandonment to Christ. As mature children of
the Father, a new way has opened up for us. It is the
way of a child, the clown and the sage in which life
glows with an extraordinary luminosity amidst the most
ordinary of circumstances.

REFLECTION

The way of simplicity is so easy and yet so very
difficult. It only asks one thing of us--abandonment to
Christ--and yet it takes a lifetime of renewed transformation. The way of simplicity asks for a "letting go"

of all "right" intentions in preference to a simple intention that is enlighted by love of God alone.

I cannot strive to attain the way of mature childhood; and yet it can only be achieved through a conscious, intentional, inner-directed activity. It becomes a way of returning to the candor and innocence of childhood while deepening in maturity because of a centeredness in Christ.

Achieving the way of spiritual childhood cannot remain a lofty ideal that is not attached to the reality of everyday life. Spiritual childhood is lived out in abandonment to Christ through the tasks that appear before us everyday. As in the life of Therese of Lisieux, the way of spiritual childhood matures and develops at the kitchen sink, rubbing elbows with others; through the hurts one experiences because of her own self-centeredness, through the pre-occupations of the business world, as well as in times of communion with Christ in prayer. My life can only become simplified in the everyday commonplace activities that emerge because of my unique combination of cultural, familial and personal factors. I have to search out my own life experience and situation to slowly unfold into mature childlikeness, into Christian simplicity. This involves taking a risk, of changing in a way that I cannot foresee because of the path that has been set before me. Mature Christian childlikeness will demand a courage greater than any other feat. The struggle will be especially acute when nothing seems to be clear, everything seems complicated. It is then when I am most surely called to abandon myself in loving trust to His ways.

Summary and Transition

The purpose of this chapter has been to formulate means by which I could see and hear the hidden message of Christ being spoken to me alone, and to discover my relationship with Him as a relationship of intimacy. First of all, I spoke of Christian faith experience as an experience of intimacy, as differing from other religious experience. For the Christian, faith is dominant. God is a God of nearness who is whispering a message that is calling me to a uniquely free destiny in His love. The Christian response to this special call of love can only be the willingness to be reborn through the grace of Baptism. It calls for a total response of surrender to Christ who, through His gift of grace, has called me to an intimate relationship with Him.

As Christians we have been called to a relationship of son or daughter to a loving Father. His message of love has only revealed to us what is necessary for us to respond to His love. Through both historical and personal key situations the gift of faith has been made known to me. With Mary and Martha I have come to realize that only one thing is necessary, that is, a listening, loving response to His invitation of love. In response to Christ alone who has formed a personal relationship with me, I am called to become transformed through a prayerful immersion into the attitude of Christ.

Through prayer and meditation I may be able to more fully mirror the simplicity of God. Through His wholeness and oneness He calls me to become whole. Out of his infinite glory He gives the power for my hidden self to grow strong so that rooted in love and built on love I may grasp the utter fullness of God.

To grow in this fullness in God, my response can only be a deepening imitation of Mary who pondered the Word in her heart, who trusted in Christ and abandoned herself to Him totally. She lived her life in simplicity, centered fully on Him. In prayer I respond to the invitation given to me. I trust in the Spirit who voices my greatest needs and I risk that I will be able to respond fully to whatever invitation is given. The essence of prayer then is obedience to the word of invitation voiced by the Spirit. The result of obedience is a reunification of life and a mature response of "Thy will be done." Thus prayer becomes a listening to the Will of God so that I may walk in His ways all the days of my life.

We found recorded in Matthew that where your treasure is there will your heart also be. If my life is centered on Christ nothing should interfere. Living with a simple intention instead of a purely "right" intention I will find my life centered on Him alone who is working in me.

In the final section the way of spiritual childhood was explained. Knowing that His love lasts forever, all

166

action, prayer and growth become simplified. Through
mature Christian childlikeness I will be able to respond to the risk of listening to His word, slowly work
through His love to change what needs to be changed and
to respond more fully to Him. In the following chapter
we will outline more concretely how the Christian ideal
of simplicity may become a way of life for me, and how
with courage I may be able to respond to the unfolding
message of Christ.

ENDNOTES

[1]Scriptural quotes throughout this section are taken from The Jerusalem Bible, Reader's Edition (Garden City, New York: Doubleday and Co, 1971).

[2]van Kaam, op. cit.

[3]Kevin O'Shea, "Enigma and Tenderness," Spiritual Life XXI:1 (Spring, 1975), pp. 8-22.

[4]Ibid., p. 20.

[5]Thomas Merton, New Seeds of Contemplation (New York: New Directions, 1961), pp. 35-36.

[6]Adrian van Kaam, In Search of Spiritual Identity (Denville, New Jersey: Dimension Books, 1975), pp. 293-314.

[7]Ibid. pp. 310-311.

[8]Adrian van Kaam, "Dynamics of Spiritual Self-Direction," Spiritual Life XXI:4 (Winter, 1975), pp. 261-282.

[9]See In Search of Spiritual Identity pp. 82-107 op. cit. for a further explanation of how scripture reading and the reading of the masters of the spiritual life offer insight into the Christian tradition of God's self-communication to man.

[10]Thomas Merton, Zen and the Birds of Appetite (New York: New Directions, 1968), p. 138.

[11]Adrian van Kaam, On Being Yourself (Denville, New Jersey: Dimension Books, 1972), pp. 164-190.

[12]St. Augustine as quoted by van Kaam, Ibid., p. 167

[13]Ibid., p. 181.

[14]Murray Bodo, Francis: the Journey and the Dream (Cincinnati, Ohio: St. Anthony Messenger Press, 1972), p. 58.

[15]Hubert van Zeller, Leave Your Life Alone (Springfield, Illinois: Templegate Publishers, 1972), pp. 55-81.

[16]Sister Miriam Louise, "Mary: R:ceiver and Witness of the Word," *Review for Religious* XXXI:5 (September, 1972

[17]Ibid., p. 767.

[18]Walter M. Abbott (ed.) *The Documents of Vatican II* (New York: America, 1966), p. 88.

[19]Sister Jean Annette, "A Simple Life," *Desert Call* IX:4 (Fall, 1974), pp. 9-11.

[20]Jacques Ellul, *Prayer and Modern Man* trans. C. Edward Hopkins (New York: Seabury Press, 1970), pp. 3-170.

[21]Ibid., p. 37.

[22]Søren Kierkegaard, *The Journals of Søren Kierkegaard* trans. Alexander Dru (New York: Oxford University Press, 1959), p. 97 as quoted in Ibid., p. 111. (Italics in the original.)

[23]Ibid., p. 107.

[24]Leonard Berstein, "A Simple Song," (New York: Amerson Enterprises, 1971). All other references to this song will be centered and single spaced throughout this reflection.

[25]Thomas Merton, *No Man is an Island* (New York: Dell Publishing Co., 1955), pp. 85-88.

[26]Ibid., p. 87.

[27]Ibid., p. 88.

[28]William McNamara, "The Recovery of Childhood," *Desert Call* X:4 (Fall, 1975), 1-3; Susan Muto, *Steps Along the Way* (Denville, New Jersey: Dimension Books, 1975), pp. 116-133; and Lawrence Sullivan, "Lisieux and the Wisdom of China," *Spiritual* Life XIX:3 (Fall, 1973), 179-203.

[29]*The Autobiography of St. Therese of Lisieux: The Story of a Soul*, trans John Beevers (Garden City, New York: Doubleday and Co., 1957), p. 133. Or see *Story of a Soul: The Autobiography of St. Therese of Lisieux*,

trans. John Clarke (Washington, D.C.: ICS Publications, 1975), p. 238.

[30]McNamara, op. cit., p. 1.

[31]Clarke, op. cit., p. 151. (Italics in the original.)

[32]Sullivan, op. cit., p. 195.

CHAPTER VII

THE CHRISTIAN RESPONSE OF SIMPLICITY

INTRODUCTION

Before we are able to simplify our response to
Christ we need first to discover what is un-simple about
our present response. In so doing we will uncover attitudes, ideas and ideals that are not Christian but that
pose under the name of Christian. We will also be able
to more fully enter into full discipleship with Christ,
that is, we will be able to live the death and dying as
well as the birth and resurrection aspects of His message. We will reflect on several authentic "ways" of
living Christian simplicity in concrete daily life.
From this foundation it is hoped that each person will
formulate his or her own response of simplicity.

WHAT IS UN-SIMPLE ABOUT MY RESPONSE TO CHRIST?

In trying to live the Christian message we cannot
deny our humanness, our tendency to "miss the mark" and
become self-centered. Keeping this in mind we become
aware of the difficulties involved in living a Christ-
centered life, a life of simplicity. Dalrymple and
O'Shea speak about the practical acceptance of our
humanness and the radical conversion that is necessary
to live fully the Christian message of simplicity.

John Dalrymple and Keven O'Shea[1]
Transforming Our Humanness

Our lives speak more loudly than our speech or our
prayer. It is all too easy to speak about God in our
lives without keenly being aware of His presence. The
person who is aware of God as a presence in daily living
cannot be cold and theoretical because there is a hidden
dimension, an infinite significance to everything that
he does as a result of his close partnership with God.
Living the Christian life then means taking God the
Father seriously in the reality of everyday situations
of life. Not to escape, but to face up to this presence
in everyday life is to live a starkly simple relationship
of complete abandonment to God. Dalrymple says that to
admit God to only the "religious" part of life, a part
that exists along side many other parts, is really not

to accept God at all.

Therefore the first step in Christian discipleship
is a stripping bare of the compromises that complicate
our response to Him. It is an acceptance of the "enigma", the restlessness, that arises from being human.
This enigma is not something we can focus on with our
eyes. O'Shea says,

> It is an experience of alienation carried to
> ultimate lengths: What is alienated from us is
> a profound and important dimension of our very
> self.
> . . . .
> We will not admit it, and we try, in vain, to
> defend ourselves from its very existence.[2]

Part of the enigma centers around our inability to master and control our very selves, our carrying the cross
of being a person. Another part of the enigma centers
around our not wanting to acknowledge God in Christ as
the central humanizing core of ourselves. According to
O'Shea, to become humanized means to allow the redeeming
grace of Christ to reach down into the core of human
existence, into the dimension of it that feels least
human, to heal it, integrate it and transform it.

Christian conversion is radical in this interior
sense of being transformed to the very roots of our being, allowing no part of oneself to be unaffected by the
demands of God. If we truly become transformed we could

> let go of our care and concern and stop organ-
> izing means to ends, and just be in each moment
> of awareness as an end in itself. We could feel
> that we could love our whole lifestory, that we
> are graced and made beautiful, by the providence
> of our own history.[3]

In the intense moment of awareness of the tenderness of
God one can claim and own his limitedness and not be
overwhelmed by the fact that he is powerless and vulnerable. The experience of being healed and transformed
by Christ is a gentle growing into a oneness that is
not of our own making. The healed person who lives in
grace is

much less defensive, much more simple and direct, more able to commit himself, more aware but less afraid of all the forces within him and around him that drive home his smallness and insignificance.[4]

After the first moment of conversion we have to settle to a lifetime of fidelity by prayer, observance, and discipline of thought and action. As noted by Dalrymple, it is not the seed which springs up straight away that produces the harvest, but the seed sown in the richest soil. The seed which took longer to sprout will yield mature fruit because its growth came from deep within the soil of the earth. The task of conversion to a total centeredness in Christ demands a transformation from our very roots, from the depths of our being. The slight glimpses of growth we perceive beckon us forward to a promised fulfillment in God, to a "condition of complete simplicity, costing not less than everything."

REFLECTION

When I respond to Christ's invitation to transform my life to His ways, I must be careful that the route of transformation I take is not merely a greater understanding of myself and my human limitations. Total transformation in Christ is much deeper. It is a sense of being totally, unconditionally accepting of the healing power of grace in my life. I may never fully understand when and how this grace works in me, but through a gradual unfolding of my life in response to grace experienced in everyday situations, I may sense my relationship with Christ in a deeper manner. Through meditative reflection on the unfolding of God's grace in my life I may be able to see glimpses of the unfolding path that lay before me.

Besides substituting a deeper self-knowledge for a true relationship with Christ, another obstacle to self-simplification may be that I try to keep Christ at a distance and not allow Him to be the centering hub on which my life rotates. I may continue to do everything in the name of Christ but not really live the conviction this entails. Or, I may consider Christ in a cheap relationship falsely termed intimacy, founded on a closeness I "feel" to Christ because every minute request (e.g. good weather or success in a football game) I have is answered in my favor.

What may be unsimple about my relationship with
Christ is the non-acceptance of the fullness of His
message. I may find meaning in the Eucharist or in the
Resurrection but am never able to enter into the agony
and death of the passion of Christ. In other words, I
only accept the part of His message that appeals to my
state of mind or my needs. I am unwilling to let go in
total abandonment in and through the whole Christ.[5]

THE CALL TO "LET GO" WITH CHRIST

The essence of Christian life is total surrender
in Christ. While it may be easier to choose our own
mortification and denials in surrender to Christ, Thomas
Merton says that it is far more beneficial and perhaps
demands more from a person to accept the "agony in the
garden" in the present moment, in the demands that issue
forth from the everyday. In the following section we
will consider both self-chosen mortification and the
"letting go" with Christ that meets us in everyday life,
calling for a simplification of our response to Christ.

Søren Kierkegaard, Thomas Merton and Dietrich von
Hildebrand Surrendering in Christ

True simplicity can only be attained through an
innermost readiness to relinquish anything if God wills
it. Paradoxically, it is only in our surrender to God
that we become wholly collected and our whole essence
becomes actualized in one all comprehensive attitude,
that is, an attitude of complete abandonment to Christ.

Kierkegaard notes that to surrender, to deny oneself, to bear one's own cross, is a slow and burdensome
task. One good deed or high minded ideal does not constitute total surrender. When Christ spoke to the rich
young man of the Gospels, he did not limit his message
to "go sell what you have and give to the poor." Rather,
he said, "Go and sell everything you own and give the
money to the poor, and you will have treasure in heaven;
then come and follow me." (Mark 10:21) Selling his
goods and sharing the profit with the poor was only the
beginning. Christ asked for more than the young man
could give--namely, the long process of a continual
bearing of the cross to follow Christ. The young man
could not face the daily denial after he had won the
treasures of heaven. To follow Christ means to walk
the way of Christ, to walk in need, in humility and in
simplicity.

Total surrender to Christ requires a deep change of heart in which we die to one level of our being in order to find ourselves alive and free on a much deeper, spiritual level. For example, fasting and other mortification can only have their proper effect of purification when our motives for practicing them arise from a deep personal conviction that we are loved uniquely by and in Christ. This is the only motive that makes denial and sacrifice seem at all worthwhile. Sacrifices that are performed merely on the external level eventually turn out to be a false and operative self-display, or self-pitying introspection.

Ironically, the sacrifices that are not chosen often have greater value than those we select for ourselves because such sacrifices that appear of themselves in daily life are not hemmed in my selfish motivations. Accepting the daily unexpected sacrifices leads one to eventually submit more and more to purifying actions that cannot be understood. In the words of Thomas Merton,

> only when we are able to "let go" of everything within us, all desire to see, to know, to taste and to experience the presence of God, do we truly become able to experience that presence with the overwhelming conviction and reality that revolutionize our entire inner life.[7]

It is only when we become divested of our sense of possession of even our very selves, that we may live in perfect openness, in a state of total defenselessness that is utter simplicity and total gift. The gift of self takes the sting out of self-emptying and turns the giving into a gentle selflessness in the presence of a deeper life, in imitation of Christ's total gift of himself.

REFLECTION

Christ's sole purpose in life was to do the Father's will, to die so that others may live. He lived in trust, convinced that the Father would never "give him a stone for bread." He took on the full burden of humanness to draw that humanness to perfection through union with the Father. He accepted the most debasing punishment people could devise only to prove that the Father's love and protection was greater still and would overcome all evil.

175

When I dare to be a disciple of Christ, I dare to risk being nailed to the cross with Him. While my cross may not be the wood of Golgotha, it may be just as burdensome and just as real. I may be asked to bear the cross of my own human limitedness, my desire to be god, or my daily struggle with tainted, complex motives. My cross may be to accept the apparent meaninglessness of the present moment or the lack of understanding I receive from those I work with every day. My cross may also be an awareness of my helplessness in alleviating the burdensome pains of another, to watch someone suffer, physically or emotionally and not be able to do anything about it. The greatest cross I may have to bear is to watch a brother or a sister become entangled in their own self-centeredness while cutting Christ completely out of the picture of his or her life.

As I discovered through my retreat experience, my life may become immensely simplified if I allow Christ to be Christ for me and accept the burden of humanness while living in the assurance of His love for me. Through the daily dying, the daily being stripped of one more layer of attempts at self-redemption, I may come to the kernel of truth in His love for me. The circumstances of my life may not change, the joys and the sorrows, the laughter and the tears may not differ. But when my life becomes transformed by the living grace of Christ, there must be a transparency and a serenity that would not exist without His love. Christ constantly, quietly calls each person to let go, to become transformed, to live in a way of simplicity that is real and active. When I carry the full load of the message of Christ as I perceive it in the present moment of my life, I cannot live complacently. I need to discover each day how Christ is calling me to die and rise with Him.

What can I do concretely in the everyday to simplify my life, to put into practice the ideal I find flowing from the call of Christ? How does the Christian life of simplicity differ from the life of simplicity lived by someone who has not received the gift of faith? And how does my desire to simplify my life influence my interaction with others? In the following presentations I will suggest several ways of answering these very basic questions about living a simple life. Initially I will present simplicity of life as a transparency shown in interaction with others.

THE CHRISTIAN "WAY" OF SIMPLICITY

Ladislaus Boros and Kevin O'Shea[8]
Transparency in Interaction with Others

In surrendering to Christ I have received myself
and all that happens as a good. My very existence becomes an expression of praise and thanks to Him. This
lived attitude of thanksgiving suggests a way of life
that is so simple that it is lived out in trust, transparency and compassion in interaction with others. It
does not try to focus on a "God" located and defined in
some way independent of our natural contact with Him in
everyday life. This attitude does not isolate the person from the normal, healthy environment and everyday
relationships. It simply calls for a greater intimacy
and a deeper honesty with all people.

In a chapter entitled "Honesty", Boros finds that
he cannot speak about honesty and transparency without
first speaking about the attitude of ultimate human au-
thenticity: simplicity of heart. He says that when we
speak of honesty we are not speaking about a merely ethical attitude, but about a quality of being. In order
to enter into the essential of being, he concludes that
we must become like children. The idea of simplicity
and transparency that characterizes children does not
yet exist in the consciousness of a child. Its consciousness is based on things, events and others--the child is
not yet aware of its own ego. In its creative youthful-
ness, the child keeps itself open, has the capacity to
grasp the essential thing and receive it without any intention toward it. For a mature adult to live the innocence of intention found in a child, that person must
live in unconditional loyalty to God in all one does.
Interaction with others must be characterized by a clarity, transparency, purity and luminosity that can rightly
only flow from a mature and deep conviction that Christ
is the center of life. Each of us must be a person with
a whole heart:

> whole in devotion, whole in honesty, whole in
> friendship, whole in love. This heart is not
> divided, it is not split. It is not dominated
> by other goals.[9]

It is said in the Gospels that heaven springs from
the hearts of the simple. It is a virtue that is not
only praised in the Gospels, but one that stands at its
center, the virtue without which a person cannot enter
into nearness with Christ, into the kingdom of heaven.
Christ has promised to each person that ones happiness
in heaven will resemble that most longed for in a concrete way here on earth. For the Samaritan woman, it
was water; for the people of Capharnaum, bread of life;
for the fishermen it was nets overflowing; to shepherds,
great herds and ever green pasture; to the merchant,
precious pearls, and to you and me, that which we long
for with all our hearts: happiness in the Lord forever.
The kingdom of heaven for one who desires to live simply
is the reward of finding all of life flowing from a clear,
transparent relationship with Christ. Using a Quaker
term, it means to "center down" with all of life's energies into attaining that one goal that will give us ultimate happiness.

Thomas Kelly[10]
Centering Down

> Prune and trim we must, but not with ruthless
> haste and ready pruning knife, until we have
> reflected upon the tree we trim, the environ-
> ment it lives in, and the sap of life which
> feeds it.[11]

Kelly develops the Quaker doctrine of simplicity in
reflecting upon the theme of centering down. But he says
before we may begin to center down we need to be aware
of where the "tree of our life" is planted, what its
strengths and weaknesses are, and what the goal of centering is to be. To center down today is difficult for
us because we don't know the answers to these elemental
questions. We are not skilled in the inner life, we try
to be several selves at once without being organized by
a single, mastering self within us. Strained by the
very mad pace of modern existence, we tend to blame our
inward uneasiness on our daily, outer burdens. We desire
to skip over into a center where all of life seems to
flow in unhurried serenity, peace and power. Reflecting
on the life of a Quaker forefather, John Woolman, Kelly
realizes that he did not struggle to achieve simplicity,
but he merely yielded to the Center and his life became
simple. His life had a singleness of eye, "his many
selves were integrated into a single true self, whose

whole aim was humbly walking in the presence and guidance and will of God."[12]

For the most part, our failure to center down does not lie in the lack of time we so often claim. For too many of us it lies in a lack of joyful, enthusiastic delight in Christ, a lack of "deep-drawing love directed toward Him at every hour of the day and night."[13] If we were truly concerned about and convinced of the love of God being the center of our lives, this love would flow over into the lives of others. We would be overwhelmed by the concerns of the world that lies before us. A deep conviction of God's love directing our lives would make us see the worlds' needs anew. In Kelly's words:

> We love people and we grieve to see them blind
> when they might be seeing, asleep with all the
> worlds' comforts when they ought to be awake
> and living sacrificially, accepting the worlds'
> goods as their right when they really hold
> them only in temporary trust.[14]

REFLECTION

'Tis a gift to be simple, 'tis a gift to be free
'Tis a gift to come down where we ought to be.
And when we find ourselves in the place just right
'Twill be in the valley of love and delight.
When true simplicity is gained
To bow and to bend we shan't be ashamed.
To turn, turn will be our delight,
'Till by turning, turning we come round right.[15]

The lilting melody of this Quaker folktune portrays both the delightful gift of being drawn to simplicity and the effort that it takes to "come down to where we ought to be." The lives of the Quakers seem to revolve around the home and hearth, the gifts of the land, and their faith in God who was the center of their lives. "When we find ourselves in the place just right," the place of love and delight, our defenses will not be needed. We can drop our defensive armor and live out of the one self that is our true self. We can drop the defensive images we hold about ourselves, about our relationship with God, and the image we hold about ourselves in protective interaction with everyone we meet, even family and friends.

In transparency and trust we won't be afraid to

"bow and to bend." The situations of life won't prove to be mountains to be scaled but stepping stones to a clearer, deeper understanding and acceptance of the meaning of life. I will not be threatened by the difference of others, but will welcome them as listeners to the will of God in ways that are different from mine. A co-worker's unique display of talents, strengths and weaknesses, her ability to flow with "the changing sands of time", will not be envied but appreciated for the complementarity her gifts bring to my own unique combination of strengths and weaknesses.

"To turn, turn will be our delight." To become transformed, to center down demands a life of constant re-evaluation of our actions, attitudes and ideals to ascertain whether they are in tune with the changing environment and demands of everyday life and in line with my unique capacities to emerge within these situations. To live the simple life one must bore ever more deeply into the essentials of life. We will "come round right" if our actions stem from a true conviction of God being the center of my life's motivations and ideals. Finding a rooting in God, finding His love to be predictable and constant, complexity that usually flows from interaction with others can be lived with and can be a source of deepening maturity for me.

In the final section of our subtheme of living the Christian response of simplicity, we will see that living the simple life revolves around one choice, that is first choosing the kingdom of heaven.

Vernard Eller[16]
"Choose First the Kingdom of Heaven"

The core dialectic within the simple life itself is essentially the believer's inner relationship with God finding expression in his outward relationship to "things."[17] Eller concludes that this dialectic leaves simplicity open to misuse by those who want credit for living it but who are in no way urged to change their present style of life. To ascertain how I am living the simple life I need to constantly reflect on my living the Gospel counsel: "Set your hearts on his kingdom first, and on his righteousness, and all these other things will be given you as well." (Matt. 6:33) To set one's heart on his kingdom is to seek, above all, to let his will be done in my life. My motivation must spring from an inner conviction of personal loyalty to the Lord with my whole heart. As Eller notes, "the eye (I) must be right if anything is rightly to be seen."[18] One's ultimate loyalty must center down and converge at a single point: an undaunted loyalty to Christ.

Eller insists that there is no deviation from a single-willed centering on God. He just as firmly contends that the outward details of its expression cannot be decreed. Each person has to rightly judge for himself how his actions speak of a firm conviction of his centeredness on God. Therefore, Eller notes that the simple life is not to be equated with the least possible consumption of worldly goods, or with the practice of the virtue of frugality. The rightful use of the goods of this world can be a greater good than sparing use of them, if these goods are used to support our relationship with God rather than to compete with it.

It is interesting to note that a style of life that is marked by the simplification of one's possessions and relationships is conspicuously more satisfying than a life which is devoted to luxury. Therefore we must recognize that the simplification of life that presently has taken on the popularity of a "fad" or cult, may be purely for hedonistic reasons. The true test of simplicity for the right reasons will show in the depth and length of the commitment to this style of life.

As shown in the life of Christ, the simple life and the ascetical life are not the same. If it were, we wouldn't see Christ joining in the wedding at Cana or dining at the home of the publican. We can only conclude that the simple life is not nearly as easy to spot and identify by its outward markings as is the ascetical renunciation of material goods. In other words, to live the simple life we must be more concerned about the inner attitude than about the outward manifestation of simplicity. This does not mean that the simple life is a life of luxury. Rather, the simple-living Christian dispossesses himself of "things" precisely that he might be liberated from them to live out his love and loyalty to God alone. Quoting Kierkegaard, Eller notes that our natural instinct is toward cunning, shrewdness and complexity. It takes a conscious, life-long effort to develop a life of simplicity. It is only through God and with his help that we can get back to the basic simplicity for which we were created.

REFLECTION

Ultimately, what Eller is saying is that the simple
life cannot be judged by external appearances alone.
"By their fruits you will know them," still rightly
applies. For someone who is simple interiorly, who has
"chosen the Kingdom of heaven first," cannot hide her
conviction in exterior actions. If we look at the lives
of those individuals who were noted for their simple
conviction about Christ's love for them and all people,
we will sense a uniqueness that ties in with the needs
of the times in which the person lives, the individual
endowments of the individual, and a full living of what
appears to be the person's unique spiritual identity in
the service that person gives to others.

For example, St. Francis of Assisi lived a life
noted for its poverty and simplicity. In response to the
vision he received, he went about repairing the ram-
shackle remains of the Church.[19] Through his life his
response unfolded in simplicity as he understood the
message more clearly. He was to rebuild the internal
community of the Church that had become lethargic and
ill-directed.

Along with St. Francis we could also list St.
Elizabeth Ann Seton, Albert Schweitzer and Mother Teresa
of Calcutta to name only a few. Each one of these persons was and is noted for living a simple life. The
only common characteristic however that we can find is
that they were firmly convinced about their relationship
to Christ and that he alone made the difference in their
lives. Each one responded to or is still responding to
the needs of the times, spending his or her particular
gifts to alleviate some lack in the world with the sole
intention of drawing others into a love relationship
with Christ.

Besides these well noted lives of simplicity, I
would also like to reflect upon the lives of two others
who have deeply affected my life and have taught me the
value of living the simple life. Though they perform no
extraordinary feat of bravery or self-sacrifice, my parents have taught me about the true value of living the
simple life because of the very way in which they lived
their lives. I see them as constantly struggling to
live their lives in response to the call they received
many years ago. The years filled with the pain and joy
of raising a family have not complicated their lives but

have drawn them closer to each other and to their God.

"The kingdom of heaven" for them has been the joy and happiness of each of their children. Through the poverty of their early years, they were rich with the simple joys and pleasures of "making do" with the little they had. Through their daily living in joy, their efforts to bring forth the fruits of the earth, their lives spoke of a deep faith in a loving, caring God. They are at peace with "prince or pauper" as their concerns lie deeper than mere appearances. Their table is always set with the fruits of their own labor, sharing with anyone who will share with them the best of what they have. Their actions seem to meet the occasion, speaking of a joy and contentment with life and a pride in even the small and the everyday.

If I were to tell them about my reflections on their lives, they would find many excuses to dispute these claims. They would probably humbly respond: "We did what we felt we could do best. We try to forget the bad that has happened and only cherish the good. We have been richly blessed; we also have to bear the cost of these riches." Their philosophy of life is not complicated. One word alone would sum it up for them: love.

Summary and Conclusion

In summary, let us recount what constitutes the Christian response of simplicity. First, in order for me to live in simplicity I need to accept the limitations of my humanness and be converted fully to Christ. Living a life of surrender to Christ has to "show" in the reality of the everyday situations of life. God cannot be approached as an independent part of life that I may choose or reject. Without compromise, He has to be the center of my life, the root and foundation of my very being. If my life becomes centered totally on Him, I will become less defensive, more simple and direct. I will not only come to a greater understanding of myself but through an on-going conversion, because of his constant gift of love, I will become healed of duplicity and self-centeredness.

Through a life-time of "letting go" with Christ I may be drawn into a relationship of deeper intimacy with Him. I will then be able not only to share in the joy filled incarnation-resurrection aspects of his message, but I will also find the strength to bear my own cross out of love for him. Through daily dying my life may deepen. I may come to understand a little more clearly my own personal spiritual identity in Christ.

The Christian way of simplicity is different from other ways in that I surrender to Christ, to the one who finds strength in weakness. A christian who lives simplicity in his life cannot be other than utterly sincere and transparent in interaction with others. As one centers life ever more deeply around the "one thing necessary," eyes become opened to the needs of others. The message of Christ appears on all levels of life.

We concluded this Chapter by reflecting upon the passage: "Choose first the kingdom of heaven." Each person that we reflected upon lived their life in simplicity; a love centered on Christ was their only common characteristic. Choosing the kingdom of heaven still involves an individual, unique response from each person. Every Christian must choose which way he is to live his response after a prayerful reflection upon needs, talents, unique identity, the signs of the times and the call one perceives showing itself in life situation. In reflection I realize that my parents have lived the simple life without extraordinary feats or special charism. I, on my part, also have to choose how to live my life in simplicity. My response will also depend upon all that I bring to the call, and how completely I "choose first the kingdom of heaven." In the following Part I will explore how the living of the vowed life in community may occasion a deepened centeredness in Christ and, therefore, a life of greater simplicity.

ENDNOTES

[1]John Dalrymple, Costing Not Less Than Everything (Denville, New Jersey: Dimension Books, 1975), pp. 17-84; and Kevin O'Shea, "Enigma and Tenderness," Spiritual Life XXI:I (Spring, 1975), 8-13.

[2]O'Shea, Ibid., p. 9.

[3]O'Shea, Ibid., p. 11.

[4]Ibid., pp. 13-14.

[5]Since it is often far easier to accept the joyfilled birth and resurrection mysteries of Christ these will not be discussed at this time. It will be far easier to remain true to the letting go theme if these mysteries of Christ's message are looked at separately in a later portion of this thesis.

[6]Søren Kierkegaard, The Gospel of Suffering trans. David and Lillian Swenson (Minneapolis, Minnesota, 1948), pp. 10-20; Thomas Merton, Contemplative Prayer (Garden City, New York: Image Books, 1969), pp. 72-89; and Dietrich von Hildebrand, Transformation in Christ: On the Christian Attitude of Mind (New York: Longmans, Green and Co., 1948), pp. 57-85.

[7]Merton, op. cit., p. 89.

[8]Ladislaus Boros, Meeting God in Man (Garden City, New York: Image Books, 1968), pp. 131-141; and Kevin O'Shea, "Enigma and Tenderness," Spiritual Life XXI:I (Spring, 1975), 20-22.

[9]Boros, op. cit., p. 132.

[10]Thomas Kelly, A Testament of Devotion (New York: Harper and Row, 1941), pp. 122-124. While it may be interesting to do an extensive study on the Quaker Testimony of Simplicity, the scope and direction of this study does not warrant it. Briefly though, the doctrine of Simplicity as it is lived by Quakers, Mennonites, Amish and Brethren does give us some food for thought. In the everydayness of their lives they strive to live simplicity in all they do. They claim as the source of their inspiration, the light of Christ. In all of their actions they strive to do God's will. While their living of simplicity is based on frugality and plainness, their basic philosophy of right use of the gifts of God

is to be admired. In the right use of times, money, food, shelter, clothing, education and speech they strive as a community to live the will of God in all things. For further study of the Quaker doctrine of simplicity see: Howard H. Brinton, The Quaker Doctrine of Inward Peace (Wallingford, Pennsylvania: Pendle Hill Pamphlets, 1948), pp. 3-30; George Peck, Simplicity: A Rich Quaker's View (Wallingford, Pennsylvania: Pendle Hill Pamphlets, 1973), pp. 3-32; and Edward K. Ziegler, Simple Living (Elgin, Illinois: The Brethren Press, 1974), pp. 9-123. (This volume also contains an extensive bibliography on the Quaker way of simplicity).

[11]Kelly, op. cit., p. 113.

[12]Ibid., p. 117.

[13]Ibid., p. 121.

[14]Ibid., p. 122.

[15]Edward D. Andrews, The Gift to Be Simple (New York: Dover Publications, Inc., 1967), p. 136.

[16]Vernard Eller, The Simple Life (Grand Rapids, Michigan: William B. Eerdmans Co., 1973), pp. 11-114.

[17]Ibid., p. 11.

[18]Ibid., p. 24.

[19]See G. K. Chesterton, St. Francis of Assisi (Garden City, New York: Image Book, 1957).

PART FOUR

THE VOWED CHRISTIAN RESPONSE TO THE CALL OF SIMPLICITY

INTRODUCTION

Recall for a moment the retreat experience, the
seed of my research on simplicity. I, as a vowed religious, engaged in my life tasks as teacher, had spiraled
away from living a life centered in Christ. Instead of
living a Christ-centered life, I had gotten "caught up"
in the work I was performing and the image I was portray-
ing to those I thought I was serving. I discovered that
I was living a scattered life in an effort to say "yes"
to all of life's demands, real or imagined.

My experience of being "caught up" is not my experience alone. Many religious are plagued with the same
difficulty and find a need to simplify their lives.
Therefore, in this Part, I will present positive means
of understanding and living Gospel simplicity that so
many religious communities claim as their characteristic
virtue but find so difficult to adequately describe and
live.

In the first section I will present the need to slow
down to re-discover my relationship to Christ as one of
intimate love and fidelity, as a response to Christ as
my ultimate concern. Special emphasis will be given to
the center-to-center relationship with Christ that must
be formed through prayer to live a life of simplicity.
The vows will be researched collectively as a means of
self-simplification--each vow being a possible means of
drawing the religious to Christ. Community life then
will offer a setting in which religious may together
move toward full Christian living in a shared simplicity
of life.

CHAPTER VIII

REDISCOVERY OF THE VOWED LIFE AS AN AID IN
RESPONDING TO THE CALL TO SIMPLICITY

INTRODUCTION

Each Christian is called to live a life of simplicity, a life patterned after the life of Christ, a life
of love and service to the world. The vowed life is but
one way to live the fullness of Christ's message through
selfless love and availability of the human person to
others in union with Christ.[1] The vowed life is then
necessarily built on an intimate relationship with Christ,
as a result of a life of faith in Christ as ultimate
concern, and on a life of prayer which is an effort to
deepen communication with Christ in the everyday.

A religious takes the vows of poverty, celibacy and
obedience as means of deepening her baptismal commitment
to Christ. Besides a deep life of faith, founded on
prayer, these vows are also a means of self-simplification because of the power each of these vows possesses
to heal the vowing Christian from the human experience
of lostness, aloneness and vulnerability. Poverty may
draw me to a more respectful use of things, to valuing
persons, events and things as they truly are instead of
focusing on how they will serve my own needs. Living in
a spirit of poverty may also free me from inordinate
attachment to persons, events and things that are not
necessary in the light of the "one thing that is necessary." Obedience implies a listening to the unfolding
of reality and a responding to the will of God as it is
made known to me in my unique, and therewith limited life
situation. It occasions an honest and sincere effort to
discover the will of God for me in everyday interaction
with others. Celibacy is a response of love based on a
centeredness in Christ--a love that purifies and simplifies my interaction with others. Despite a continuous
effort to live out the Gospel message of love, I may at
times fail, but through the loving support of a community
of religious with the same basic goal in life, that is,
a life centered in Christ, my life will slowly unfold in
greater simplicity. Let us begin the considerations of
this chapter by first presenting the faith dimension of
the vowed life as being an intensification of the Christian faith experience.

THE VOWED LIFE AS A RESPONSE OF FAITH

J. M. R. Tillard[2]
Centrality of Faith in the Vowed Life

What is the central core around which the religious
life becomes integrated and value filled? Tillard remarks that it can only be the hard core of faith itself.
In religious life, the very life itself centers around
the faith element. Faith comes first. It is like the
thread on which one's entire existence depends. Without faith religious life falls apart, it becomes absurd.

Therefore, when we speak of renewal in religious
life today, we cannot get caught up in the accidentals
of religious life that can and should change; but we
must begin by searching out what constitutes the heart,
the central core of the Christian mystery. If the Gospel
is truly to remain a call which the Lord addresses to
Christians throughout the ages, and which transcends all
the meanderings of human history, then we must discover
the essentials of that call. Only then will religious
who profess to live that call to the full be able to
live a more adult Christian life, one that is free from
minute prescriptions that often overshadow life and have
nothing to do with the essential core of faith on which
it is based.

To say that religious life has its center in faith
is to believe in Jesus Christ, to offer to Him an unconditional "YES" with one's entire life. Then all the
concerns of a religious life, the ideals, questions and
even the shortcomings become embraced by God's steadfast
mercy and love. With this "yes", a religious both
chooses to center the essential part of existence on
Christ, and chooses to anchor apostolic activity and
commitment to the world within that same Christ. Religious vocation has as its prime motivation, something
other than seeking for merit, an exaggerated desire for
austerity, a self-centered striving after perfection, a
flight from the world, or even a willingness to serve
the Church. On the contrary:

> . . . it aims at being, in its basic motivation,
> an inwardness, a centering of one's existence
> on what represents, in the strictest sense of
> the term, the proper and determining element of
> the Faith, the specific affirmation of the

189

Christian mystery: in Jesus Christ, God Himself
entered into the mystery of man to lead him to
his full completion, which opens him up to the
Other and to other human beings.[3]

The religious freely chooses to live in a state in
which one's entire existence is centered on the perception and demanding value of choosing first the kingdom
of heaven. That person freely chooses in the here and
now situations of life, in regard to one's own personal
fulfillment and use of the goods of Creation, to pay as
little attention as possible to the captivating values
of this world.

Everything that has some connection with his
own use of created goods, his own joy in living, his own fulfillment, his own social existence, his own involvement in the world, what
he could take for himself, from his temporal
commitment to the service of the Kingdom, will
be submitted to the absolute role of what seems
to him to be the one thing necessary.[4]

That person wishes to have this concern for the
transcendent stand out in bold relief in everyday life.
In response to the Word of God who alone can reveal the
content of this action, the response to the "one thing
necessary", that person is going to:

. . . live in a state of separation in regard to
personal wealth, in the search for which the
shadow of Mammon is often mingled, and in regard
to the love of man for woman, and in regard to
the personal planning of the acts that rule his
personal destiny according to his own standards,
and in regard to the use of amenities for earthly
comfort.[5]

This religious person will strive in the humdrum existence and immediate situations of everyday life to witness to that dimension that cannot be measured in terms
of this world. This person freely chooses to center
one's "personal" existence on the Kingdom of God. In
Christ Jesus a total response is made to the essence of
Christian mystery: the love of God implanted in baptism
and the Eucharist.

Concretely, all that one does is permeated and invigorated from within by a free choice to follow Christ. This choice should absorb the person so totally that it permits no dichotomy in behavior, no splitting of life into compartments. All that one attempts, experiences, accomplishes and becomes will thus become valuable for "the kingdom of heaven."

If we are really in earnest about penetrating to the heart of our religious commitment, to the core of faith, we cannot help but seriously ask ourselves what is essential to this life of faith, and what is absolute within that life. For a Christian, the only motivation that could justify living "according to the vows" is a plan to arrange one's entire life around this central core. And the most expressive way of recollecting oneself around this core is through a life of prayer that attempts to revivify and re-express one's conviction about the centrality of God to all of life.

REFLECTION

In the "Decree on the Appropriate Renewal of Religious Life," we read:

> Since the religious life is intended above all else to lead those who embrace it to an imitation of Christ and to union with God through the profession of the evangelical counsels, the fact must be honestly faced that even the most desirable changes made on behalf of contemporary needs will fail of these purposes unless a renewal of Spirit gives life to them. Indeed such an interior renewal must always be accorded the leading role even in the promotion of external works.[6]

Since a religious vocation stems from the initiative of God, the main thrust of renewal must be interior; it must be a setting of the heart and mind wholly on God. Religious renewal must be a re-evaluation and a re-commitment to the life of faith that alone makes the lives of religious meaningful. The internal renewal must flow from a full turning toward God, a centering on one's will in response to the special gift of grace given in a religious vocation.

When religious life becomes centered on the essentials, those attitudes and beliefs that are not merely

191

accidental, then the whole of a person's life may be
lived in a deep conviction of the love and care extended
by God to one who tries to imitate Christ in a limited
human way.

A life of faith requires a double response, that
is, God must first give the initial call; then a response to this call has to come from the receiver of
this gift of faith. When God is the primary agent of a
religious vocation, he chooses someone "for the sake of
the kingdom" so that he can draw that person closer to
himself, so that he can make that person his own totally
and unconditionally in a form of life which resembles
as closely as possible the lived attitudes that his son,
while becoming human, adopted for the sake of the kingdom. On the part of those who are being called, we can
speak of a response that is characteristically simple if
the eyes of the one being called are fixed on the divine
initiative. That is to say, when the person's only concern is doing the will of God and all actions flow from
a life of faith.

When I pause to reflect upon how seriously my community has responded to the call of internal renewal,
I realize how far we have yet to go. In theory, each of
us professes to live a life of faith, trusting in the
goodness of God and finding God's love and concern enough
to make religious dedication possible. But, in practice,
when I look at the daily response many religious give, I
realize that dedication is sometimes resting on shaky
ground.

In reflecting upon my retreat experience, I realize
that I was doing all the "right things", I was exteriorly
living a deeply religious life. I put my time in prayer.
I used all of my energies in service of the children and
the parents of the school in which I was teaching. There
seemed to be nothing really wrong, nothing that had to
be changed. And yet, I felt pulled apart and scattered
by the apparent meaninglessness of all those activities
in the name of religious dedication. Through the experience I came to realize that external behavior, or even
having the right attitudes and ideals was not enough. I
had to meet face to face the question: who is really
the center of my life?

I had to find out for myself where my "treasure"
lay, on what my heart was centered. I had to find out

192

whether the "good" that I was doing as a somewhat dedicated religious was only being done to develop a good image of myself . . . to appear to be a good teacher . . . to be doing a service for others. What <u>really</u> was my motivation? Did I feel so dissipated because everything that I was doing, I did for the wrong reasons? On what was my life founded?

I realized that my whole stance as a religious person had to be re-evaluated. I realize that no matter how definitively my community decided on renewal in depth, I myself could not come to that renewal unless I personally became healed of the brokenness that seemed to dissipate my life. I realized that my life would only become simplified, clarified and integrated "for the sake of the kingdom" when I seriously sought out my response to the gift of faith I had received through God's intervention and initiative. I realized that my heart could only be set rightly when every joy, fulfillment and success is centered on the "one thing necessary," in service of the kingdom. Every good action would then become purified of its self-centered motivation and gratification when with the whole of my strength I would do all in the name of Christ. The failures, the disappointments and my own experience of not being able to do enough would not be troublesome for me. These failures should merely convince me that I am in real need of the Father's guiding hand.

Centering my life on a true conviction that God does love and care for me and all of mankind, may at times make the day to day living of a faith life a little easier. But listening for the will of God and trying to live that will out in my own unique way is often not very clear. God remains a Mystery. He keeps himself in hiding when I feel like I am most in need of his direct intervention because of my humanness. The more firmly I believe in the hidden mysterious love of God, the more integrated and simple my life will become. My life will not be scattered and split into unrelated compartments but will flow in one continuous effort to find all experiences and situations under the one motivation: for the "sake of the kingdom."

Since the renewal of my life and of religious life as a whole stems from internal renewal, our lives must return to an inwardness, to a life centered in faith before we can share that faith life with others. In the

following section we will consider the life of prayer
for religious as a means of deepening one's conviction
of the love of God.

THE LIFE OF PRAYER AS A MEANS OF DEEPENING MY
COMMUNICATION WITH CHRIST IN THE EVERYDAY

Herbert Smith[7]
Prayer as a Center-to-Center Relationship

The process of personal growth and the integration
proceeds spontaneously and unconsciously, but it also
goes forward consciously and with deliberate struggle.
If God is the center of this struggle, we must reach
out to him in our conscious life. That conscious
effort to reach out to God who is the center of life is
called prayer. It is in prayer that many of the critical decisions in behalf of growth are made and without
prayer they may not be made at all. Smith remarks that,
"sin pits me against God and my own true self, but
prayer is the struggle to end the dissidence of sin, and
confirm God's plan for me and for the whole universe."[8]
Prayer is the time during which I align my heart, mind
and energies with the One who gives meaning and direction to life.

For the religious man or woman, much of the struggle
to come to a personal relationship with Christ consists
in the effort to be faithful to the search for the Presence of God, and the struggle to remain in his Presence
once it is found. Faith is always operative in a life
of prayer. The more purified and simplified prayer
becomes, the more essential is the "faith-contact" with
God. Prayer is a continued search for God because we
never fully meet him. It is an experience of God
because he is never fully absent. Because prayer is a
faith-contact between the one who prays and God, it is
a strenuous listening more than a dialogue. In prayer
we listen for the "Uncreated Word, and there is nothing
to add, nothing to subtract, nothing to correct."[9]

While prayer is so unique, personal and mysterious,
it is important to formulate certain directives that
will keep one's life of prayer on the right track. To
avoid infantilism and stagnation in prayer, each person
must unfold a unique prayer life according to the laws
of growth in prayer. Smith lists these laws as seven.

1. Prayer must be conducted according to the law of center-to-center relationship.

In prayer I must find my own center and God's center. If my prayer comes forth only from my peripheral concerns instead of from my spirit core, I will never be fully involved in that prayer. I must daily, constantly search for and find God in a warm-hearted, personal, intimate way. "He must be sought out in my life and my prayer as the God of providence and destiny, the mysterious Lamb of the Book of Revelations who alone can break open and read the meaning of the scroll of time."[10] By being in touch with my own daily life, the heritage of my community as well as Scripture and tradition, I will be better able through this prayer to find my place in the plan of God.

2. We must daily relate our ongoing affairs to the UNUM.[11]

By daily relating what we are seeing, experiencing and becoming to God as the Integrating Force of our lives, we will discover a growth in intimacy with Him.

3. Our prayer must call on the growing resources and developing nature of our personality.

We should be content that prayer makes for a more intellectual, spiritual and selfless communication with God. The absence of feeling does not mean an absence of love. Rather, it may mean a deeper love, a more spiritual love, a more stable and faithful love. The secret is to bring to prayer our total selves, all our qualities as well as deprivations as they exist here and now.

4. In prayer we must respect the specific laws which govern the stage of prayer we have currently reached.

This calls for an honest appraisal of where we really are along the road of the spiritual life. We must prudently become aware of the stages of prayer as they have been studied and described by spiritual authors throughout the centuries.

5. Our prayer must be supple enough to respond to the Spirit.

We must daily listen to the Holy Spirit as well as to our own spirit. We must daily question ourselves: Who am I now? What do I really want? Where am I going? How should today's prayer affect tomorrow's? Through a prudent questioning of self in light of an ever deepening relationship with God, we may become more able to faithfully listen to God communicating his will to us.

6. Our prayer must remain prayer.

Prayer is communion with the Lord. While reflections, insights may be a result of prayer, they are not in themselves prayer. They could remain only on the level of communication with self instead of with the Lord.

7. Our prayer should have a guide other than self.

The guide other than self who is experienced in the life of prayer brings an objective view that I alone cannot have toward my own prayer. As Smith concludes:

> The spiritual director is a force in prayer--he pours the cold water of reason over us when we begin to expect prayer results that do not come from prayer but only from work, study, training, good food, rest, spiritual directors, doctors, psychiatrists--or miracles.[12]

REFLECTION

For a religious person, a life of prayer is the only guiding and supporting force that makes that dedicated life possible. Prayer is the conscious effort to come to intimacy with God, to respond to the invitation God has extended in a unique way to each Christian, but in a special way to each religious. As a religious I need to constantly ask myself how my life of prayer and intimacy with God differs from other Christians; how my life of prayer and relationship with God differs from my own brother's and sister's life of prayer. Is my relationship with God something that is relegated to times in prayer alone? Or does my response to God's invitation of intimacy come forth from every minute of the day--from the busy moments of teaching the reluctant student to communicating with adults I find unjust and troublesome. Does my prayer draw me to be more myself,

to be more receptive to God's love as it shows itself
in the normal situations of the day? Do my relations
with others show that as a result of prayer I am daily
trying to become less self-centered, more honestly
sincere?

Because I am a vowed religious, one who has chosen
and been chosen to make more explicit my intimate relationship with God, do my daily interactions with others
show that transparency and simplicity that characterizes
a "faith-contact" with God? Do I honestly believe with
the whole of my limited self that God truly loves me?
Can I live with God's mysteriousness without trying to
correct, or add, or subtract anything that He wills in
my life? Am I willing to continue to search for a
deeper understanding and communion with Him because I
have experienced Him as being the Guiding and Integrating Force of my life? Or do I do all the talking and
commanding of God because I am afraid or unwilling to
listen to what His call of love might entail? Each of
these questions should draw me to a humbler, more transparent relationship with God and in turn, aid in simplifying my interaction wtih others.

I cannot find immediate answers to any one of these
questions. The test of time and effort will alone prove
to me that God will be God and that He allows me the
freedom to respond to Him or not. How can I be sure of
this? How can I discover if I am "on the right track"
or not? Let us examine the seven directives given by
Smith. In applying them to my own life and to the lives
of spiritual authors who have come to a degree of
intimacy with God through prayer, I may be able to deepen
my prayer life and allow that prayer life to show itself
in interaction with others.

Center-to-Center Relationship

When my life of prayer is a constant search for the
living God and a continuous effort to discover my own
true spiritual identity, my life necessarily will be
drawn to simplicity. I will not try to run from this
relationship as Francis Thompson did when the "Hound of
Heaven" pursued him. Rather, through prayer, through
meditation on the Scriptures, and the study of tradition,
I will become convinced of God's love for each person as
I read of failure, our turning from God, and God's constant pursuit of limited human beings.

Along with St. Teresa of Avila I will become convinced of God's love for me despite my failures to discover Him or to relate to Him in others:

> However quietly we speak, He is so near that
> he will hear us: We need no wings to go in
> search of Him but have only to find a place
> where we can be alone and look upon Him
> present within us.[13]

When I relate to Him who is more intimate to me than I am to myself, to paraphrase St. Augustine, this relationship cannot help but overflow in simplicity in relationship with others. My prayer life as well as my apostolic life as a participative religious will be an outpouring of His love in its utter simplicity.

Daily Relationship to the UNUM

The child who doesn't understand the help I am trying to give him in learning Math, the religious who doubts the sincerity of my deep concern for her, the exciting news of the birth of a nephew, as well as the spark of joy that has been seen on the face that is usually sullen—each of these experiences can be God's way of making Himself known in the disconnected moments of the day. When my life in prayer is related to Him, no incident, person or place can be without meaning. When I experience God as the integrating force in my life, my life cannot be other than simplified and unified even in its apparent disunity. Speaking of God as the one who draws meaning from the scattered and sometimes jolting or unnerving events of the day, St. Teresa says:

> His majesty knows all about this, as I have
> said; intervention on our part is quite
> unnecessary; rather we must serve His Majesty
> with the humility and simplicity of heart and
> praise Him for his works and wonders.[14]

Prayer as Related to Deepening Resources

Prayer can never be the same from day to day or else it will be stagnated and infantile. Prayer, like a vine, will only deepen and become fruitful as it searches daily for the life-giving substance that can only be discovered through struggle. My prayer will only unfold as I emerge as a person, as I try to unleash

the binding power of my own self-centeredness, and as I
try to discover the strengths of my own true identity.
Using the analogy of a bird tied by a fine thread, St.
John of the Cross tells us:

> It makes little difference whether a bird is
> tied by a thin thread or by a cord. For even
> if tied by thread, the bird will be prevented
> from taking off just as surely as if it were
> tied by cord--that is, it will be impeded from
> flight as long as it does not break the thread.[15]

If I accept my strengths and acknowledge my limitations as I discover them because of a regular prayer
life, my prayer cannot be a lifeless, compartmentalized
experience. It will unfold and deepen as I am able to
live the unique limitations of my life. St. John again
says:

> If a person will eliminate these impediments
> and veils, and live in pure nakedness and poverty
> of spirit his soul in its simplicity and purity
> will then be immediately transformed into simple
> and pure Wisdom, the Son of God.[16]

The absence of feeling or the lack of mountain-top
experiences should not disconcert my best intentions.
When I approach prayer with my total self--my strengths
and defenses--I cannot help but be drawn closer to God,
whether I experience it explicitly or not.

Stages of Prayer

To grow in and mature in a life of prayer, I must
have some notion of the stages of prayer that have been
experienced and recorded by masters throughout the centuries. I must prudently become aware of the state
that I am in, learn of its particular characteristics,
its fullness or lack of feeling, its desolation or
consolation. Through a careful study of St. Teresa of
Avila, St. John of the Cross, and St. Therese of Lisieux
to name a few, I will be able to experience the stages
of growth and struggle as they appear in my concrete
everyday life. I will not be tempted to compare my
prayer life with others, nor to pretentiously talk about
my prayer life as being without difficulty.

Responsive to the Spirit

How ready am I to say: "Let it be done to me according to your word?" Through a daily questioning and pondering of the Word as it appears in my life, the Holy Spirit and my spirit may be drawn into closer unity. My spirit may be able to respond to the Holy Spirit. The author of the Cloud of Unknowing states:

> But most of all, he must learn to be sensitive to the Spirit guiding him secretly in the depths of his heart and wait until the Spirit himself stirs and beckons him within. This secret invitation from God's Spirit is the most immediate and certain sign that God is calling and drawing a person to a higher life of grace in contemplation.[17]

Prayer Must Remain Prayer

As a vowed religious I must not delude myself into thinking that reflection and spiritual insight is prayer in its fullest meaning. Reflection may just be a greater self-knowledge; or insight a seeing clearly my own desires and deepest needs. Prayer, to be prayer, must be communication with Christ and not merely a deeper communication with myself. Likewise my work cannot become my prayer. My work will be affected by a deep prayer life but not vice versa.

Guide in Prayer

As an aid in discovering the "trueness" of my relationship to God in prayer, I may have to have an outside, objective inspiration. During certain stages in my life this guide may be a spiritual director who is trained and experienced in leading others. At times, the guidance I receive may come from an attentive listening to homilies and retreat conferences will be sufficient. At other times, a return to Scripture and a study of the traditions of the spiritual life will be most helpful. My life will only be drawn to a greater simplicity as I approach any of these means as aids in coming in touch with my own needs and with the will of God for my life.

In the following section I will further clarify how the right approach to Scripture, spiritual reading and study of the heritage of one's community may be aids in

folding my life in simplicity and in a deeper relationship with Christ.

Sister Florette Amyot[18]
Religious Call to Listen and Respond to the Word

If we were to summarize the explicit council directives in regard to religious renewal, we would find the
total message in just one phrase: return to the Gospel.
The Council Fathers, guided as they were by the Holy
Spirit, sensed that religious needed above all else to
gather their spiritual energies and simplify their lives
to the one thing necessary: listening to the Word of
God.

The author suggests that we review several conciliar
passages that verify the necessity of religious returning to the Gospel:

> Since the fundamental norm of the religious
> life is the following of Christ as proposed
> by the Gospel, such is to be regarded by all
> communities as their supreme law.
>
> . . . .
>
> The refore, drawing on the authentic sources
> of Christian spirituality, let the members of
> communities energetically cultivate the spirit
> of prayer and the practice of it. In the first
> place they should take the Sacred Scriptures in
> hand each day by way of attaining "the excelling
> knowledge of Jesus Christ: through reading these
> divine writings and meditating on them."[19]

In responding to the directives, many religious
experienced the difficulty of making the Scripture a
meaningful part of the day. Often times, more recent
spiritual works appeared more inviting that the "too
familiar" Scripture passages. Many religious faced on
the one hand, the frustration of not finding meaning;
and on the other hand, a certain uneasiness because of
their lack of joy in reading what so many spiritual
writers had spoken of as bringing joy and delight.

Reading with a "Converted" Heart

The author suggests that perhaps we need to return
to reading Scripture not merely with the mind, but with

the "heart", prayerfully in the presence of God. The message of the Gospel should not be read for mere information out of intellectual abstractions that are often separated from the real meaning of life. Rather, it should be read as the Good News of Jesus Christ, alive among us today, our hope and glory.

When we come to the Word in the obedience of faith, we are open to receive the Spirit, which is life. The Word does not remain static but becomes creative as Isaiah wrote: "The word that goes out from my mouth does not return to me empty, without carrying out my will and succeeding in what it was sent to do." (Is.55:11) Our task in responding to the Word is to free ourselves from the entanglements that threaten to divide the heart and rob it of inner peace. "Any thing that prevents my being wholly intent on pleasing the Lord, will disturb my inner peace and prevent me from hearing the Word spoken in my heart by the Spirit."[22]

I may need to be cleansed of my refusal to love anyone, of my using others as a compensation for the absence of the One love that can alone fill my heart. I may have to re-evaluate how I use my leisure time, what I do for pleasure, and what importance work plays in my life. I may be an idol for myself, seeking my own will, living a life of comfort, immersed in meaningless trivia. The burden that the Lord said would be light and sweet begins to grow progressively heavier. Living anything but complete surrender will drown my life in mediocrity.

Peace, Perseverance and Simple Desire

Unless religious take their lives in hand and seriously direct its course, they will not survive, they will live in absurdity. To find a quiet time or place of prayer may be difficult in today's craze of active involvement. A religious who is deeply convinced of the necessity of quiet time for prayer and reflection may have to "seek God" despite the difficulties. Through a fruitful use of quiet time, others will hopefully be drawn to also seek Him with their whole heart. To seek Him with reverent love and simple desire is to trust in His word to Isaiah; "I will heal him and console him, I will comfort him to the full, both him and his afflicted fellows, bringing praise to their lips. Peace, peace to far and near, I will indeed heal him, says Yahweh." (Is. 57:18-19).

REFLECTION[21]

Reflecting upon the vowed life, Andrew Cusak made the following statement:

> Sisters, unless we're willing to write on every page of the Scriptural life of Jesus, (unless we are able to fully accept every aspect of Christ's life) then we're not able to write on the personality that is Jesus within our own inner journey. Unless we are able to say "yes," to the inner experience of all that He is, then we're not able to say "yes, I have an identity that only has God as its answer; I am what I am by the life of God."

To live a deeply convinced Gospel life is not only our prerogative as religious; it is the command of the Council and the only kind of living that will make religious life meaningful. But before I can live the Gospel in a concrete way in the everyday affairs of my life, I have to be willing to "waste time" with Scripture, to discover what Gospel living entails. Perhaps, by a special study of the characteristics of women in the Gospels, I may find helps on making my life a total consecration to God. I may find direction for my life of intimacy with Christ by patterning it after the example given by the simple women of the Gospels.

First of all, the Gospel speaks of women who are lovely interiorly. By their actions they are selfless, concerned about others, and simple. Our Blessed Mother made sure that the needs of others were taken care of-- "do whatever He tells you." She also accepted the seeming disobedience from Christ when he stayed in the temple because he was "about His Father's business." The woman who was content to merely touch the hem of Christ's garment showed the utter simplicity of her faith. And there's a very delicate simplicity about the widow of Naim who had lost her son.

Secondly, there seems to be a difference in their lives once they have met Christ--they become lovers in a special way. In the life of the Samaritan woman we find a problem of love. And for the woman caught in adultery, we discover a misdirection of love. Once they experienced the love Christ had for them, despite their behavior and reputation, their lives became as deeply loving as they were self-centered before. They could

love because there was meaning in their love. The
Mother of Christ also expressed her love, perhaps most
beautifully at the foot of the cross.

A third characteristic of a Gospel woman is that
she is a life-giver. Mary gave life to her son; Mary
and Martha gave him life-sustenence when he visited
their home. Elizabeth gave life when she was long past
the years of childbearing because of her great faith
that anything is possible with God.

Fourthly, a Gospel woman is a light-giver, not in
the sense that she gives light to her child's eyes, but
more importantly that she gives light through faith.
Mary gave Christ as the light of the world when she presented Him in the temple to Simeon. The Samaritan woman
brought the light of Christ to the people of her village.
Mary Magdalen spreads the light of Christ's resurrection
to the apostles.

The last characteristic of the Gospel woman is that
she is lonely. Mary was lonely when she could not share
in the mysterious life of her Son, what He was doing,
the parables he preached, and the way He spoke of his
Father. She certainly must have been lonely at the foot
of the cross when everything she had hoped for her son
seemed lost. The adulterous woman who came to Simon the
Pharisee's house for dinner must have been extremely
lonely searching for a kind of love that would satisfy
her yet-unfilled needs.

If we know and understand the way in which Our Lord
dealt with the women in the Gospels, we may come to a
greater realization of how he loves us and how his love
draws us to simplicity, just as he drew these women to
a simplicity in love. We may then see how those three
notions, that is, selflessness, service and simplicity,
that were characteristic of Gospel women may find expression in our lives.

If I love the Lord and have Him as the center of my
life, my effort to love others is greatly enhanced. The
way in which I teach the students, or care for the poor
and aged in the neighborhood, would speak of the love
that I experience from Christ, and in Christ, because I
find the love of Christ shining forth from them. I have
to be more than a good teacher, more than a Christian
who can only partially share Christ's love with others

because of family responsibilities and so on. By my
very life I have to share the light of faith with those
I serve. I need to be the best instrument that I can
be to share the light of Christ with my limited world.
My life should mirror the simplicity of the love of God
in my care and concern for those around me. I can only
remain in-touch with the love of God by communicating
with Him, by discovering His designs in Scripture, in
the special love He has shared with the persons He met.

As another means of communicating more fully with
Christ as a vowed religious, we will explore the implications of spiritual reading for the spiritual life as
a whole.

Susan Annette Muto[22]
Spiritual Reading as an Aid to Simplicity

Spiritual reading is both an aid to living a deeper,
more spiritual religious life, and a means whereby a
religious may grow in simplicity. As an aid in developing a richer, fuller spiritual life, spiritual reading
first of all helps to build an intellectual reflective
life. A reflective life is not cut off from the workings of the spirit, but aids in discovering the true
identity of the spirit, by providing input that will
broaden the present horizon of the person, and will aid
in providing a simulus for further growth. To develop
an intellectually reflective life, a religious needs to
know how to synthesize, to bring together the scattered
readings of the day into meaning. Through this synthe-
sis she will be able to sort out the false from the true
"prophets" and will be able to deepen her life commitment
through the constant effort to emerge ever more fully
into the person she is called to be in religious life.

Spiritual reading also possesses the power to bind
celibate energy.[23] Because the religious lives in a
community, she is not bound by details that the single or
married Christian has to be concerned wth. The energies
that are there need to be channelled into thoughtful
reflectiveness. And since religious are no longer bound
be a time schedule that provides for spiritual reading,
each person has to build fundamental inner structures
of freedom to set time apart to do spiritual reading and
the other growth producing aspects of spiritual exercises,
such as meditation and meditative reading.[24]

205

Whatever spiritual task I am about, it is important
that it aid me in returning to or in remaining close to
the Sacred, to dwelling with the holy Word of God. Muto
speaks of spiritual reading as being a three-fold return
to the sacred life. First of all, it is a return to the
Word as the source of spiritual unfolding. It aids me
in making distinctions between living and loving, between
friendship community and faith community. In other
words, it aids in drawing unique and individual religious
into a common life form based on a common goal of living
in communion with Christ. Spiritual reading also is a
means of returning to our roots, our roots in our faith
and in our community. In this way, spiritual reading
may be a prelude to prayer.

Lastly, spiritual reading may be an aid in returning to the simple. Through spiritual reading the funda-
mentals of religious life, faith and the spiritual life
may again become clear as the human "camps" that so
often divide us are under-cut. Through a return to the
word in all its simplicity, messages of the One who is
the Way, the Truth and the Life may be more clearly
heard.

When simplicity is gained the old is ever new.
The selections I read from Scripture as well as from the
spiritual masters hold a new message each time I read
them reflectively. I sense that humanity today is really
not very different from times past. I try to become one
with the oneness of humanity, knowing that I too have
limitations, failures, blindness. When I approach
spiritual reading with the attitude that this reading
holds something for me, each word takes on a newness
and an intensity that would not be there without my
full attention being drawn to it.

In the same sense, as the person grows in the
spiritual life, she grows in "healthy relativization,"
a term inspired by the thinking of Adrian van Kaam. In
the ultimate horizon, a simple person never allows
anything to become too much. Neither aridity nor good
feelings seem to make that person overly depressed or
elated about the "feeling level" of her spiritual life.
Spiritual masters have called this attitude "holy indifference." T. S. Eliot expressed this paradoxical
attitude as "to care and not to care."[25] It is a lived
attitude of leaving something up to God, an attitude of
dependence in which God will give what is needed when I
am most in need.

For the simple person, the end is the beginning. Each moment remains pregnant with meaning. The simple person accepts the special gift of a "life time burning in every moment." A simple person is able to live the rhythm of the everyday. She is freed from waiting for the spectacular as she realizes that this moment holds meaning of its own, that it may have greater meaning than any spectacular event.

REFLECTION

The spiritual life is not something that is disconnected from the rest of my life. Rather, it draws meaning from that life and brings a stilling and a quietedness that would not be there without time spent in reflection on the meaning of my life, on the meaning of my relationship with Christ. As a result of my retreat experience, I came to realize that doing all the "right things" was not enough. There had to be a right way of doing all the right things. One of these right things is spiritual reading. Spiritual reading could be a dead, lifeless task to perform, a task that has nothing to bring to the rest of my life. The seeming lack of meaning draws me to question how and why I was doing spiritual reading and what I had hoped it would do for my spiritual life. Spiritual reading may be that one task that draws my life into meaning and allows it to become really simple.

Reflecting on his present life, T. S. Eliot notes in "East Coker":

> So here I am in the middle way, having had twenty
> years--twenty years largely wasted, the years of
> l'entre deux guerres
> Trying to learn to use words, and every attempt
> is wholly a new start, and a different kind of
> failure
> Because one has only learnt to get the better of
> words
> For the thing one no longer has to say, or the
> way in which
> One is no longer disposed to say it. And so each
> venture
> Is a new beginning, a raid on the inarticulate.[26]

Eliot describes his life to be a venture, a task of struggling to find meaning. "Twenty years were largely

wasted." He tried to make the words say what he was
experiencing and yet they seemed to be without meaning,
without life. His life seemed to be a "mess" of indecision, a struggle to capture what was lost, and found,
and lost again. Instead of each new venture being a
beginning, the "new" seemed to draw him deeper and
deeper into meaninglessness. Words wouldn't completely
say what he was searching for.

> . . . And what there is to conquer
> By strength and submission, has already been
> discovered
> Once or twice, or several times, by men whom
> one cannot hope
> To emulate--but there is no competition--
> There is only the fight to recover what has been
> lost
> And found and lost again and again: and now,
> under conditions
> That seem unpropitious. But perhaps neither gain
> nor loss.
> For us, there is only the trying. The rest is
> not our business.[27]

Do Eliot's reflections hold any meaning for my
life? Maybe I too need to stop searching for the way in
which I can imitate perfectly the life of someone who
seems to have made the most of her life. Maybe I need
to merely try to discover for myself the way in which I
can best live my life and leave it at that. Maybe I
need to search for the one or two things necessary that
will help me to regain what I once possessed. In other
words, maybe I need to find those things that would
simplify my life, those things before which all else
fades. Perhaps I need to listen to what is really
important in my life and then direct my energies to
attaining that or at least being ready for them when
they do happen to come. "For us, there is only the
trying. The rest is not our business."

Through spiritual reading I may discover what is
really important in my life, on what my life is actually
centered. Over and over again that which is most important to me may issue forth. This is one clue to attaining simplicity: spiritual repetition.[28] Trying, in
this sense, is not an obsessional delving into everything
in search of meaning, or a self-centered searching for
fulfillment of my desires. Instead, the spiritual

208

repetion that is spoken of here is a spirial movement,
a standing in word and action over and over again to
bore more deeply into the meaning that is there without
me. It is a going deeper into the profound message that
is held in store for me, even in the everyday situations
of life, even in the selections from Scripture that I
thought I fully understood, in the message that I "once"
received from reading the works of the spiritual masters.
Boredom, in this sense, is a spiralling deeper to allow
all things to fall into place, to come to meaning on
their own.

Boring deeply into the text before me may aid me in
discovering that I am more than just the little "ego
empire" I so often revert to in daily life. I may discover a little more clearly who I am in the core of my
being. Spiritual reading may awaken me to that part of
me that is utterly without guile, that spirit core
within me that is without pretense, that is without
striving in the sense of ego-functional "getting something done."

Since there are no easy directions on how to develop
a spiritual life, the words of a spiritual writer function only as an invitation for me to look and listen,
to see and hear the challenge that God issues to me
uniquely in my life through these words. The words of
Eliot again give me food for thought:

> Men's curiosity searches past and future
> And clings to that dimension. But to apprehend
> The point of intersection of the timeless
> With time, is an occupation for the saint--
> No occupation either, but something given
> And taken, in a lifetime's death in love,
> Ardour and selflessness and self-surrender.
> For most of us, there is only the unattended
> Moment, the moment in and out of time . . .[29]

". . . in a lifetime's death in love, ardour and
selflessness and self-surrender." This too is the
occupation of the religious. Through a lifetime of
boring more deeply into the love relationship I have
with Christ, the intense moments that often appear to
be without meaning are intensely meaningful. God is
experienced as being very near even when he holds himself in darkness. In selfless love and self-surrender
to His way of working in and with me, the "trying is

all that matters, the rest is not our business."
Religious life demands a life of love, a life of self-surrender to the One who is really the center of that
life dedication.

Often times, spiritual reading brings me to the
realization that there are deeper meanings to my life
that I often realize. In the following section I shall
consider my motivation for living religious life, and
clarify how that motivation is often unclear and complex.
Through these considerations I may discover what is un-simple about my present way of living religious life,
and how these motivations may become simplified in
developing attitudes and "ways of being" that speak of
a simplicity of life.

CLARIFYING THE MOTIVATIONS FOR LIVING THE VOWED LIFE

Reginald Masterson
Re-evaluating Motivation for Living the Vowed Life

While secularity has often been downgraded because
of its "this world" pre-occupation, it has exercised a
prophetic critique on the Christian communing by calling
it back to the mission given to it by Christ: to bear
witness to the unchanging love of the Father for all.
True secular values have pointed out the wrong emphasis
that has been placed on the style of religious life in
response to previous historical times. In other words,
in the past the Church witnessed to the Father's love of
the world by performing acts of charity for the poor of
the world. Most of the time the task of aiding the poor
can be carried on by other agencies, such as the Peace
Corps, which brings the necessary care to the poor.
Masterson notes that though acts of charity will <u>always</u>
be an important witness, they will not be the uppermost
way in which religious will bear witness to the Father's
love for the world.

According to Masterson, the Church today must strive
to see that the light of the Gospel is brought to all
areas of life. The Church must in our age bear its
witness in guiding people, for example, in using his new
found powers over nature for the service of people rather
than for further exploitation or annihilation of creation.
Secular society cries for a witness to transcendent
values. A pure secularist's views are characterized by
an opaque world view:

Rather than letting in the light of the Transcendent which alone gives ultimate meaning to the world, the world is self explanatory; it has value without any reference to the Transcendent. . . and can see no further than "the wall of this world."[31]

Precisely because our culture is without a transcendent Christian reality, the Christian community needs the eschatological witness of the religious community.[32] To bear witness to the primacy of heavenly goods, "for the sake of the kingdom," has been and always will be the primary purpose of religious life.

Therefore, the task of future religious is to reassess their personal commitment to bear witness to the unchanging nature of the Father's love, to live the faith experience of a personal relationship with Christ. The challenge has been issued to the Christian Community as a whole, but most especially to the religious community, to demythologize their cultural "works of mercy" which served well in previous ages, and which gave a direction for the witness of the Gospel message. The challenge today is to continue to serve the needs of the world, which in a sense are greater today than ever before, while still being true to the Gospel message as it is in its deepest essence. In a world that fails to see beyond the horizon of its own scientism, a community without the ability to bear witness to the deeper reality of the message will indeed appear to be an anachronism.

To serve the greatest needs of today, to bear witness in a world that denies the Transcendent mystery in everything, a religious person by her very life has to witness to this deeper reality. One way of bearing witness is through a deeply committed living of the vows. Authentic religious obedience is an efficacious antidote to the drive for false autonomy which characterizes the modern drive for individualism. At the heart of the Christian message stands the conviction that true freedom for people can only be realized in and through Christ. "Nothing less than intense personal communion in love with the Father in and through Jesus Christ by the power of the Holy Spirit can motivate true religious obedience."[33] Only the religious who has experienced intimacy with Christ can know the freedom which results from it. If the religious is truly animated by a spirit of loving dedication of the Father in Jesus Christ, the tasks to which the religious are assigned are indeed fulfilling. The call for authentic religious obedience is not a cry for "law and order." Rather, it stands against the reactionary trends of today, while being motivated by a search for freedom in and through a personal encounter with Christ. Without this "transcendent" motivation, neither reactionary demands for rigid external observance, nor excessive permissiveness will solve the identity problem many religious are faced with today.

Similarly, when we speak of the celibate life, we need to stress the positive value: a total dedication in love to the person of Jesus Christ, instead of emphasizing the negative aspects of celibacy as merely freeing us from family life. Without an ultimate goal of living a life dedicated in love to Christ, religious may become easy prey to the satisfaction of artificially induced desires and needs. A religious may become passive, bored and undirected when the soruce of unchanging values is denied, ignored, or given something much less than ultimate concern.

Authentic religious poverty would also provide an antidote to the present day over-exaggeration on sense satisfaction. In our consumption-orientated culture "the challenge to sacrifice will fail in religious life if the individual does not have a personal and total commitment to Jesus Christ."[34]

REFLECTION

The mass of men lead lives of quiet desperation. What is called resignation is confirmed desperation. From the desperate city you go into the desperate country, and have to console yourself with the bravery of minks and muskrats. A stereotyped but unconscious despair is concealed even under what are called the games and amusements of mankind. There is no play in them, for this comes after work.[35]

Even though Henry David Thoreau lived over a century ago, his description of the plight of people is very fitting for today. Many Americans live their lives in desperation, searching for those things that will give their lives meaning. All of their actions seem desperate because their values are based on something

212

that is less than ultimate. The cry is often heard
today: Why can't we simplify our lives? Why does there
have to be this rash of racing around, this constant
activity to gain "the more." The "more" for us today
often ends up being more possessions, more security,
more fullfillment, more military buildup of peripheral
needs that often substitute for the ultimate needs.

Religious are a part of this modern culture too.
It is very easy to get "caught up" in the desperate
search for the "more" in peripheral concerns. Ultimate
concerns are often substituted for my lesser concerns
such as, merely offering the best education for young-
sters, merely alleviating the physical needs of the poor,
merely offering material consolation to the elderly.
Often the ultimate concern of bearing witness to the
unchanging love of the Father for all is not born out.
The service we often give is no more than the service
that could be given by other agencies who are merely
moved by humanitarian concerns.

Questions have to be seriously asked in regard to
the meaning of religious life today and the motivations
by which we serve the needs of people. Thoreau offers
further wisdom for our consideration:

The best works of art are the expression of
man's struggle to free himself from this condition, but the effect of our art is merely
to make this low state comfortable and that
higher state forgotten.[36]

Do we as religious perpetuate the "arts" while ignoring
"the kingdom" for which we have dedicated our lives?
Does the service we give bear the mark of a personal
relationship with Christ who is the grounding and rooting of all true involvement in the name of Christianity?
Do the actions of "modern religious" bear the marks of
a deeply dedicated life?

In considering the services we are giving to the
world today, in judging whether our actions are bearing
witness to the unchanging love of the Father for all
mankind, it may be worth our while to reflect upon the
witness that has been given by our sisters in times
past. In reading ther heritage of my community, I
realize that the "pioneers" of my community used the
best of their talents to aid that section of society

they felt was in the greatest need of receiving the message of God's love. Since to Mother Theresa[37] the education of female youth was most wanting in early nineteenth century Europe, she founded a community that would service that need. And when many from her country migrated to America in the 1840's, she sent five of her small band of twenty to accompany them and to service their greatest needs. After a short while they discovered America's needs to be different than the European, so education was to include those poor of America, both male and female.

While the service these sisters performed was monumental, Mother Theresa was more concerned about the spiritual welfare of her sisters than about the service they were giving to the poor. She realized that her sisters really had very little to offer to uneducated poor girls unless they had a deeply spiritual life, unless the motivation for their labors was based on an intimate relationship with Christ.

If we look at the early history of most communities we would find the same strong emphasis on a deep prayer life in order to give service to the needs of society. In conversing with the senior members of my community, I am struck by the utter simplicity of their faith. Many of them performed few extraordinary feats, but their lives glow with a success that is deeper than any success in teaching, or nursing, or care for the aged. Their success lies in a deeply personal relationship with Christ, in a life based on simple faith.

Even though today we cannot perform the same tasks that our founding sisters performed, we are asked to bring the message of the Father's unchanging love to a world scared by nuclear buildup. How will service to the needs of the times take form today unless we too have a deeply personal relationship with Christ? The role of religious life has not changed as drastically as we sometimes think. The way in which we meet the needs of society has and should change. But if we don't have the personal relationship with Christ that would be the grounding motivation of all our actions, we are doing little less than perpetuating the "arts" as referred to by Thoreau.

Other words of Thoreau come to mind:

It is something to be able to paint a particular

214

picture, or to carve a statue, and so make a
few objects beautiful; but it is far more
glorious to carve and paint the very atmosphere and medium through which we look, which
morally we can do. To affect the quality of
the day, that is the highest of arts. Every
man is asked to make his life, even in its
details, worthy of the contemplation of his
most elevated and critical hour.[38]

Perhaps our task in today's world is to "affect the
atmosphere" with a concern that is deeper than the
"arts." It seems that the task of religious today is
to "paint the atmosphere" of the day with concerns for
the ultimate. If we truly take this as the direction
for our involvements the task we will perform will be
based on an utter simplicity of faith, on a deep conviction of a personal relationship with Christ who
really "paints" the atmosphere with our lives.

Since simplicity of life for religious is often
synonymous with poverty, in the following section I
shall consider how simplicity is rightly related to
poverty and how our attitude toward poverty needs to be
changed from a concept of material deprivation to a
true poverty of spirit. Through these presentations I
hope to show how simplicity and poverty of spirit can
only flow out of a deep relationship with Christ, and
how an attitude of simplicity will make possible the
services we perform in the name of Christ.

Johannes B. Metz and Cornelius van der Poel[39]
Simplicity and Poverty of Spirit

Metz refers to the temptations of Jesus in the
desert as representing the three assaults on the
"poverty" of Jesus, and on the self-renunciation he
chose to live in redeeming us. To become human, Metz
remarks, is to become poor, to have <u>nothing</u> to brag
about before God. "To become man means to have no support and no power, save the enthusiasm and commitment
of one's own heart."[40] To become a person is to pro-
claim the poverty of the human spirit in the face of a
Transcendent God.

The cross of Christ is the proof of God's fidelity
to each of us, and is what gives us courage to be true
to oneself. The cross is the sign that one person

remained true to humanity and bore the burden in full obedience. We on our part, always remain at a distance from our own selves, and never fully sound the depths of our being, we always remain a promise, never quite fulfilled. We have but two choices in response to never being able to be ourselves totally: we may either obediently accept our innate poverty or become a slave of anxiety. For us to accept our innate poverty is to hand over our lives to God and pledge ourselves to the mystery of God's all-pervading presence.

When we encounter the person of Jesus Christ:

We become sharply aware of innate poverty as human beings. We see then the dire want of a man who lives on the bread of eternity, whose food is to do the will of the Father.[41]

Did not Christ live here on earth in continual dependence upon the Father? So too, our innate poverty must be lived from the depths of our being where our existence is unified and harmonized in dependence upon the Father. "To be able to surrender oneself and become 'poor' is, in biblical theology, to be with God, to find one's hidden nature in God."[42]

According to vander Poel, the best way to live this internal decision to live in total dependence on God, is to live an external sign of this inner conviction. Our presence in the material world implies that we must express ourselves in a material sense, and that our spiritual reality must come to life, act and develop within and through our material existence. Thus through human activity, the whole of creation may glorify the Creator. In this sense, it is not material possessions that make us selfish. We by our nature have a tendency to make ourselves the center of our world and we often express this selfishness in our attitude towards possessions. "The more man finds security and power in the material dimension of his life, the less he will be inclined or able to recognize the deeper spiritual value of his own being."[43]

Religious life of the past at times gave the impression that "not-having" or "possessing-in-common" were virtues, but religious were usually provided with everything they needed, once permission was obtained from the superior. The focal point for religious today must

therefore be based on a correct understanding of poverty
as it is understood in our culture. According to vander
Poel, it is extremely important to understand the meaning
of poverty, for the concept of poverty has changed over
the millenia:

> . . . in early Old Testament writings, pros-
> perity was considered a blessing from Yahweh,
> while poverty was a curse and punishment.
>
> . . . .
>
> The /later/ Scriptures often indicate that
> the poor seem to have the preferential concern
> for Yahweh. This preference is not a rejection
> of the rich, but a rejection of the misuse of
> power which their riches have imparted to them.[44]

Therefore, the status of "being poor" seemed to be
a more acceptable condition for Yahweh. van der Poel
notes that:

> This again was not on account of "not-having"
> but rather because the state of material
> poverty became in a certain way the visible
> manifestation of man's vulnerability and
> dependence. Poverty if correctly understood,
> can indeed become a sign in which total
> dependence on God is manifested in human terms.[45]

Christ noted in the Sermon on the Mount, "Happy are the
poor in spirit, theirs is the kingdom of heaven."
(Mt. 5:3) Christ seems to see nothing wrong with
material possessions, provided that the person does not
put ultimate trust in them and retains a sensitivity to
the needs of people.

According to van der Poel:

> It is not the lack of ownership that makes
> poverty a reality, nor does the use of less
> expensive material goods express the sign of
> dedication to God. It is rather that approach
> to life in which all the material goods that
> the religious person has and uses becomes part
> of his own personal self-expression which
> manifests the transcendent perspective of
> human existence. This commitment does not

exclude personal possessions, but it includes
a personal detachment.[46]

In other words, it seems that poverty for us is mainly
a "poverty of spirit." According to Metz, poverty of
spirit is lived in the everyday acceptance of our limitedness and our dependence upon God. Metz speaks
specifically of several forms of poverty of spirit.

The average person in the world, who performs no
extraordinary feats lives what Metz calls the "poverty
of commonplace." In imitation of Christ who was a
frighteningly simple person, whose only talent was to do
good in the name of the Father, the simple person today
lives dependence on God in the concrete everyday. In
imitation of Christ:

He has no talent but that of his own heart,
no contribution to make except self-abandonment, no consolation save God alone.[47]

Likewise, the person who does not choose to live in
poverty in the sense of doing without material possessions, lives a "poverty of neediness and misery" as a
sacrament to others. Exceptional people carry within
their hearts another type of poverty of spirit, that is,
their "poverty of uniqueness and superiority." Each
great person carries an exceptional mission that is
without parallel and without security.

Other "poverties" that can be lived are the "poverty
of our provisional nature" and the "poverty of our finiteness." Each person is here on earth only for a
limited time. There are only certain possibilities
because of this time. Our possibilities are even further
limited because of each individual's finite possibilities.
Accepting these poverties, that each person faced, is
to admit our dependence on a God who is Infinite and
All-pervading.

REFLECTION

"We on our part, always remain at a distance from
our own selves, and never fully sound the depths of our
being, we always remain a promise, never quite fulfilled . . ." These words speak to me about the poverty of
being human and our inability to perfectly live the
fullness to which he has been destined through all of
time. van Kaam says that "simplicity is a courageous

fidelity to what is really authentic in us, to what is
in accord with God's plan for us."[48] To live our individual lives with each person's individual limitations
is to live in simplicity, in a courageous faithfulness
to what is in God's plan for us. I may never fully
understand the extent of God's plan for me; I will
never be able to "mirror" completely the simplicity of
God. This should not disturb me if I live in dependence
upon his love and care for me.

To live in obedience to the poverty of being human
is to live in childlike dependence upon God while trying
to be faithful to what is authentic in life. St. Francis
de Sales uses an analogy to clarify this concept in
regard to poverty:

In all your affairs rely wholly on God's
providence through which alone you must look
for success. Nevertheless, strive quietly on
your part to cooperate with its designs. You
may be sure that if you have firm trust in God,
the success that comes to you will always be
that which is most useful for you whether it
appears good or bad in your private judgment.
Imitate little children who with one hand hold
fast to their father while with the other they
gather strawberries or blackberries from the
hedges. So too if you gather and handle the
goods of this world with one hand, you must
always hold fast with the other to your heavenly
Father's hand and turn toward him from time to
time to see if your actions are pleasing to him.
Above all things, take heed that you never leave
his hand and his protection, thinking that thus
you can gather more or gain some advantage.[49]

Francis de Sales speaks of the concrete, active
dependence on God. If correctly understood, this dependence is not a passive "leaving everything up to God."
It is an alive using of the gifts of the earth to further
the Father's love for everything created. Our poverty
lies in using these gifts and not claiming them as our
own.

The poverty that we live as religious is a concrete
sign of our dependence on God. Since we don't live in
a vacuum, but in a concrete material world, our poverty
and dependence upon God should "show" in our use of
material things. As was pointed out by both Metz and

van der Poel, "not-having" or "possessing-in-common"
may just be external manifestations of a missing internal attitude, because we don't place our ultimate trust
in God. The external is a sign of an internal conviction. External sign without internal conviction is
empty deprivation that is really without meaning. It
does not express our dependence upon God.

How do I know whether or not I am living "poverty"
in the true sense of dependence upon God? Perhaps it is
best to re-focus our attention from "having" material
possessions, to the spirit of personal detachment with
which we use the materials of our professional world.
What is my reaction when I am asked to "share" a
treasured personal possession such as a teaching unit?
How ready am I to share this project with others who
don't have their heart and soul involved in "making"
this project work? How willing am I to share my time
with others when I would like to relax in front of the
T.V. at the end of a busy day? Can I be equally
"dispossessed" of personal "knick-knacks" as I can be
of sharing the community funds? Where does my poverty
hit me the most?

Perhaps my poverty lies in accepting the very
ordinariness of my life. I may not have received great
talents, nor a superb intellect. Can I accept the
poverty of being an ordinary human being who strongly
feels my dependence upon God, or do I try to become
superior in inferior, trival ways? Does my life become
complex because of my struggles to deny my dependence
and smallness?

My poverty may be just as great in accepting the
unique talents and superiority that often place me in
the lime-light. Do I try to deny these talents, "keep
them hidden under a bushel basket," or do I share them
with others, being mindful that perhaps these talents
are part of the unfolding plan of God for me?

My greatest poverty may lie in bearing sickness,
weakness and failure. Do I accept these also as
possibly being a part of God's plan for me, or do I
"thrash around" by trying to deny that they may be God's
way of calling me to become dependent on him. Can I
accept the help of another, the support of another? Am
I open to the advice of another or am I closed-up in
my own little world?

"Your treasure is where your heart is" again comes
to mind. If my heart is centered on the love of God
for me and in trying to emerge within the plan that God
has destined for me, the "poverty" that is unique to my
life will aid and not hinder the unfolding of this plan.
If my heart is based on "treasure within", I will be
like the man who sold all he had to buy the pearl of
great price. I can only accept the limited, finiteness
of my life if I possess the "kingdom of heaven within."
Only then will my life be governed by a gentle, peaceful disposition, a disposition of simplicity.

Through a daily commitment to accept our poverties
in the light of the unfolding plan of God, we may perhaps become healed of the poverty that keeps us from
admitting our total dependence on God. Only then will
we be able to respond in true "in-dependence" in trying
to be faithful to what is really authentic in us. In
the following section we shall consider briefly the
positive powers the vows possess to heal us of our lostness, aloneness and vulnerability.

Adrian van Kaam[50]
Healing Power of the Vows

The path of religious life is an exploration of
God's continually unfolding plan of salvation. van
Kaam views the vows as enhancing the process of emergence
by healing the vowing person of self-centered tendencies
toward power, possessiveness and exclusive love. He
says that anything that goes counter to personal honesty
and consistency denotes a lack of simplicity. When a
religious is heroically faithful to a unique vocation,
that person may appear to be proud while in reality is
living in dialogue with the unfolding plan of life.
One should not "conterfeit simplicity by escaping into
the security of the life of a 'regular fellow'; he
should not attempt to be safe at the expense of his
integrity."[51] With these thoughts in mind, let us explore how the vows will aid the person to unfold simply
and how the right living of the vowed life will enhance
the unique unfolding of the person in simplicity.

"Obedience is the willingness to listen to reality
as a revelation of possibilities to be actualized by
man as the creative center of his life situation."[52]
Obedience thus invites me to listen to the unfolding of
reality while being mindful of the unique limitations

221

of my personality and life situation. The healing power of obedience is most necessary today when we are tempted to be disobedient, to organize life around tasks and preoccupations that exclude anything not relevant to single-minded projects of life. The vowing person should be able to live a more perfectly obedient life if one's vision is not clouded by concerns for status or possession.

Likewise, "chaste love is a love purified from ego-centric impulses which threaten to use self-love or love of others as means of dominating self and others."[53] It heals the vowing person from violating the spiritual, psychological, or physical integrity of self or others. Through living the vow of chase love, an atmosphere of mutual love, respect and esteem radiates to all, and will hopefully hasten the time when true personal and communal love becomes a reality for most people. Chaste or respectful love means that I respect myself wholeheartedly, and love others within my unique life situation without this love becoming exclusive in the sense of marital love or exclusive friendship. Thus the vow of celibate love heals me from excluding anyone from my care and concern, and from dominating the life of another to the detriment of their self-unfolding.

"In poverty I may select that which fosters my unique call in this world and detach myself from all that can obscure and destroy my fidelity."[54] Poverty enables me to become healed of my possessiveness that has been substituted for true self-presence and respect. In poverty of spirit I may discover the style of life that is most in tune with my unique set of talents and limitations.

The more I experience a respectful listening and presence to myself and all that is, the more healed and at home I will feel with the whole of creation. The more I grow in intimacy with the Holy, the less I am liable to become seduced by excessive and ultimate concern with structure; and the less apt I will be to "use" others to my advantage.

REFLECTION

Living the vows as described by van Kaam heals us of our lostness, aloneness and vulnerability. That is, they heal us of the poverty of being human. Living obedience may heal us of the tendency to draw everything around ourselves. Through a willingness to listen to the unfolding plan of God as it shows itself in the everyday situations of life, I may discover a little more fully my unique set of limitations and talents and how to use these to the best advantage in bearing witness to the Father's love for the world. Instead of centering my life around a single-minded preoccupation with tasks, my whole self may become centered in fulfilling the will of the Father in my life. Being healed of my self-centeredness I will be more able to responsibly bring the breath of God's love to others.

With a detached heart, I will become healed of the tendency toward possessiveness. When my heart is centered on and dependent upon God, I will be less likely to use others to my advantage, or claim "things" that are really not important in the light of my ultimate concern for God.

Through the healing power of celibacy I will be able to more wholeheartedly respect each person in their uniqueness. I will not be as apt to try to dominate others, nor to claim anyone exclusively for myself. Being healed of my fear of loneliness, the transparency of the love of God will show through more clearly in my interaction with others and in my respect for all of creation.

Through my saying "yes" to the Father's love for me, I am in effect saying "yes" to my deepest self. I respond more fully to the deepest mystery of my life, and allow it to unfold in simplicity because of his invitation extended to me to emerge as responsibly and authentically as I can in the everyday situations of life. Each day I will then be able to utter more fully the promises I have made.

Summary and Transition

The purpose of the Chapter has been to clarify the ways in which a vowed Christian may more fully live the Gospel call to simplicity. As in previous Parts, faith again seemed to be the centering core that alone would make religious life meaningful. Religious life will be kept from absurdity only by an unconditional "yes" to Christ, to live totally in Him. This complete self-abandonment, patterned after the life of Christ, opens the vowing person to a deeper relationship with God and others. For a religious, concern for the Ultimate meaning in life should stand out in bold relief. That is, a religious should witness to successes that are not measurable in the eyes of the world. But, through a full turning toward God, the religious freely and simply lives her choice to follow Christ.

The more firmly a religious believes in the hidden, mysterious love of God, the more simple life will become and the more fully will be realized the importance of internal renewal in preference to external change. Through a deepening life of prayer, ones heart, mind and energies will become fixed on the Divine Initiator, who alone makes this life meaningful. To grow in simplicity, it is essential that the vowed person renew "faith-contact" with God through a deeper understanding of oneself in relation to God. In using Smith's "formulary for prayer," we pointed out the necessity of the center-to-center relationship of prayer, how God must be found in the daily affairs of life, how prayer must be in tune with a deeper self-knowledge, how one must study the stages of prayer to know the particular characteristics of the present state, the necessity of responding to the Holy Spirit through my own unique spirit, the importance of prayer remaining a communication with Christ, and lastly, the importance of having a guide other than self.

Besides prayer we pointed out the necessity of returning to the Gospel to appropriately renew religious life. While more recent writers may offer much food for thought, there is no substitute for the Words of Scripture themselves. Through a reading of Scripture with a "converted" heart, one's life may unfold in imitation of the Gospel women whose lives were characterized by simplicity and selfless service. Spiritual reading was also presented as a means of synthesizing and relativizing the affairs of everyday life. Spiritual reading also aids in a three-fold return to the life of the spirit: a return to the Word, to our roots in faith, and to a simplicity of life.

Secular society has also pointed out the purpose of religious life: to bear witness to the primacy of heavenly goods. Religious must seriously re-examine the ways in which they serve the needs of mankind and how appropriately their vowed life aides in making their service more than mere humanitarian concern. Through obedience they offer a counter witness to the false autonomy of today; through celibacy they witness

positively to a life of intimacy with Christ and against
the fulfillment of false needs and desires; and through
poverty they witness to a society that is engulfed in
consumption the value of non-possessiveness. Through
reflection on the words of Thoreau, we pointed out the
necessity of religious to "paint the atmosphere" with
an awareness of the unchanging love of the Father for
all of creation.

Poverty of spirit as related to simplicity was presented as a possible way for religious to witness to a
dependence on God through accepting the poverty of being
human. Poverty for religious should be a visible sign
of an acceptance of an innate vulnerability, lostness
and aloneness. Through a detachment from "things" and
persons, a religious witnesses to childlike dependence
upon the Father. Through the healing power of the vows,
we pointed out that simplicity can only be attained by
selling all to "buy the pearl of great price," by centering one's heart on the full and authentic living of one's
deepest self in tune with the unfolding plan of God.

When I deepen my "faith-contact" with God, I constantly renew my life of prayer in tune with the Gospel
message. I realize that I cannot center my life on God
in isolation from others. Therefore, in the following
chapter we will stress the importance of a community in
unfolding my life in simplicity.

ENDNOTES

[1]William F. Hogan, "The Vowed Condition,: _Sister Formation Bulletin_ XVI:1 (Fall, 1969), 13-14.

[2]J. M. R. Tillard, "The Theological Viewpoint: Religious Life, a Choice Rooted in Faith," _Donum Dei_ No. 17 (1971), 13-36.

[3]Ibid., pp. 30-31.

[4]Ibid., p. 27 (Italics in the original.)

[5]Ibid., p. 29.

[6]Walter M. Abbott (ed.). _The Documents of Vatican II_ (New York: America Press, 1966), p. 49.

[7]Herbert Smith, "Prayer and the Maturing Sister," _Sisters Today_ XLII:8 (April, 1971), 439-453.

[8]Ibid. p. 448.

[9]Ibid. p. 447.

[10]Ibid., p. 441.

[11]Smith uses the term UNUM as a short form of "Unum Necessarium" which refers to God as the "necessary one," the core of life.

[12]Ibid., p. 443.

[13]St. Teresa of Avila, _The Way of Perfection_ trans. E. Allison Peers (Garden City; New York: Image Books, 1964), p. 184.

[14]St. Teresa of Avila, _Interior Castle_ trans. E. Allison Peers (Garden City, New York: Image Books, 1961), p. 101.

[15]_The Collected Works of St. John of the Cross_ trans. Kevin Kavanaugh and Otilio Rodriguez (Washington, D.C.: ICS Publications, 1973), p. 97.

[16]Ibid., p. 149.

[17]William Johnston (ed.). _The Cloud of Unknowing_ (Garden City, New York: Image Books, 1973), p. 177.

[18]Sister Florette Amyot, "Listening and Responding to the Word of God," Open to the Spirit (Ottawa, Ontario: Canadian Religious Conference, 1970), pp. 40-46.

[19]The Documents of Vatican II, op. cit., pp. 468-471.

[20]Ibid., p. 42.

[21]This reflection is based on ideas gleaned from a retreat conference given by Rev. Andrew Cusak at Good Counsel Hill, Mankato, Minnesota on June 11, 1972. (Mimeographed.)

[22]Susan Annette Muto, Unpublished Class Notes, Center for the Study of Spirituality of the Institute of Man, Duquesne University, Pittsburgh, Spring, 1974.

[23]See also Adrian van Kaam, The Vowed Life (Denville, New Jersey: Dimension Books, 1968).

[24]In her book, Approaching the Sacred, Dr. Muto clearly defines the differences between these three spiritual exercises. Spiritual reading is the foundational discipline of the spiritual life that gives a frame of reference within which to meet God more personally. It also teaches how to live the truths of Christianity in day to day life. Meditative reading, on the other hand, is considered to be a variant form of meditation in which the text, for example Scripture, or the writings of a Spiritual Master, substitutes for mental prayer. In meditative reflection I dwell on one or several passages from Scripture and direct questions toward my own life: What in the text applies to my life? How does the experience of the spiritual writer coincide with my own experience? How is God communicating with me through these words. The amount of material I cover is not as important as what meaning it has for my life. Meditation is that period of time I set aside for more personal communion with Christ. In preparation for this reflective time, I may read a passage from Scripture that tells me of an experience in the life of Christ. In meditation I may place myself quietly in the presence of Christ and become fully involved in how that same situation may be lived in my life. For example, how does Christ's example of doing the will of the Father find meaning in my life? For a clear presentation of the art and discipline of spiritual reading see Susan Annette Muto, Approaching the Sacred (Denville, New Jersey:

Dimension Books, 1973), pp. 15-78.

[25]T. S. Eliot, "Ash Wednesday," in *Selected Poems* (New York: Harcourt, Brace & World, Inc., 1964), p. 84.

[26]T. S. Eliot, *Four Quartets*(New York: Harcourt, Brace, & World, Inc., 1971), p. 30-31.

[27]Ibid., p. 31.

[28]For a clear distinction between spiritual repetition and blind repetition see: Adrian van Kaam, *In Search of Spiritual Identity* (Denville, New Jersey: Dimension Books, 1975), pp. 224-229; and Susan Annette Muto, *Steps Along the Way* (Denville, New Jersey: Dimension Books, 1975), pp. 134-167.

[29]Ibid., p. 44.

[30]Reginald Masterson, "Religious Life in a Secular Age," *Cross and Crown* XXLL (June, 1970), 133-147.

[31]Ibid., p. 136.

[32]Ibid., pp. 140-141.

[33]Ibid., p. 140-141.

[34]Ibid., p. 143.

[35]Henry David Thoreau, *Walden and Other Writings* (New York: Modern Library, 1950), p. 7.

[36]Ibid., p. 33.

[37]Mother Mary Theresa of Jesus Gerhardinger founded the Congregation of the School Sisters of Notre Dame in Bavaria in 1833 with the purpose of instruction and training of youth.

[38]Ibid., p. 81.

[39]Johannes B. Metz, *Poverty of Spirit* trans. John Drury (New York: Newman Press, 1968), pp. 5-53; and Cornelius van der Poel, *Religious Life: A Risk of Love* (Denville, New Jersey: Dimension Books, 1972), pp. 67-85.

[40]Metz, op. cit., p. 14.

[41]Ibid., p. 27.

[42]Ibid., p. 34.

[43]van der Poel, op. cit., p. 74.

[44]Ibid., p. 78-79.

[45]Ibid., p. 79.

[46]Ibid., p. 83.

[47]Metz, op. cit., p. 37.

[48]Adrian van Kaam, The Vowed Life (Denville, New Jersey: Dimension Books, 1968), p. 359.

[49]St. Francis de Sales, Introduction to the Devout Life trans. and ed. John K. Ryan (Garden City, New York: Image Books, 1966), pp. 172-153. See also sections in this thesis on the childlike qualities.

[50]Adrian van Kaam, op. cit., pp. 279-314.

[51]Ibid., p. 359.

[52]Ibid., p. 281.

[53]Ibid., p. 285.

[54]Ibid., p. 301.

CHAPTER IX

COMMUNAL RESPONSE TO THE CALL OF SIMPLICITY

INTRODUCTION

Religious community's main purpose is to draw together those who acknowledge their common bond of being called by Christ. This shared life goal has the possibility of calling each member to fuller spiritual and human growth based on responsible love and respect for each other's limitedness. The process of self-simplification, a process in which each person is engaged in answering a unique life call, is broadened and enhanced because of the mutual support and love shared among the members. Together then, the members of a religious community may be able to live a shared simplicity of life, discovering in each other the Christ each one has been called to serve. Each individual's communing with Christ, to discover his will, can be strengthened by the community's centeredness in the Eucharist.

At times true encounter in community may become distorted, resulting in childish dependency, inhibiting conformity, and self-centeredness among the members. An atmosphere of honesty, concern, and transparency needs to prevail in order to draw the members to child-like dependency, free-responsiveness and Christ-center-edness. Only then can a community be a center in which the value of Christ-centeredness, lived in simplicity, can be radiated to others as each religious goes out to serve the broader world community.

ROLE OF COMMUNITY IN SIMPLIFYING LIFE

Adrian van Kaam[1]
Purpose of Community Life

The purpose of community life is to be the background from which individual men and women can emerge ever more fully into the cultural world in which they will serve. Their aim is not to serve for the glory of their community, but for the glory of Christ who is the center of that community. We all share in common the inner call to "live a celibate life of religious worship and witness, and we all feel the necessity to live that life sustained by some type of community."[2] If it were not for community, says van Kaam, it would be very difficult for someone who is not exceptional to avoid the idiosyncracies of a unique personality. A person alone could not, with limited talents and capabilities, create the spiritual and material conditions for religious freedom. In van Kaam's words:

> What is more beautiful than a community of unique individuals living serenely in profound respect for one another's individuality, a respect which is expressed and symbolized by the gracious style in which they allow one another to be.[3]

Therefore, the first condition of community life is to "put up with" the imperfections and limitations in myself and others. By so doing I may grow in silent adoration of the hidden glory of God in the unpleasant, temperamental, anxious, or weak members of the community. Though we are different in temperament, in talents and in outlook, the deepest possibility of coming to a oneness in community is to realize the glory that God has given to each one of us in a hidden way, a way that often taxes our imagination and forces us to look at one another in faith. To be able to begin to speak of unity in community, we can only build on the fundamental ground of faith. Only then can we live with each other's diversity in unity. Only then can we live community in the creative tension that individual diversity may bring.

Besides being an abode for the adoration of the hidden glory of God, community is a nurturing ground for the building of childlike trust among the members. Through a life of trusting, we are more able to bear with one another's burdens without letting gripes and troubles overrun us. In spite of all adversity, our trust must be in the Real Presence of God among us. He is at the heart and the center of our community.

It was said of the apostles and early Christians, "see how they love one another." And still we know of their diversity and idiosyncracies, their struggle for power, for love and for possessions. What was it that "held" them together and gave their community life meaning? It was more than any natural bond, it was a common bond of love of God. So, too, our love in diversity can only be a measure of the common bond of our love for God as the ultimate concern in our lives, even though at times our witness is far from perfect.

The ultimate aim of community life is not community itself. Rather, its aim is to promote in individual members an increasing freedom for the pursuit of their personal religious presence in the social structure to which they have been called by grace. But, we must keep in mind that:

> In community life, the fundamental principle of respectful promotion of each member's uniqueness far from being whimsical and individualistic, leads to rules, customs and unwritten encounter structures which limit and discipline our individualistic, egoistic needs and desires.[4]

Community encounter also implies developing within the individual members the ability to be alone. When I dare to be myself, and become aware of my unique call in life, I experience that I am somehow not like everyone else. I am alone. This solitude prepares me for the courage to stand alone in the world when the situation calls for a witness that I alone may be able to bring. This aloneness implies an openness toward the Divine who is working in me uniquely. Therefore, my community should offer me a rich opportunity for prayer, recollection, silence and spiritual self-renewal in which I may come to discover my deepest self and in turn witness to the transcendent dimension of my life in whatever cultural enterprise I am engaged. Essentially, the religious community's task is to create an atmosphere in which religious may more easily live on the level of the spirit and be able to more fully witness to this transcendent dimension in the culture.

REFLECTION

When the life of a community is centered on Christ, that shared life may lead naturally to a promotion of simplicity within the individual members. When the shared life is an adoration of the hidden glory of God, present within each person, there is a respect that is deeper than respect for the individual. It is a respect for Christ hidden within the individual members.

In imitation of the life of Christ, a community lives together and fosters the individual growth of its members, in the everyday hidden life of the community. Through faithfulness to the small and seemingly insignificant common understandings, a community creates an atmosphere for the unfolding of each person.

Through mutual support in the diversity of living within the structures of a particular community, each person will hopefully emerge because of the creative tension that will naturally spring from truly accepting diversity. We stress <u>creative</u> tension, because the attitudes, ideals and each person's unique talents and limitations can be a source of harmony or disharmony in a community. When the natural tensions that exist because of our diversity are accepted as building a different part of the mystical body, this diversity, though at times painful, can be creative. When individual diversity is not accepted, not used as a basis of our search for unity, it can be destructive of the very foundation of our common life shared in faith. Our shared life together may become either very complex or an unfolding of simplicity, depending upon how willing we are to allow each person to unfold in her uniqueness.

Our love for one another will only grow when we trust in the good will of another, when we honestly and sincerely allow each person to be oneself while calling each person to a further growth and full conversion to a life of faith in Christ. No one person should be allowed to stagnate, to stop emerging into the fullness of the person one has been called to be. No one should be forced to build a protective shell around oneself, that would keep one from emerging into full, authentic personhood, that is, into simply being the person one could best be.

Through my retreat experience, I came to realize the support that a community can give in aiding each person to grow into the fullest imitation of Christ. Community life provides me with the time to heal from the brokenness that had dissipated my life. My respectful community allowed me the space and privacy through which I could grow to accept more fully myself and to accept my true relationship with others in Christ.

When individual lives become more centered on Christ as their ultimate concern, the community provides the necessary atmosphere in which each person may unfold in the uniqueness and simplicity that should characterize a life centered on Christ. Community life will then be the nurturing ground out of which the individual can bear a fuller and richer witness to the Father's love for all creation.

233

Adrian van Kaam[5]
Community: Center for Value Radiation

        van Kaam says that in the light of Christ's revela-
tion, we know that individuals have defected from the
ultimate meaning of culture, that is, from presence to
the Father and in cooperation with the Holy Spirit in
the unfolding of creation.   Therefore, religious should
bear in mind that:

        the presence to the Father as revealed by Jesus
        is not only the fundamental mode of life that
        should inspire, purify and deepen our service,
        but it is also the kind of presence that is
        easily lost, forgotten, and repressed because
        of the original sinfulness in which we all share.[6]

Therefore, in preparing for cultural participation, each
person must discover daily moments in which to find and
experience oneself as a participant in the process of
humanization and spiritualization of humanity.   Through
these moments she will become more present to the Sacred
and less preoccupied with certain areas that usually
engulf a functional society.   The participative religious
is called to help withdraw the opaque veil from the
Sacred by a selfless, deeply religious manner in which
one serves the cultural unfolding of people and creation.
Through honest dialogue with the authorities of the
community, the religious person attempts to discover in
what way as a unique individual that person may best
participate in some area of the culture without doing
harm to oneself or to that segment of society served.
As a participative religious, one should share the
cultural dedication of all Christians so deeply that
they will often fail to recognize that person as a reli-
ious:

        A religious shall not be among them as an
        example of pure perfection, but as someone
        whom they can see and touch, whose weakenesses
        and foibles they can observe, and whose life
        is involved in their lives of cultural dedi-
        cation.[7]

        Participative religious life should always structure
itself in such a way that it protects and fosters the
highest possible unique religious-cultural unfolding of
each religious within a particular community.   It should
also foster the lived unity of personal unfolding,

of each religious within a particular community. It
should also foster the lived unity of personal unfolding,
cultural participation and true service. Without a
stress on this lived unity, a religious may become
overwhelmed by the variety of problems, both personal
and cultural, that clamor for attention and solution.
The more complex the society in which the religious is
engaged, the more aware the community as a whole should
grow in preserving the individual integrity of its members. For no matter how nobly meant and generously
planned it is, every form of service has at its heart the
possible taint of human selfishness which affects this
service as a whole, which may make it deteriorate, and
which renders it far less efficacious than it could be.

REFLECTION

The ultimate goal of religious life is to foster
the individual religious' presence to the Father as a
witness to the love of the Father to all. Witnessing
to the presence of the Father presupposes an intimate
relationship with Him, a relationship that is lived
out in a selfless and deeply religious sharing of one's
unique potential. Witnessing to the culture has to
become concrete in some task or occupation. But this
occupation doesn't have to be anything grandiose. To
witness to the love of God in the culture, a religious
must simply be faithful to what is most authentic in
the concrete dailiness of life. It may be instilling
Christian values to one's students across the cafeteria
table. By example, by efforts to live in tune with God's
unique love for all, the love for students will shine
through and will influence the love they bear for one
another. An individual may not have the ability nor the
temperament to do innovative teaching, but, if efforts
speak of a love for each unique child, instruction will
bear richer fruit than the best developed curriculum
that is without the touch of Christ's love for individual
students. Another person may be a brilliant lecturer.
This person may witness to the utter simplicity of Christ
shown in concern for all people, by using an ability to
understand philosophical phenomena to bear witness to
Christ. An administrator may witness the love of Christ
to a hospital staff by concern for the spiritual as well
as the physical needs of each patient. In an age when
the right to life is denied to so many, the value of such
a witness cannot be measured. Likewise, a person engaged
in social work may merely "fight the establishment" for
the poor; or she may also simply witness to the love of

Christ for them and aid them in living with their
poverty. Through dialogue, each person has to be mindful of the message of God's love--how can this message
be best lived, and how can that message be fostered in
those served?

Through witness to the culture as it is unfolding,
the religious shares the simplicity of God's love with
others. By the transparency with which love of God is
shared, a religious walks the same path with all people,
sharing the love that that person uniquely has received
from God. In realizing that service is most natural
and most in tune with capabilities these services are
performed in response to Christ's love. This person
also realizes that simplicity and freedom happen when
that person is free in her ability to respond with a
community to the one thing that binds their efforts with
meaning--the power of Jesus in their hearts.

At times, even with the best of intentions, the
community life that should simplify our lives becomes
distorted and motivated by peripheral concerns. In the
following section, we shall briefly present several distortions that may cloud a community's goal to live in
reflection of the love of Christ.

DISTORTIONS IN COMMUNITY

Adrian van Kaam[8]
Distortions in Community

True encounter in community implies the courageous
acceptance that in many dimensions we are not the same;
that we should be different; and that these differences
at times may distort community life as a whole. If I
cannot tolerate creative tension in community, I may fall
into relationships of pseudo-encounter, relationships in
which I am robbed of my freedom and rob other of theirs.
Identifying with fellow religious who blindly agree with
all I think, or those with whom I fuse indiscriminately,
is one type of pseudo-encouter of sentimental in-being.
On the other hand, a total rejection of mature religious
who manifest that they disagree with me or cannot accept
or understand all that I am, may lead to another pseudo-
encounter of counter-being. Both types of psuedo-encounter
may foster a devastating, closed attitude of rejection,
negativity and condemnation, among the members of a community.

236

Individual reactions may also tend to distort community encounter. The more tightly I cling to my own personal structures of religious, cultural and social life, the less I shall be able to experience my uniqueness which makes me aware of my identity. "If I wish to be safe from all disapproval, rejection, misunderstanding, conflict, or decrease in popularity, I must repress all awareness of my original selfhood."[9] The more I deny my individuality, the more anonymous I become, the more likely I am to be absorbed in a numb collectivity that substitutes for community.

Someone who was overly protected as a child will unconsciously select those symbols, images and metaphors of community that symbolize the possibility of living as a warmly loved child who receives boundless care, tenderness, and understanding. Superiors are then expected to be as understanding mothers who are warm and sweet. In the same situation, someone who has become the constraining, controlling personality will regress to anxious conformity to structures lived obsessively and defensively in early childhood.

A third type of personality van Kaam describes as the creative personality. The creative, open transcendent person has overcome fixation on the two levels of childhood just described. This person has the most effective and serene attitude toward community structures. This person is able to bear patiently with superfluous structure which cannot be changed for the time being and still lives wholeheartedly within those structures. A person who is creative is able to constantly go beyond those structures that don't fit the contemporary situation and live in the presence of the Holy, which is an ultimate concern.

REFLECTION

Distortions in community happen most frequently when religious do not accept diversity, when they do not accept the individuality and uniqueness of each person within the community. Distortions occur because we, in our humanness, have the tendency to draw all things around ourselves, and use defensive tactics that often close us up within ourselves. In our pseudo-encounters we sometimes play "games" with each other, games that deny the person of the other in community. One such game could be called, "Pick and Choose." In this game we choose those we will love. We ignore others. Another game may be, "Let's Make a Deal." If you do this . . ., I'll do this for you. If the other person does not respond in the way we want them to, we give up on that person and cut them out from any love at all. Another possible distortion could be called, "The Half-way House." In it a person may come only "half-way" in her love for another member of the community. It is also hard for her to love any one first. In this distortion we just tolerate people, we co-exist. A fourth game that we sometimes play could be called, "Hot and Cold." In this game we deal with others according to our mood. Each of these games is lived by all of us to some extent, in some situations. This is a reason why we need to struggle together to make communities what they should be. This is why it is extremely important to know ourselves and to know our tendencies in relating to others.

Besides playing games with my community, I may be caught in childish dependency. I may cry for love, tenderness and compassion from my community without being willing to give unselfish love and understanding in return. Through childishness I may mask my fears by hiding behind the superior, or hiding behind structures. I may never come to freely accept responsibility for my own life nor allow that life to unfold in its fullest potential.

I may become shackled by conformity to rules, the opinion of others, or the image that I have set for myself as a "good" religious. Through my retreat experience I discovered that my "yes" saying entangled me in the clutches of meaninglessness. My life was not inner-directed; it was only lived superficially. Through the support of a community that allowed me to emerge to become myself, I could eventually transcend this fixation. I learned to live with structure, and to accept others as real graces in my life. Because I was struggling to turn more fully to God, I could more easily see that mere conformity did not allow me to see the transcending power of God in my life or in the lives of others.

I realized that the ultimate strength of community comes from complete abandonment to the ways of the Father. I discovered in imitation of Christ that I too could make others more loveable by loving them, as Christ made Mary Magdalen and Zaccheus loveable through his love. Community life may never be easy. Developing loving relationships at times calls me to suffer through the relationship. Christ cried when his friend Lazarus died; he also must have suffered through Peter's denial. Persevering in love for others implies a more mature response, one that is always unfolding as I come to understand and accept myself more fully in relation to Christ.

After briefly looking at several distortions that can occur in a community when each person does not honestly and sincerely try to center life on Christ, that is, try to simplify life by having Christ as the ultimate concern, it is important that we look at several communal aids that may foster simplicity in our communities.

COMMUNAL AIDS IN FOSTERING SIMPLICITY

Adrian van Kaam[10]
Communal Fostering of Simplicity

When I discover in certain periods of my life that I am more than usually irritated by structures in my community, and find that my life has lost some of its meaning, these are the times to question myself about my prayer life, my recollection, my hours of waiting silence, my spirit of intimacy with the Lord. In recollection I come to myself--the self I have come to know through a variety of human encounters of the past. However, recollection is more a looking at Him than myself. As van Kaam says:

> The only way to come home to myself is to remove myself from the externals of identifying encounters, to bring myself to rest, to empty my mind of preoccupation, to let go the flow of experiences, to be responsive in peace to whatever the Holy allows to well up in my heart, and then to find out who I am.[11]

Along with individual recollectedness, it is sometimes helpful to develop means by which a community may draw itself together and communicate about the life of the spirit. Spiritual reading together is one solution. A number of sisters may select a spiritual book that they choose to read together. Everyone in the group reads the book meditatively. At times this group may come together to freely share their response to the book. It is important in using this tool to foster community that no one feels forced to share, to bare one's soul, to fall into the trap of excessive emotionalism. Through a

relaxed sharing of ideas and insights, individuals may
be drawn to see that their lives need to be converted,
that they need to find out more about themselves and
about their relationship to Christ in prayer. Another
means of communal fostering of simplicity is to use a
method of communal reflection that has been developed
by Paul Roy.

Paul Roy[12]
Communal Reflection

One of the tremendous implications of religious
life is that we must be permeated with a sense of the
presence of God to whom we have committed our lives. We
do not just occasionally place ourselves in His presence,
we ARE always in his presence. When we pray we attend
to this presence in a special way. Roy understands the
term "contemplative in action" as meaning that we are so
caught up with the realization that we live in God's
presence that all of our actions are carried out under
the influence of and with an ever-increasing consciousness of that presence.

The Examen of Consciousness as explained by George
Aschenbrenner, is a reflection on how we have grown in
our awareness of the presence of God in the activities
of everyday life.[13] The idea of communal reflection adds
another dimension, that of how a community as a group
has become aware of the presence of God. According to
Roy, communal reflection is other than "shared prayer."
It is "shared-time-in-prayer." When a group comes together for communal reflection, it is understood that
they are not coming together to "render an account to
one another." The group does not come together to give
a progress report.

The group comes together: a. to remember that
we do indeed live in God's presence; b. to reflect on our own consciousness--during a day or
a week with all of its varied activities--of
the Divine Presence, and to reflect on the
influence that this presence has had on our
way of acting; c. to share, if we are so moved,
the Good News with our community; God at work
in my life, redeeming me, making Himself known to
me and to those around me; d. to seek the support
and help of my community if I have found it
difficult to be aware of the presence of God

during the day, or if I have been unable to
recognize it in myself, in others, or in the
gifts of creation; e. to reflect together on
how we as a group have been able to witness
to the saving presence of God in the world;
f. if we consider the fact that God's own
description of Himself was in terms of presence
(Ex. 3:14) maybe our communal reflection can
help us grow in the way we are present to one
another and really live the command that Jesus
gave us to "be perfect just as your heavenly
Father is Perfect." (Mt. 5:48)[14]

The main purpose of communal reflection is to help us
discover the Presence of God and his expectations of us
in all aspects of our life. Through shared-time-in-
prayer we may develop a common openness and may bring
ourselves to a more total giving of ourselves to God.
Together we may look at our life and examine what Jesus
is calling each person to do. Sharing-time-in-prayer
also presents an opportunity for a community to express
one another's expectations, to learn the needs of others,
and to share in the grace experience of another.

REFLECTION

Through a reading of Scripture or the writings of
a spiritual master with a group of other religious, I
become convinced that "I am not in this alone." I will
more realistically see that our lives are bound together
by a common search to become more present to Christ as
He appears in my life. Through this shared reading, we
are in effect supporting each other in our inner journey.
Communal sharing may also aid my personal response to the
question: How deeply do I allow others to enter into my
life?

If rightly approached, shared reading may be a way
of allowing the deeper concerns, the more central aspects
of another's life to emerge into my consciousness. I may
"see" a deeper aspect, a more profound and wholistic
picture of the other. Deeply trusting in the good will
of everyone in the group, there will be no need for anyone to do a "surface performance", or a pretentious presentation of where one is in life. In respect for the
uniqueness of each person, some may want to share their
insights; others may realize that on a particular day the
interaction of the group gives one enough inspiration to
continue on through a present state of darkness.

Shared reflection on the readings will aid me in becoming more centered on others and on Christ acting within each person, than on my own self-centeredness and my individualistic searching for meaning. In other words, sharing spiritual reading may aid me to simplify my life as I realize that it is the quality with which I bring myself toward life that determines the depth to which people may come into my life. When I am able to share in the depth experiences of another, I may become more empathic, more loving of the other in search for meaning, in efforts to come to intimacy with Christ, to find life centered on Him.

For example, during a particular time of the year a community may decide that they will place special emphasis on the liturgical readings. When they gather together in the evening to communally reflect on their day, they would read the Scripture selections for the following day. Tomorrow the first reading is taken from James 2:1-9. Through a reading of this selection the community may discover that this reading strongly emphasizes the concrete living of faith. St. James tells us that living faith and making distinctions between groups of people do not go together. He cites an example of two men, one rich and one poor, who walk into the temple. Then he says:

Listen, my dear brothers: It was those who are poor according to the world that God chose, to be rich in faith and to be the heirs to the kingdom which he promised to those who love him. (James 2:5)

Perhaps the community could stop with just these few thoughts and reflect upon how their individual lives of faith make them heirs of the kingdom. Through shared reflection they may realize that this particular community, serving in a middle class area of a large city, does not meet the "poor" in the sense of those who lack material possessions. How can they place special emphasis tomorrow on treating everyone justly? Who are the "poor" that they do serve? Could it be the child who is "poor in love" and causes constant upset in the classroom? Could the poor be the person sitting next to one of them who is in special need of concern, who is trying to work something out and seems to be constantly "against" what the community is striving for? What special awareness of poverty can this group work toward for one day? Through these reflections, the Gospel message

of the day may become more concrete for them and may be
the unifying factor for their good works. Consciously
being aware of a communal effort to live just one small
aspect of the Gospel may draw each individual to a concrete living of that message in her activities of the
day. Sharing the Eucharist together, hearing the message
together may give my prayer life and time in reflection
an impetus that I could not have alone. Perhaps when
the community gathers together again the following
evening, I may say that each person I met was more real
to me because I was concerned about serving the "poorness"
in that person. I may also have to say that today I was
not able to keep this part of the Gospel in mind; I may
have been too preoccupied with my own concerns.

    Through communal reflection we continually call to
mind that our main purpose in religious life is to
attend to the God in our lives. Through communal reflection we become more aware of the need to call to mind the
presence of God throughout the day, to be contemplatives
in action. In sharing our time with one another, we
share the struggles and the joys of the day. The presense of God in our lives can be seen to permeate through
every moment of the day, not just in the moments that we
spend in formal prayer, as important as these are to our
lives of intimacy. Communal reflection is not to be
approached as a checking system; we are not merely gath-
ering together to render an account of one another. The
main purpose is to make more concrete our shared search
for God in our lives. Recalling together His presence,
reflecting on how our lives are different because of this
awareness of His mystery in life; finding support in a
sometimes fruitless struggle to be in God's presence--
each of these steps in communal reflection will aid a
community in concretizing their faith life as a community.
Through an unforced sharing of things that really matter,
each person may be encouraged to unfold uniquely in relationship with Christ.

Summary and Conclusion

    The purpose of this Chapter was to clarify the role
of community, the distortions that sometimes cloud the
good that a community can do, and the means that may aid
in the fostering of simplicity through communal sharing
of spiritual reading and reflection on the presence of
God in our lives. Religious community's main purpose is
to aid in the full spiritualization of its individual

members, to aid each religious in fully turning toward God. Though at times a community may fail, though the best intentions may become distorted in working through anxieties that were formed in early childhood, a community may also aid in the true conversion of heart that alone will bring us to simplicity in our relationship with God and with others in the concrete everydayness of life.

Religious are discovering that they heal (return to simplicity) best when their inner journey is spiritually wealthy. Because of the care, concern, and understanding shared among religious and witnessed among the people with whom they work, others may discover that they too are called to live the vowed life. Through the simplicity that shines through the lives of religious who are deeply convinced in Christ as the center of their community, young people may be called to make their lives of equal simplicity. In the following I will propose ways in which the novice may begin the inward journey of self-simplification to come to one's own unique spiritual life within the religious lifestyle.

ENDNOTES

[1]Adrian van Kaam, Personality Fulfillment in Religious Life (Denville, New Jersey: Dimension Books, 1967), pp. 103-122.

[2]Personality Fulfillment in Religious Life, op. cit. p. 139-140.

[3]Ibid., p. 255.

[4]Ibid., p. 287.

[5]Adrian van Kaam, Personality Fulfillment in the Religious Life (Denville, New Jersey: Dimension Books, 1967), pp. 73-129; and The Vowed Life (Denville, New Jersey: Dimension Books, 1968), pp. 315-363.

[6]Ibid., p. 337

[7]van Kaam, op. cit., pp. 97-98.

[8]Adrian van Kaam, Personality Fulfillment in the Religious Life, op. cit., pp. 205-230; and The Vowed Life, op. cit., pp. 207-278.

[9]Personality Fulfillment in the Religious Life, op. cit., p. 283.

[10]Adrian van Kaam, "Spirituality in Community Living," op. cit.; and Personality Fulfillment in Religious Life, op. cit., pp. 302-304.

[11]Ibid., pp. 304-305.

[12]Paul Roy, "Communal Reflection," a talk given at Good Counsel Hill, Mankato, Minnesota, August, 1973. (Mimeograph.)

[13]Refer to George Aschenbrenner, "Consciousness Examen," Review for Religious XXXI (January, 1972), 14-21.

[14]Ibid.

PART FIVE

THE NOVICE'S MOVEMENT TOWARD SIMPLICITY

INTRODUCTION

The period of formation prior to full commitment to
religious life is a time in which the novice can begin
the never-ending process of discovering who one is and
what place is held in the plan of God. Because the
novice comes from a society in which self worth is based
on the ability to function in a given task, the person
needs time to grow and to unfold into a fuller human and
spiritual person. There will be a need to find worth
based on who one is and not on what one does. In this
Part I will present ways in which the novice can discover
what is authentic, and how one's life can unfold
according to God's unique plan.[1]

CHAPTER X

UNFOLDING IN SIMPLICITY IN THE
NOVITIATE SITUATION

INTRODUCTION

A whole new way of life is slowly unfolding for the
novice introduced to religious life. Gradually the new
novice becomes aware of a different way of looking at
life and approaching one's own life. Through regular
journal keeping, spiritual reading and fruitful periods
of silence and solitude, the novice may come to sense
the deeper meanings of the hidden presence of God within.

The novice may discover that a functional way of
life is not the fullness to which a person is called. A
discovery of a need to let go of personal means by which
life has unconsciously been complicated needs to be dealt
with to come to discover a self dormant within. The
period of mourning associated with the embodying of a new
life form is heightened by this inner need to let go.
Through wise direction and prayerful consideration, the
letting go process will lose some of its sting. Slowly
each novice will become dependent upon God and upon His
will for life. Life will then become less self-centered,
more true to self, and much more simple in interaction
with others.

The novice comes to a community brimming with life,
eager to give of oneself completely to the living of
religious life. The attitude of giving without counting
the cost, of almost forcing oneself to "externally" be
the perfect religious is common. Methods used, bay be
questioned but usually this person trusts in the good
judgment of the director. It is the task of a wise
director to temper this enthusiasm into a realistic,
unique, and "interior" embodiment of this particular life
form. Through the example and teaching of the director
an atmosphere in which the novice can slowly unfold, may
allow the novice to come to an ever fuller view of who
one is and what the will of the Father is.[2]

To better understand the role of the novitiate in
leading a novice to a fuller spiritual and personal
unfolding let us begin by clarifying the purpose of the
novitiate as it has been outlined by Adrian van Kaam.

Adrian van Kaam[3]
Spiritual Initiation in the Novitiate

Central to the purpose of the novitiate should be
a worshipful initiation into the two great transcendent
mysteries of the faith: Trinity and Incarnation. The
novitiate program must be Christ-oriented, Church-
oriented, and Scripture-oriented, not in the sense of
theological discourse, but in the sense of a lived
awareness of the transcendent dimension in the everyday
lives of the novices. The novitiate as a whole should
foster personal spiritual formation in prayerful presence
and living faith contact with the transcendent meaning
of reality.

The novitiate is a time of discovery of the transcendent dimensions of faith. What happens to the
novice in this full presence of faith? The novice
forgets about oneself and small concerns and participates
in a deeper reality that literally transcends and absorbs
that person. This prayerful presence in faith fosters
within the novice a transcendent spiritual outlook and
spiritual life style. It must therefore facilitate the
practice of this living faith by creating conditions that
may be used by God to grant the novice a sense of His
divine presense within life. Through spiritual direction,
rules, environment, courses, conferences, readings, prayers and exercises, the novitiate situation leads to
moments in which the novice may at times penetrate into
the mysteries of faith that are formulated in the spiritual doctrine of the Church and in the writings of acknowledged spiritual masters.

The novice who desires to make more explicit a
relationship with the divine presence through meditative
reflection, becomes increasingly aware of one's own
graced potentialities and desires for at oneness with
the Divine as He makes himself known in everyday life.
The novice begins to understand how ordinary daily life
is spiritualized in a special way by Christ who became
man in the ordinary life of Nazareth. Through reflection
on the hidden life of Christ, a novice may participate
more fully in the deeper meanings of daily life in the
novitiate.

It is of crucial importance for the novices to understand that the life of transcendence is trustworthy to the
degree that it is faithful to the everyday manifestations

of God's will. The life of the spirit should be lived
in a kind of mindfulness that keeps in touch with the
flow of an experience of God in the midst of daily life.
Keeping in touch with daily life also implies a kind of
forgetfulness of the transcendent as the novice is
reimmerses repeatedly in the natural flow of daily life.
Without this healing forgetfulness, the novice would
become alienated from the divine presence in the midst
of daily activity, and as a result, experience life as
being compartmentalized instead of unified because of a
spiritual life. One's prayer life would not be connected
to daily life. Spiritual life would become cut off from
growth through daily experience.

With the purpose of the novitiate clearly in mind,
we may now proceed to delve more deeply into concrete
ways in which the novice director may lead the novices
to a fuller spiritualization of their individual lives.
To do this we will follow the same format as in previous
Parts, showing that our lives may become simplified only
as they become centered on God as our ultimate concern.
We will first present ways in which the director may educate the novices to a life of faith to allow them to be
open to the gift of grace in their lives. Following this
we will be able to more clearly delineate a novice's
response of faith with growing sensitivity to the mystery
of life and of God that is operative in life.

Paul Molinari[4]
Education for Living in Faith

According to Molinari:

Religious life is a "life" of personal love for
the Person of Jesus Christ: a life of love that
leads one to share whatever is His, to live the
kind of life He chose to live, a life He Himself
lived with others.[5]

Considering both the social and ecclesial context in which
the life of faith of religious should evolve, we need to
ask ourselves: how concretely can we teach novices to
make a loving response to God in faith, to share one's
total life with Christ?

First of all, if we correctly understand the meaning of formation, we must begin with the idea that it is
God Himself who forms. The novice director must respect
the action and the plan of God in the lives of those

directed. By being attentive to His action, by remaining
on the same "wave-length" with God, the novice director
may aid the novice in unfolding in a deep life of faith.
God is himself the one who takes the initiative and is
the Real Master and Inspirer of our life of faith.

Having a great respect for God's work within an
individual person, implies that the director cannot hope
to discover the ways and designs of God by having some
preconceived plan or blueprint. Preparing the way for
grace implies that the director should be able to adapt
to the infinite variety of personalities that may be
encountered, as well as be mindful of the mysterious and
always deeply personal ways of God's providence.

> Teaching a loving response to God in faith
> means, therefore, constantly listening to
> our brothers, constantly listening to life
> itself; listening in a humble and poor
> attitude that is compounded of a respect
> for the other and a searching for the ways
> of God.[6]

The main task of the novice director then is to
build an atmosphere in which the faith life of those
directed may reach its highest potential. The task is
to be there gently to help the individuals to discern,
to see what God expects from them. The director essentially aids the novice in the formation of the "heart,"
the vital center of one's being and personality, so that
the beginner may come to a more personal interior
knowledge of the Person of Jesus Christ who is the center
of our lives. Therefore, the director must not force,
but create situations which will help the novice to
become more aware of God's ways as they are operative in
one's special personality, the circumstances and situations of one's past and present life, and according to
the measure of His freely given grace.

To educate the novices, to lead them to a deeper
life of faith, it is important that the director aid
them to discover the richness of the Word of God as contained in the Sacred Scripture and tradition. It is not
enough to present ready-made formulas that explain the
essence of our faith. More importantly, we must challenge
them to translate the words of Scripture in such a way as
to integrate the saving message of God into personal
experience in their lives.

251

Formation of this nature must be oriented to an integration, a transformation from within, so that the novice may truly become what one ought. We are to foster the novices' spiritual self-discovery, so that they may respond to the design of God's plan for their lives, under the action of the Holy Spirit. This type of formation must lead the novice to a deeper understanding of one's own unique vocation which is a total self-giving to God.

Response of Faith

Molinari notes that what God asks, even at the beginning of religious life (and the novitiate truly is the beginning) is not an intellectual assent to theological truths; rather, what God expects is a wholehearted acceptance of the Divine Person and His right to ask the complete gift of oneself in return. Faith commits the entire person: intellect, faculties, potentialities, and attracts the heart until it becomes completely committed in love, sympathy and affection. Just as Christ called each of His Apostles as he was, He draws each one of us today in way that is suited to their particular individuality. In turn, he asks for a response that is typically his own, each in a way that is perfectly in tune with his own personality.

For Christ, an invitation that is addressed to the entire person calls for an unconditional response. God can make increasingly exacting demands upon His creatures, and the only acceptable response to this total gift of love is a heartfelt "yes" springing from unbounded love and trust in the Wisdom, Power and Goodness of God. How is this invitation of love experienced? Molinari says that, first of all, there is a constant, growing attraction to intimacy, a strong desire for Him alone. Sometimes this desire takes the form of a great nostalgia, a feeling of solitude that makes us yearn for Someone. This Someone is God, even if one is not conscious of this, or even if one does not acknowledge God as the giver of the invitation. He seeks us by touching our hearts. If we reply by seeking Him, this seeking soon develops into an attitude of loving expectation, an attitude of dependence on the beloved.

Christ asks a response of an understanding heart. To respond to the words, "Come and see," is to run the risk of allowing Him to reveal Himself and to make us share His views, His way of thinking and loving. Molinari quotes an ancient proverb which expresses this well: "Give me your heart and I will give you my eyes."[7] Accepting Christ's invitation means to allow his loving gaze to penetrate to the depths of one's heart. This intimate contact with Him urges us to go to Him with all our defenses down. It means to enter into an adventure that transforms one's entire existence, to trust ourselves to His love so that He may lead us where He wills. Allowing oneself to be led creates in us a disposition of vulnerability, trust and self-surrender in the light of Christ's love.

If a person dares to respond to Christ in total conversion to His love, that person discovers endless new insights into Him who causes this following. We must be willing to take the first step, to become sensitive to the mystery of His love, to accept what one may discover, and to risk a deepening love at every stage of the journey in becoming more deeply related with Christ. van Kaam speaks of the necessity to become sensitive to mystery to allow God full play in my life.

Adrian van Kaam
Sensitivity to Mystery

van Kaam notes that today there is a lack of sensitivity to Divine mystery as Christians are beginning to move out of the monolithic subculture which has encapsulated us for centuries. We are affected by the rapid rate of change and are not accustomed to using quiet time to become sensitive to any level of mystery in our lives, much less to the Divine Mystery. That is why it is especially important in the novitiate to stress this sensitivity, otherwise the novices will be missing out on the Mystery that surrounds them, and the Mystery to which they desire to dedicate their lives.

As has been stated earlier, the spirit self in us is the ability to become aware of the Beyond. We feel that some mystery permeates us and allows us to be. When a person's faith is ultimately, even on the natural level, founded on one's spirit self, we are able to live in basic faith, hope and love. When one is graced, this natural ability is enhanced and becomes the ground of the graced and spiritual life. This means that when we experience God as being absolute, intimate and all-penetrating, we have this experience according to an intensity and clarity that is in tune with our natural experience. The intensity of the faith experience depends, first, upon a minimum of faith intuition, an intuition that is not necessarily loaded with emotionality, and secondly, on natural intuition. That is, the faith experience could co-vibrate with one's personal and vital self. The intensity of the experience of my unique, personal intimacy with God Himself is the experience of wonder, the marvel of undeserved grace. In other words, grace deepens the natural ability in a person to be sensitive to mystery in life.

Applying these thoughts to the novitiate situation, a novice who comes from today's social structure, may have to develop a sensitivity to religious experience by doing the things that momentarily may not be meaningful. She has to live in the assurance that what she gets out of the experience is not the ultimate intention; doing the will of God should be a motivating force. Because each person has a own life call, a unique mystery, that is totally in the hands of God, each person can only cooperate with this mysterious plan and allow Him to organize life.

If faith is real for the novice, if one truly believes that God is intimately related, to each person, there may be a better preparation to experience God as being very near. According to van Kaam, a person can acknowledge the personal being of the God of Mystery without betraying or denying the mystery aspect of this personal God. That is, a person tries to avoid the pitfalls of anthropomorphism by refusing to reduce God to the merely human image of personhood.

If a person does not explicitly experience the mystery of God, that person does not have the option to deny the existence of God either. On the one hand, giftedness and sensitivity to mystery may be present, although it may be underdeveloped according to the culture, situation, or a person's own present inability to quietly become present to the mystery. On the other hand, van Kaam notes, that an ego-person approaches mystery as being irrelevant, useless, impractical and far away. Mystery for this person is anything that cannot be control. The ego-person loses oneself proudly and busily in the things that can mastered, dominated, manipulated or penetrated intellectually. In the back of ones mind the conviction is held that sometime in the future,

someone will find out what the mystery is all about.
Because the experience of what presently escapes understanding may keep bothering a person, rites such as
astrology and fortune telling seem appealing.

Someone may grow in sensitivity to mystery by trying to live up to one's own experience and simply responding to the will of God as is seen in small ways. One
tries to live up to the experiences of others while at
the same time realizing that ones sensitivity may never
equal the sensitivity of the one admired. Because of
the present religious fad in regard to approaching
experience, it is important for the novice to realize
that though religious experience, or a deep sensitivity
to mystery, is helpful, it is not the center of the
spiritual life. Central should be the personal desire
for and openness toward the mystery. For the novice,
energies should be channelled so that one's natural
ability to perceive mystery is deepened, so that the
value of the Transcendent may be realized in an age
where mystery is something that everyone tries to manipulate.

REFLECTION

Something which has existed since the beginning,
that we have heard,
and we have seen with our own eyes;
that we have watched
and touched with our hands:
the Word, who is life--
this is our subject.
That life was made visible:
we saw it and we are giving our testimony,
telling you of eternal life
which was with the Father and has been made
visible to us.
What we have seen and heard
we are telling you
so that you too may be in union with us,
as we are in union
with the Father
and with his Son Jesus Christ. (I John 1:1-3)

St. John's words express the deep conviction of
Christ's love. The Word who was made flesh has existed
for all time and especially exists in each person today.
The task of the novitiate is to aid each young person to
discover for oneself this deep love of Christ that has

been experienced by others. It is a special time in which the novice may come to a clear perception of Christ as he is seen operative in her life, and through listening with attentiveness to how the will of God may be sensed in life.

Leading Another to Spiritual Unfolding

The task of the director is to bear witness to the One that is seen, heard and touched--to bear witness to Christ as His presence is made known through the affairs of present day life. To bear witness to Christ in this manner, the director must first be aware of what motivates one's interaction with the novices. Is the director truly convinced of Christ's unique presence in each person's life? Are the novices allowed to unfold according to each one's own graced potential and desire for Christ? Are interactions with the novices motivated by a keen awareness that it is Christ who is truly forming and guiding each novice, that the director is only an instrument in the hands of God? Only the Lord can call us to a personal intimacy with Him; only the Lord can teach us how to pray.

I need to place my trust and confidence in Him, being a John the Baptist who will lead the novices to discover Christ for themselves. Humbly I need to be taught what the Lord told his disciples: "Do not let your hearts be troubled. Trust in God still, and trust in me." (John 14:1) In this trust, all I can do is to try to attain the capacity that Christ has given to me both in deepening my own spiritual life and in drawing the novices to a deep, personalized spiritual life. Reflecting on the life of St. Therese of Lisieux, especially when she was asked to work with the novices, I realize with her that my only task is to help each novice to discover a unique path to a deeply spiritual life.

> Never was my hope mistaken, for God saw fit to fill my little hand as many times as it was necessary for nourishing the soul of my Sisters. I admit, Mother, that if I had depended in the least on my own strength, I would very soon have had to give up. From a distance it appears all roses to do good to souls, making them love God more and molding them according to one's personal views and ideas. At close range it is totally the contrary, the roses disappear; one

feels that to do good is as impossible without
God's help as to make the sun shine at night.[8]

St. Therese found that her task of leading the novices to a deeper spiritual life was most severely tested
when her sister, Celine, was under her care. Celine took
liberties that the other novices dared not. Therese's
affection for her was naturally greater than for the other
novices. She had to constantly evaluate how she was leading each novice, but especially her own sister, in coming
to understand her relationship with Christ.

As director, I may find it difficult to work with a
particular novice. I may try to "change" the novice to
fit my "image" of what a perfect religious should be.
Ways in which the novice may doubt my good will, a rightful defensiveness as I impose myself, may be clear signs
for me that I am not allowing God to take the initiative
with this unique life. Though I must continue to confront, my confrontation must become more sensitive and
adaptable to God's mysterious ways. I realize that
perhaps the only way I can allow God to work with each
novice, despite our differences, is to build an atmosphere in which the grace of God may work uniquely in
each life.

Evelyn Underhill in Practical Mysticism uses an
analogy that may clarify for us the task of the spiritual
director in leading the novice to a deeper spiritual life:

> "No-Eyes" has fixed his attention of the fact
> that he is obliged to take a walk. For him
> the chief factor of existence is his own move-
> ment along the road; a movement he intends to
> accomplish as efficiently and comfortably as he
> can. He asks not to know what may be on either
> side of the hedges. He ignores the caress of
> the wind until it threatens to remove his hat.
> He trudges along, steadily, diligently, avoid-
> ing the muddy pools, but oblivious of the light
> which they reflect.
>   "Eyes" takes the walk too: and for him it
> is a perpetual revelation of beauty and wonder.
> The sunlight inebriates him, the winds delight
> him, the very effort of the journey is a joy.
> Magic presences throng the roadside, or cry
> salutations to him from the hidden fields.
> The rich world through which he moves lies in

257

the foreground of his consciousness and it
gives up new secrets to him at every step.
"No-Eyes", when told of his adventures,
usually refused to believe that both have
gone by the same road. He fancies that his
companion has been floating about in the
air, or beset by agreeable hallucinations.
We shall never persuade him to the contrary
unless we persuade him to look for himself.[9]

Aiding the novice in looking for herself, in experiencing the joy, the beauty, the fullness of God's presence in life is the task of the director. Aiding one
in seeing and experiencing the gift of grace in life
implies walking the same path, patiently working to
broaden one's perception, to help the novice to see that
God works uniquely through each personality, the circumstances of life that are sometimes difficult, and through
the gift of His freely given grace. To allow the plan
of God to unfold freely, the novice director must be able
to distinguish between what is essential and crucial in
the religious mode of existence and what is merely a
personal preference. In other words, both the novice
and the director must become aware of how each is called
to respond to the gift of faith in life. van Kaam says
that:

Initiation, without a steady education to self-
knowledge, can never lead to spiritual wisdom
and maturity. We must know what is moving us.
Do we behave in a certain manner because we are
compulsive, overanxious, hysterical, perfection-
istic? The director must educate his initiates
to self-understanding before God, a process
which, like initiation, is never complete; it
can always go deeper.[10]

The task of the novice director is to lead the
novices in the discovery of Sacred Scripture, to incarnate that Scripture in their lives. The best way to
educate the novices is through a personal living of
Scripture in daily life. Through this spiritual initiation the novice may be led to accept the gift of oneself,
intellect, faculties, and potentialities. Through a
delving deeply into a living Scripture the novice may
come to discover how to respond to Christ's unique love.

The Novice's Unique Response to Mystery

A novice may slowly realize that one's heart may need to be transformed by the loving presence of Christ. One may experience a yearning to respond to this invitation. The novice may eventually become aware of a dependence upon Christ. When giving oneself completely to Christ, an awareness of the defenses used, many of the blindnesses along the path of life will be known as weak attempts to keep Christ at a distance. Trusting in the transforming love of Christ, one's life may begin to unfold in simplicity. The mysterious workings of God in life may unfold as a willingness to unconditionally trust in His ways.

The new experiences of the novitiate, the stress on discovering one's own path in life, may be a frightening process to a novice who has always been in control of life clearly and efficiently. The different level of relationships may test an ability to relate with others who are different from one's own family. An ability to do scholarly research may not seem important, and at times may even be a hindrance, in coming to meditative reflection on the mystery of life. A novice may come to discover that it may be important to presently bear with the feeling of uprootedness in order to allow a dimension of life that has been dormant to awaken in the new emphasis placed on living in mystery, in coming to a deeper level than personal and vital life. Maybe to wait in darkness means to center one's very being on the good things that the Father has done even though the novice presently doesn't understand and cannot control feelings of uprootedness. Perhaps the advice given to a disciple by the author of The Cloud of Unknowing may give some direction:

> Lift your heart up to the Lord, with a gentle
> stirring of love desiring him for his own
> sake and not for his gifts. Center all your
> attention and desire on him and let this be
> the sole concern of your mind and heart.[11]

By trying to live the mystery of God's will a novice may discover that His will is not as harsh as presently experienced--it is just not one's own will. God may purify one's will by giving little pleasure in doing what one wants. A person may be more limited by the limitations placed upon one's own love than on the

limitations God has allowed in a unique identity. A
response of simple faith to the Will of the Father thus
entails an ever expanding self-knowledge. Each person
needs to know just how far one will follow the will of
God, just what one's capacity is, and how willing one is
to be led by God. A person of faith needs to set one's
will on what He wills. The experience of freedom that
comes from this letting go prepares the person of faith
to persevere in doing the Will of God, no matter how
vague it seems at times, no matter how trying the ordinariness of life may be.

The mystery of God's love is not something that is
revealed only in ecstatic experiences as a newcomer to
religious life may have so often thought. One may find
a blindness to the mystery of nature all around, to the
mystery of each person. Or a person may slowly come to
realize that there is more to nature than how aesthet-
ically pleasing things are to one's eyes. The sunset's
beauty, which has given an experience of serenity once
or twice in life may be the open window for a realization of serenity experienced in the mystery of God's
love. The delicate completeness of a newborn child may
atune a person to the loving care and concern of God for
all of creation. The words of Scripture, which at times
appear only as riddles that confuse and trouble, may be
openings by which the novice may gradually see how God
is working in life, calling one to freely respond to His
love through words that at times are not inviting. The
monotony experienced in the sameness of the novitiate
may be God's mysterious way of calling to deepen one's
love for Him. It may be a way for Him to purify one's
images of God as the fulfiller of needs, or the Father-
image in life.

A novice may need to begin asking oneself questions
similar to these: What requests am I most able to
respond to? Why do some things seem easier than others?
Is what I do really what I have been asked to do? In
reading Scripture, do I resist what I read there; do I
say that the requests of God for the people of times
past is only for them and has nothing to do with my
present condition? Do I begin each day by preparing
myself to listen to the will of the Father by spending
quiet time just listening in prayer? Do I respond more
in fear of what I think God is asking of me, or is my
response moved by a sense of loving care and concern
for God? Am I contented in prayer only when I feel good
about these experiences, or can the dryness and my

inability to sense God's mysterious presence in my life be accepted as well?

In the following section we will discuss how prayer is one way of growing in sensivity to the mystery of God's presence and love in my life. As Egan states: to pray is to wait; to pray is to be simple.

Keith J. Egan[12]
Waiting in Simplicity through Prayer

Through an attitude of waiting we develop a deep respect for the mystery of God's love. Each person has some notion of the mystery of love and friendship and realizes that we are formed gradually by the quality of love we have for others, and by the quality of love that others have for us. This growth in love takes time. We have to wait while growth takes place silently within us. Living an attitude of waiting is a realization that life is a mystery. It is not a passive sitting back and doing nothing. Instead it is a quieting of the senses so that the inner openness to mystery may be awakened. Through waiting in prayer, we become more conscious of the mystery of God's love for us. We come to know God as the source of life. In waiting, Christ discovered the will of the Father for his life. His waiting was fruitful in that it brought him to accept his suffering, death, and resurrection. It also aided Him in responding to the needs of those whom He came to serve.

According to Egan:

This waiting is a call to realize that most basically we depend upon God and upon his love. Yet, it is a waiting in which we are active and alive and responsive. This waiting is an openness to all that might be in our lives, to all that may be the outcome of God's love and of our honest responses.[13]

Therefore, we wait in prayer with eyes open, minds alert, and our hearts ready to respond to others and to God who has formed and shaped us with his love.

To Pray is to be Simple

Prayer, according to Egan, is a preparation of the heart so that it may have the wisdom to know when to

emphasize one or other aspect of life and how to integrate the seeming contradictions of life. As we wait
in prayer in the presence of a loving Father, we have
no need to be anything but ourselves. To be conscious
of God as our Father, is to have the freedom to approach
him in utter simplicity because he knows, accepts, and
loves us as we are. Simplicity in this sense is an inner
sincerity that cannot help but express itself in outward
actions. The simple person achieves a sense of values
and lives according to those values. In our changing
culture where established values are being challenged,
there is a special need for this inward honesty.

To be as simple as a child in prayer is to open
oneself to the discovery that God has loved me first.
When this awareness sinks deep in our hearts, we become
free to respond to God quite simply whether in word, in
silence, or in action. Egan says that prayer with others
often makes sense, but

> simplicity in prayer may also lead us to seek
> out a quiet corner, a shady spot under a tree,
> a grassy place near a lake or river, maybe a
> favorite pew in an empty Church. From time to
> time we may find wisdom in the advice: take a
> little water and a chunk of bread and go off
> alone to be before the Lord who loves and cares
> for you.[14]

The test of the simplicity of our prayer is growth in
love for God and for our neighbor. Through prayer we
become aware of Christ's challenge to turn from selfishness and to turn to God and to others in love. It
brings us in touch with the center of ourselves and aids
us in our ability to respond out of this love. "Simplicity is a gentle acknowledgement of the reality of the
way things are and the way life is really being experienced. To be simple is to be in touch with the real."[15]
This is true whether the real is suffering or ecstatic
joy. To grow as a loving person is then to become
simple in mind, in heart, in word and in deed. Egan
concludes these thoughts on simplicity by quoting from
the Prophet Micah:

> --What is good has been explained to you:
> this is what Yahweh asks of you:
> only this, to act justly,
> to love tenderly
> and to walk humbly with your God. (Micah 6:8)

REFLECTION

Waiting in prayer may be one of the most difficult
tasks for a novice who has never had to wait in the
sense of allowing the mystery to unfold. Referring
again to Evelyn Underhill's analogy of "Eyes" and "No-
Eyes", we may be able to more concretely show how an
attitude toward life that is similar to the attitude of
"No-Eyes", does not allow the novice to come to prayer
in expectation and openness to mystery.

For "No-Eyes" the chief factor of existence is one's
own movement along the road of life. The intention is
to accomplish this task as efficiently and comfortably
as possible. Everything one does has a clearly defined
goal and process to meet that goal. Prayer is approached no differently. There are set methods, set procedures
that must be followed meticulously. Efforts soon become
frustrated because the novice discovers that there is
nothing tangible to hang on to. Growth in prayer cannot
be measured. Neither can a more personal intimacy with
Christ be experienced. With unbending effort to develop
a spiritual life, God is not allowed to work in a way
that is not clearcut, definitely outlined, or entirely
describable.

As in the case of "No-Eyes", a particular novice
may only be able to experience a deeper prayer life when
the person is able to look for oneself, able to wait in
prayer without striving to attain anything in particular.
At first a beginner in prayer may find it difficult to
quiet down bodily, just to be in the presence of Christ
without striving for anything, without having a set goal
in mind. A particular temperament and life experience
may make it difficult to remain selfless, to discipline
oneself in a relaxed sort of way. To sit quietly without reading, without trying to be filled with just the
right inspiration which must surely be in the next verse
of Scripture, may be extremely difficult for a person
who has always been praised for an ability to quickly
absorb meaning from anything one reads. Waiting in
prayer may especially be difficult on a particular day.
In developing an attitude of waiting in prayer, a process
that is often slow, and inefficient in the light of
getting something done, seems often to be without perceptible results. One may eventually realize that the
slowing down and waiting cannot happen with energy alone.
An experience of dependence upon God, realizing that

efforts alone will not bring results in spiritual
growth, may be painful but real. Spiritual masters
refer to this relationship of dependence as spiritual
childhood. In this relationship the Father is allowed
to show his love, and the pray-er as child is able to
respond in freedom. What for me characterizes this
relationship? As the author of The Cloud of Unknowing
remarks: in a childlike relationship to the Father "you
will seem to know nothing and to feel nothing except a
naked intent toward God in the depth of your being."16
A child comes to the Father expecting nothing in particular but the love that the Father freely gives. The
response of the Father to one who comes as a child is a
response of love: "For like a father frolicking with
his son, he will hug and kiss one who comes to him with
a child's heart."17 Or as St. Therese of Lisieux says,
"Jesus deigned to show me the road that leads to this
Divine Furnace, and this road is the surrender of the
little child who sleeps without fear in its Father's
arms."18

     At times a novice may resist being a child. Not
wanting to be dependent upon anyone one may try to
become mature without any help. However, the person
may also realize that one's eyes, mind and heart are
shaped more by his love than by sometimes weak efforts.
Little by little as one slowly wakes to life, a return
to that childlike simplicity may happen.

     The quiet beauty of the everyday may slowly begin
to penetrate. An appreciation of the uniqueness of
the other novices, the ability to share deepening experiences with them, and the renewed capacity to say
yes and no meaningfully, may begin. The future may be
faced with new eyes, totally being oneself, waiting upon
whatever happening the everyday might bring. Just as
the pearl of the oyster can only begin to grow if it is
disturbed by the tiny grain of sand, so too, a novice
begins to grow to a greater awareness of who one is as
the complacent, common sense, controlling self is disturbed.

     Prayer may become the unifying force in a person's
life. When one's actions flow from a stilled inner
peace, life becomes characteristically simple. When
prayer, community exercises of the novitiate, spiritual
direction with the novice director, interaction with the
other novices, or even the monotonous routine of a

typical novitiate day is approached in an attitude of expectant waiting, there may be a gradual turning toward God. More often there is a need to seek out a place alone, and to have time to understand oneself in a new light as a greater relationshp to Christ is slowly coming to be.

In the following section we shall show how spiritual reading and journal keeping may be aids in deepening and concretizing the novice's slowly unfolding spiritual life.

Susan Annette Muto[19]
Spiritual Reading and Journal Keeping

According to Muto, spiritual reading may be a way to enter more fully into the mystery of Christ in my life. The spiritual masters affirm the value of hiddenness for the person who wants to imitate Christ by recording their own experiences of quietly waiting upon Christ to penetrate into their everyday lives. The life of the simple is the life of the everyday, the life in which the hiddenness of Christ can be waited upon in stillness and quiet. Like the growth in nature which goes on quietly but steadily, growth in the spiritual life often goes on unnoticed for years. Spiritual reading is one way in which a person can become more attuned to that hidden growth by identifying life experiences with that of a spiritual writer. Muto gives several facilitating factors that may aid the reader in identifying more fully with the spiritual writer.

Fostering growth in the spiritual life implies returning to my inner self. This return to my inner self suggests that I develop my inner senses, especially the sense of listening with the inner ear. While to the outer ear the sense of the Gospel message or the message of the spiritual writer seems almost nonsensical, when I listen with my inner ear I remove the veil that prevents the clarity of the spiritual word from illuminating my soul. The inner ear hears best in silence and stillness. Instead of the compulsion to be current, listening with the inner ear has the desire to dwell quietly upon the word.

Spiritual reading depends on my capacity to be still. My thoughts, feelings, emotions and perceptions have to be gently disciplined in such a way that my whole inner self slows down and becomes more silent. The more slowed down I become, the more patient I will be with the unfolding of the hidden meaning of the words and experiences of the masters. When I allow the text to take the initiative I can wait patiently for it to speak today, or to remain silent. I will not try to force meaning, but will be ready to find meaning if today the writing will speak to me. This quiet waiting Muto refers to as maintaining a vacation mood. Maintaining this inwardly if not outwardly leads to simplicity and increases the possibility of my hearing the message of the spiritual master.

Spiritual reading is also a risk. It may open up questions about my life that I may not want to reflect upon. In one sense, these questions may lead to pain. In another sense, they may lead to a rebirth in Christ, a deepening of my relationship with Christ. "The question is, am I willing to walk alone down a road that leads to simplicity and possibly to pain?"[20] Am I willing to open myself to failure and repentance, to detachment from myself and from what others may think of me? Am I willing to utter some kind of yes in the reconciling presence of Christ in whom all contradictions seem to cease?

While the inner attitudes and sensitivities are most important, there are also several facilitating conditions that may make the experience more beneficial. First of all, I try to create the right atmosphere in which to read. The room in which I do my reading is a quiet place; a room in which there is a certain order and beauty that may enhance my efforts to slow down. For a few moments I sit quietly, breathing deeply, trying to feel at home in the room while the distracting thoughts of the day are allowed to quietly slip into the background. A centering down begins to take place by quieting my busy mind, by recollecting my dispersed emotions. Inwardly I am still while outwardly I seek stillness by regulating the time, place, and style of slowed down reading that foster recollection.

The spiritual words may draw me into reflection upon my own experience as being related to the experience recorded by the author. Writing down my reflections may also be a way of slowing me down further, of aiding me in concretizing in my own life the experience of the spiritual master. Writing down my thoughts helps to shape the blur of ideas and notions, and helps me to recall past experiences. It helps to give a focus to the meditative life.

Like spiritual reading, journal keeping must also be done in a disciplined way. I need to set aside a time for doing the writing, choose a familiar place, and do the writing whether I feel like it or not. My writings may be a log of the day's experiences. Writing down the events of the day allows me to get in touch with the realization of where I am, what affects me, how I react in various situations. It may also be a record of the stepping stones of my life: the significant persons, relationships, periods of my life, the work I am called to do. My journal may also contain a record of the spiralling movements of my life: significant personal experiences, a deeper awareness of the unique me, those touching moments of my life that may be mine alone or may be universally accepted experiences. The spiritual journal may contain an interplay of all three: a rich collection of events and experiences that fosters a keener awareness of myself.

Journal keeping offers several incentives that may make the risk worth taking. It offers a possibility of an interior adventure. I may discover things about myself that I didn't know existed. It may be a means of making concrete what I have learned from life by having lived it. It may also aid me in remembering the flaws of the past and help me to realize that my life has not been chaotic or without meaning. It may be a means of making concrete what I have learned from life by having lived it. It may also aid me in remembering the flaws of the past and help me to realize that my life has not been chaotic or without meaning. It may make me face the low level of my spiritual life by the thoughtless and idealess way in which I go through life. Journal writing may also be a safety valve, allowing me to voice my deeper concerns to the patient ear of the paper.

REFLECTION[21]

The task of the novice director is to facilitate the full spiritual unfolding of the novices. One does this most especially by providing an atmosphere for the gentle, inward unfolding. A well developed spiritual reading program may be an aid. When the program evolves from the needs of the particular novices, spiritual reading may draw the novices to depth that conferences, individual direction and informational reading may not.

A novice director may choose a spiritual journal such as <u>Letters from the Desert</u>. As stated in the Publisher's Preface:

> <u>Letters from the Desert</u> was written in the form of a diary-epistle, to the many friends whom Carlo Carretto had made during his twenty years as a leader of both Italian youth movements and Catholic Action in the tense years before and after the Second World War. (xiii)

This gives us a clue to the kind of person Carretto was. He was deeply involved in social action; he was deeply committed to spreading the Gospel message to the youth of his time. A novice who may have similar aspirations of wanting to do something, of wanting constantly to be in control, might well benefit from a slowed down reading of this journal. The time for spiritual reading in the novitiate could perhaps be in the early evening hours when the necessary activities of the day seem to have been accomplished or could wait until tomorrow. There is nothing active that has to be done. Finding a quiet spot in the novitiate, one may pause for a few minutes just to recollect oneself to really be present to the reading of this journal. In the Introduction we read about Carretto's call to life in the desert. These particular words may ring true:

> This time I said yes without understanding a thing. "Leave everything and come with me into the desert. It is not your acts and deeds that I want; I want your prayer, your love." (xvii)

A man who had for forty years lived his life in service of others experienced a deeper call. Maybe this call is somewhat similar to the call that this novice has experienced in life. One's activities may not be like Carretto's, but a voice within may call: Come and see. I don't want your busy activity or your pragmatic concerns. I want you. I want your love. I want you to be the person I have destined you to become.

Reading these words in the experience of another may make one's experiences more believable. Through the time given in the novitiate one may realize that answering the hidden call is not easy. One's normal stance, and compulsive listening is not enough. Waiting

developing an inner ear that is more attuned to the
hidden message of God veiled in the words of the
spiritual writer is demanded:

> That is the truth we must learn through faith:
> to wait on God. And this attitude of mind is
> not easy. This "waiting" is "not making plans"
> this "searching the heavens" this "being silent"
> is one of the most important things we have to
> learn. (22)

Through practice of the art of being silent, of
listening with the inner ear, the novice may realize
the special call of one's life. The novice director
may also realize that listening with the inner ear may
help one to more fully hear the needs of each novice:

> One must be able to hear the inner questions,
> the unspoken ones; the inner hopes and mis-
> givings and dreams and timidities and poten-
> tialities and stupidities. One must listen
> carefully in order to serve as a proper midwife
> to the birth of consciousness in the other.
> The world is always bigger than one's own focus.
> And as we bring ourself into center where we
> are, the more of that world we can bring into
> service, the larger will be the capacity of our
> action and our understanding.22

Carretto speaks at length about his desert experience. How does this apply to a novice's life when
desert is not something this person has experienced?
How do Carretto's words affect life?

> . . . if you cannot go into the desert, you
> must nontheless "make some desert" in your life.
> Every now and then leaving men and looking for
> solitude to restore, in prolonged silence and
> prayer, the stuff of your soul. This is the
> meaning of "desert" in your life. (73)

The novitiate itself may be a desert. Another desert
could also be this time each day of going apart in the
early evening as Christ did in his earthly life. Or
desert could be an experience of our inner emptiness,
an inability or capacity to be still. The discipline of
keeping to this time in reflection, even when nothing
seems to be happening, may be difficult. The words of

Carretto could offer an impetus to keep with it:

> This is crucial: as long as we pray only when
> and how we want to, our life of prayer is bound
> to be unreal. It will run in fits and starts.
> The slightest upset--even a toothache--will be
> enough to destroy the whole edifice of our
> prayer life. (12)
>
> . . . .
>
> Deep down the soul has understood that it
> must let itself be carried, that it must abandon
> itself to its Saviour, that alone it can do
> nothing, that God can do everything.
>
> And if it remains still and motionless, as
> though bound in the faithfulness of God, it will
> quickly realize that things have changed, and
> that its progress, though still painful, is in
> the right direction. (68-69)

The desert silence was not something static
to Carretto. He learned of different silences as he
lived in the desert:

> Here, living in perpetual silence, one learns
> to distinguish its different shades: silence
> of the church, silence in one's cell, silence
> at work, interior silence, silence of the
> soul, God's silence . . . (11)

Through reading of Carretto's slow discovery of
dynamic silence, a novice may find that silence also
plays an important role in spiritual growth. Novitiate
is not an experience of perpetual silence as the desert
is, but daily experiences are filled with silence: in
church, in work, in prayer, in oneself. Along with
Carretto one may realize that there are many things
that keep silence from becoming meaningful: not experiencing anything in silence, being too tired to become
stilled and quiet, silence that loudly forces her to ask
questions about life.

> Now I don't fight any more: I try to accept
> myself. I try to face up to myself without
> illusions, dreams or fantasies. It's a step
> forward, I believe. And if I had made the
> step while I was still learning the catechism
> I should have gained forty years. (134)

Silence may allow one to give up the fight, to quit trying to do it all alone. Through reflection on life, a novice may be able to record her life without illusions, without pretext and without reverting to introspectionism. Powerlessness in the face of the powerful love of God may cause a conversion. One's smallness and unworthiness may be experienced in a new way in God's greatness. Through reading of Carretto's struggle with fatigue, with haunting memories of the times he had failed to be charitable, and with his efforts to allow God to be the center and ultimate concern of his life, the novice may begin to accept failures, and meaninglessness. The words the novice master spoke to Carretto might offer some insight:

> . . . my novice master told me with the perfect calm of a man who had lived twenty years in the desert: <u>It faut faire une coupure, Carlo</u>--(You have to make a break, Carlo) I knew what kind of cutting he was talking about and decided to make the wrench, even if it were painful. (xviii-xix)

He clearly decided to allow God to be the deciding factor in his life. Could this novice do the same? Can important goals be let go of as one's spiritual life awakens? When conversion becomes focal, life will become pure and simple.

Spiritual reading of Carretto's desert journal and written reflection on it, places the novice in a risky situation. These exercises lead to questions one might not have otherwise faced. These questions lead both to simplicity and pain; to joy and abandonment. Reflection may draw a person to a growing detachment from peripheral concerns and false-images about oneself. In attempts to protect oneself, to keep from being hurt by anyone coming too close to the real self a rare beauty in life may be covered over.

The joy and peace experienced in the letting go, puts the novice face to face, as it did in Carretto's life, with darkness and unknowing.

> . . . In order to hinder our spiritual indigestion God offers something radical: bare faith, simple hope, love without sentiment. The man who after his first steps in the spiritual life, throws himself into the

struggle of prayer and union with God, is
astounded at the dryness of the road. The
more he goes on, the more bitter and insipid
everything becomes. He derives little comfort
from the recollection of times past when God
seemed to make his spiritual path easier. (64)

Lack of consolation and good feelings may act as the
purification of heart of all selfish motives and
strivings. Efforts still can be governed by success.
One may even begin to question the pleasure received
from beautiful liturgies or community living. Are
these meaningful only because they give me pleasure and
a feeling of worth, or are they beautiful because they
truly are a worship of God and a respect for the
individuality of others? Each person may have to ask
what motivates one's actions, prayers, or following
rules. In evaluating decisions and actions a person
may gently unfold into a simple person who is always on
the road to understanding oneself and a relationship to
God more fully. Despite the dryness experienced, a
novice may discover a growing desire to consecrate oneself totally to Christ.

Adrian van Kaam[23]
Life Call and Commitment

When the formation program has been geared in such
a way that each novice is helped to give the best of
oneself, commitment to religious life becomes a possibility. van Kaam says that this yes to the gift and
burden of selfhood is at the root of our spiritual life.
This yes must be incarnated in the concrete modes of
life in which I live out my calling within everyday
situations. I may discover that some modes of incarnation are interwoven with my unique spiritual identity.
Other modes no longer seem essential and are therefore
replaced by lasting incarnations that are essential to
my living in faithfulness to the Word who lovingly calls
me.

As I live in prayerful presence to what is happening in and around me, a line may slowly emerge, that is,
I sense a certain direction, a hidden consistency making
itself known. The more this line clarifies itself, the
deeper becomes my conviction that this is my way. The
more a novice faces oneself in the solitude of the novitiate, the more attuned will that person be to the

inner voice, to inner convictions.

We must begin this process slowly with a minimum of knowing. In the hiddenness of Christ a slow self discovery happens. The answer to questions are deeply personal and therefore each person can only find them in listening to the Spirit speaking within. After long deliberation in solitude, my spirit may tell me what to do. I may not like my call on the vital or ego level and I may try to ignore or to fight it. But, it will keep returning. On the spirit level, there will be a strange conviction. Only by answering that call, as I perceive it today, will I be at peace.

The life call that I experience is the mystery of an all-embracing divine call. It is a unique call that encompasses the meaning of my whole life. It is a call that enables me to go beyond the finite, here and now situations and circumstances of my life. Being present to my unique life call means being present with my full personality. Full presence is the basis of commitment and consecration. I can only find out if my life commitments are in tune with my life call if I find myself again and again before God in liturgy, prayer, recollection and Scripture reading. Out of a growing awareness of the divine hidden direction of my life, the ebb and flow of daily experiences will become more meaningful.

However, spiritual life is not merely the discovery and growth in spiritual identity; it implies the incarnation of that eternal call within the whole of my life, in all action and modes of being.

Incarnation means accepting my limits; it means affirming the reality of foregoing ways of life because I am called to another life style, of giving up talents never to be realized, places and persons never to be met.[24]

van Kaam says that my unique combination of reaction and response is an incarnation of my fundamental life style. Incarnation has a dual purpose: to adapt to my environment, and to give an expression of my selfhood, the specific incarnation of who I am. The more harmonious are my adaptations to the environment with my unique self expression, the more integrated and consistent I will become.

273

I live out my fundamental life style within a particular life form. The religious celibate life form is
but one of three fundamental life forms. My personal
life is deeply interwoven with my chosen life form. I
cannot spiritualize myself unless I live my life form
as an expression of my life call. Having a vocation to
the religious life form is not synonymous with having a
vocation to a particular job. Vocational and professional styles however, may be modes through which my daily
life may become spiritualized. According to van Kaam,
in the spiritually harmonious person, there is a deepening integration of fundamental, vocational and professional styles. The more a person searches for,
discovers, and incarnates one's unique combination of
life call, life style and life form in the everyday modes
of life, the more simple will life become.

Adrian van Kaam[25]
Call-ability and Vow-ability

When I experience myself as "vowability", I find
the whole of my life related to the Sacred within one
of the fundamental life forms. I choose that life form
and vow myself to it with the awareness that that life
form is the way in which I will live my primary life
call. At first the call to vow my life is mysterious.
It may become clearer as my life proceeds and unfolds
through successive life events. Most often though, I
must live in semi-darkness, in the humble awareness that
I am following my life call though I cannot know in
advance the full reason I am called. My only certitude
is a certitude of faith. The call may invite me in ways
I never expected, ways which are new and original, though
still in harmony with my former ways of being and acting.

Vowing is not merely a matter of "thinking" but of
"willing" the limitations and the possibilities of this
lasting form.

Such commitment implies a creative configuration
of my whole style of thinking, perceiving,
desiring, feeling, expecting and imagining into
a rich consistent interiority which deepens and
intensifies with the passing of time.[26]

A person can only begin to enjoy the possibilities and
limitations of a life form when limitations are freely
chosen and accepted. The attitude of serenity is an
expression of the receptive celibate component of my

life. The attitude of celibacy creates the setting in
which I can be alone long enough to <u>listen</u> to my unique
life call. This listening receptivity will aid in the
meaningful direction of my life. It will keep my life
from the danger of becoming meaningless, scattered, inconsistent, and dispersed in everyday functionalism.

REFLECTION[27]

How does a novice begin to concretize a yes to a
unique life call? Perhaps one may begin to actualize a
response by firmly believing that part of this call is
to affirm the presence of Christ in life. As Lefebvre
notes:

> To believe is to let it become everything to
> us. A presence which is everything to us and
> essentially secret.   This double nature of
> his presence shows us the sort of attention
> we should pay to it. The more it means every-
> thing to us, the more there will be something
> which is always there, whatever the darkness
> and we should never doubt it. (89)

As a novice begins to recognize Christ as the heart of
one's desire, the freedom to search out a unique call,
the ways in which unique talents and limitations may
be used will draw the person closer relationship with
Him. Through prayerful consideration, a clear direction
may slowly emerge. One's unique call cannot be clearly
defined nor described, so the novice may only be able to
sense what this call is, by attempting to incarnate it
within a unique life style. For example, this novice,
may slowly discover that a controlling attitude, and
self-righteousness is only a defense to ward off the
possibility of being hurt by the comments of another.
Through prayerful consideration, a realization of how
one might be more free by gently listening to the opinions of another, and allowing the other to express
concerns without immediately being judged. One may
realize that God in his simplicity asks for very simple
attitudes: "Humility, a sense of our poverty, confidence,
inner peace, the feeling that we are not alone." (87)

Because of remembered past experiences that have
left a mark on one's life, a person may have to follow
the voice of one's spirit even though it feel uncomfortable on the ego or vital level. By uncovering the
obstacles to full spiritual living that show themselves

in one's temperament, imperfect prayer, and the limited present situation, one may experience a restlessness. Through quiet reflection on these obstacles as stepping stones and not as walls to spiritual unfolding, this open person may be more able to wholeheartedly say yes to the drawing, though hidden, love of God. Through reflection on the following questions a novice may uncover a unique thread in life. When was my last stepping stone? When did this period in my life begin? What highlights this period in my life? Knowing that this period in my life has taught me a great deal, what direction do I see my life taking? Where do I sense my life leading me? What new awareness and new attitudes do I see emerging from the past? The words of Lefebvre may give an individual the strength to be open to whatever maybe discovered:

> We should have a simple desire to offer to him
> who can satisfy it. A desire that is greater
> than our heart. We can guess at it beyond
> what we are conscious of. And if we find that
> we do not know whether we really want what
> remains so dark, we can be confident in him
> who calls us to him. We must simply desire
> what he invites us to hope for in an act of
> faith in him alone. By turning towards him
> we will find a remedy for all our ills. We
> belong to another. (99-100)

I, as novice director, may find that the best way in which I can help this novice through the painful process of self-discovery is to set the right atmosphere in which the slow emergence of the fullest, and the simplest person may happen. I should become aware of my own pre-reflective attitudes and style of life so that I will not be a hindrance to this self unfolding. My way of interacting may make this person depend upon me for direction. I should be cautious that this novice does not live in the illusion of taking responsibility for one's life when performing duties well, or spending time in prayer only because it is the right thing to do. I should instead, foster within this and the other novices a free and spontaneous self-exploration to help develop within them a deep sense of responsibility for their own growth in attitudes of honest openness to their own motives, feelings and desires. Through group conferences I may be able to speak more generally about developing these attitudes, and through individual direction I may help each novice to reflect in a special way on life. Leading the novices toward a discovery of their own fundamental life style necessitates a refined sensitivity on the part of the director. There has to be a finely balanced interplay between leading the other to new awarenesses through confrontation and a respect for the individual private lives of the novices.

The more concretely each novice is able to unfold a fundamental life style within the religious life form, the more integrated and simple will one's life become. Without a doubt, to live in this manner entails conflict and tension, misunderstanding and failure. For this person, these conflicts and tensions will not be viewed as blocks to full unfolding, but will be the birth pangs of further growth, stepping stones to a fuller understanding of oneself, world, and the aspects of life that seem to be most in conflict with present goals and ideals.

In the following section we shall briefly present the special birth pangs that a novice may experience in letting go of former ways as one begins to live a fundamental life style within religious life. We need to keep in mind that simplicity means that we have achieved a priority of values. It means that we have become persons who know what to hold on to, and what to let go of. We may have to let go of things and people, not because they are bad, but because they are no longer in touch with our response to the call of our destiny. In a particular way a novice becomes aware of what one needs to let go of in order to fully live the religious life. van Kaam speaks of this experience as mourning.

Adrian van Kaam28
The Experience of Mourning

van Kaam says that when a person enters the novitiate the interesting things and persons of the past are not turned away from completely. Outwardly a novice may cut oneself off from these, but they still continue to be present inwardly. The novitiate is the time in which a novice must be brought to a spirit of poverty. Poverty of spirit is an attitude of inward detachment. It is an inner poverty of mind and spirit, in order to be open to God. In order to come to this inner poverty, van Kaam says that a novice must go through a period of mourning.

When a person comes into the novitiate situation, former ways of acting, important goals and interest, no longer seem important. With the added stress on the spiritual life, one feels uprooted, strange and somewhat inadequate. How does the novice try to control this flood of feelings and not be overcome by them? van Kaam says that pyschologically and unconsciously one tries to control these uprooted feelings by retarding or delaying the process of loosening, a process of letting go a grasp on the past and the familiar. Mourning is a gradual working through the pain of this loss. It is not a question of repressing or denying the past; it is an acknowledgement and putting aside, an acceptance of the pain of mourning and yet an understanding that this pain too will pass.

A novice may tend to over-simplify the task of loosening. A novice often unconsciously tends to substitute something to replace the person or object given up. van Kaam says that three things happen there: the loved object becomes objectified; through introjection or incorporation the loved object enters the ego; and the person identifies with the incorporated object. For example, a novice may become attached to someone who has helped her with the decision to enter religious life. The cutting-off period in her life is delayed as she continues to hang on to that person instead of coming to her own free choice to personalize religious life. Another novice may feel a particular attachment to one's family. Familial love may be sought within the community. van Kaam notes that these are usual occurences. Mourning often proceeds through the introjection of what has been lost, and then the gradual loosening of the binding of that introjected object.

In other words, van Kaam says, that mourning is a work of inward mortification. It is not enough to exteriorly detach oneself from friends, home, parents. These outer loosenings will take care of themselves in time. But the inward closely associated ideals, fantasies, memories, images, and desires are much harder to let go of. In a novitiate program it is more important to watch for the inner detachment than for the external letting go. The inner letting go is far more difficult because of all kinds of bindings of the past. Therefore, a quieting of the mind and a stilling of the imagination is the primordial task. This is not to negate outer detachment. To witness to the life of vowed poverty, we need both internal and external detachment.

van Kaam also notes that once the work of mortification or mourning is accomplished, the person is free for new attachments. To the degree that a person's life force is re-oriented through mortification, it is turned toward the presence of God which will evoke an even greater surrender. This new orientation does not mean that the novices give up loving or associating with family and friends, but it means loving them in a new way. It means that the novice respects and relates to them in their own right, free from possessive or defensive love of them.

REFLECTION

A novice comes to the quiet of the novitiate out of the teeming activity of the postulate and intense college work. A taste of social work during the summer months has increased a desire to serve the needs of people. Excitement of finally reaching the point where one is accepted into the community is almost overwhelming.

The quiet of the novitiate, the uprooting from everything that has become familiar, the inner intensity of life that substitutes for the more exterior activity of the postulate are all overwhelming. One is beset with questions like: have I made a mistake in coming here: Why does it seem that the bottom has fallen out from under me? Why do I feel so tired, so pulled apart when everything I have ever hoped for is almost at my fingertips?

The task of the novice director is to be sensitive to this natural feeling of uprootedness. This does not mean that the novices are given false securities to hang on to, or false hopes that ease the uprooting. Instead the director allows them to remain in this state of uprootedness for a time, allowing them to adjust to the strange new atmosphere and the new intensity in the spiritual life. The novice director is to set the atmosphere of a slowed down settling into life. There is often a tendency to keep the novices busy to the point where they have no time to face their own uprootedness. If the novice director desires to lead the novices to a deeper spiritual life the tone of the novitiate has to free them to gently, squarely and lovingly face themselves within an atmosphere of silence and solitude.

When the initial shock of the novitiate loses its sting, a novice may be ready to wholeheartedly detach oneself from former loved objects. At first giving up a car doesn't seem too difficult, but giving up the small Guatemalan earthenware jar received for a friend as a gift may be more difficult, to say nothing of giving up inner attitudes. She may have to hang onto this for a while. Giving up a colorful wardrobe at first seems hard as she switches to the basic blues of the community, but somehow her room becomes the symbol of self expression, a private domain that no one else enters into. Another novice may substitute for the friends left behind. Perhaps for this novice the hardest thing was to be separated from family, especially from a three year old brother, but now the community has substituted for that detachment. In other words, the novice may find that alot has been given up but each one of the objects given up has been substituted for by a lesser object, an object or person that is acceptable within the novitiate. At first it may appear that this person has really come a long way in embodying the religious life and the detachment that this particular life entails. van Kaam says that this is a normal procedure. But the detachment must go deeper, it must begin to touch the core of where this individual really lives life.

When one is ready to see that exteriorly the letting go of many things has happened but inwardly still hangs onto them, the point of acknowledging these lesser attachments is reached. These attachments are not denied or repressed, but with the help of grace and wise direction, one may be able to fully mourn the loss of these attachments.

In order to help another to become detached inwardly, a novice director has to be able to acknowledge one's own introjected objects. One needs to work through attachments to be able to hold on to one's own convictions when the novices need help in facing theirs. If the director doesn't, a novice's questions may evoke unresolved attachments; one's life and work will become threatened and ineffective. On the other hand, the director has to be able to give up one's own world to empathically be with the novice, to enter cognitively, emotionally and bodily into the world of the novice to aid the novice in the loosening process.

Another aspect of empathically leading the novices to mourn the past, is the care and concern with which the director tries to help the novice come to an acceptance of life situations as they are. Paradoxically, the care and concern can lead to a transference. In my efforts to help the other, I may become the lost mother or father image for the novice, and the novice a child who will try anything to keep from losing that love. The transference seems to creep up slowly like the binding tendrils of a vine. If the care and concern is not disciplined, the transference becomes firmly anchored before I realize what has transpired. My immediate response may be to thrash and flail, trying to throw off the binding hold of the novice. In the process of loosening it too quickly or uncaringly, the vital life surging in the other is often marred. Care and concern in this situation takes honest and humble admission of what has happened, and only then is a slow gradual removal possible.

At times, care and concern calls for a waiting upon the right time, waiting for the novice to come to an acceptance of what she sees or cannot perceive clearly. This waiting upon allows for the unexpected to take place. It is not a programming or deciding what should be clarified, or what should have meaning for the novice. Waiting upon allows for more freedom as the director walks together with the novice down the path of life.

As can be seen from van Kaam's theory and the above reflection, detachment must take place inwardly. This inward loosening will allow outer attachments to take care of themselves. Inner detachment is the slow, gradual process of letting go of anything that takes the place of true love and respect for persons and things. True inner detachment does not mean the giving up of persons, events and things, but it means loving and respecting them in a new light, respecting them as being loved by God. In true detachment, a novice will become attached to loved ones in a new way. Interaction with these loved objects will become cleansed of possessiveness and defensiveness. Inner detachment is both a preparation for living the vowed life, and a deepening attitude that should characterize religious life. In respectful use of material goods, a novice may be willing to give up the Guatemalan earthenware jar as well as the car, if it is needed; giving up the colorful wardrobe may be a freeing experience instead of a restriction of individual choice. In living celibate love, the novice may eventually be able to love the other novices as they are without associating them to previous, no longer acceptable love of friends. Eventually one may be able to listen to the will of God as voiced by superiors instead of living in one's own controlled realm of room and individuality. Support and encouragement to others will be possible in community without seeing the community as a substitute for the familial love that has been transformed in life. Most of all the novice will be able to let go of interior attachments that continue to complicate life.

Again, the task of the novice director is to help each novice to clarify motivations and to appropriate personally, and renew creatively the habits, customs and devotions of this particular community. In the following section, I will consider the director's task in leading the novices to true community living.

Marie Beha[29]
Formation for Community

Formation for community should help the novice come to grips with the demands and rewards of living in community. In a real lived situation, one's vocation to live religious life could be tested with such realism that the decision to commit oneself to religious life in preference to family life, can be based on personal experience of living religious life.

One of the signs of a realistic decision to live in community is a willingness to put aside one's preconceived notions of a perfect and instant community. Unless the novice learns to accept the limitations of others with patience, one will not be permitted, nor permit others to risk being themselves. Failures in community are often the result of an inability to be open to the needs of others. Instead of aiding another with a task, a person may substitute sympathy; instead of entering into responsible relationships with others, a person may defend oneself by "serving" the needs of others.

Beha remarks that one of the skills most needed in community is a capacity for communication. Communication is based on an ability to leave behind one's own

preoccupations and prejudices to enter into the world
of another person. To communicate with another is to
try to understand the world of the other and show this
understanding in words and gestures, or in any way that
seems appropriate to the given situation. A responsible
person can also answer for oneself. This means that a
person can take a stand or modify a stand without feeling
threatened by others; one cares for oneself, while at
the same time admits dependence on others.

Besides being able to communicate, each member of
the community must have the capacity to be alone, to
be comfortable with oneself.

The rhythm of withdrawal and engagement, of
reflection and expression, is an essential
humanizing aspect of community structure.
The proportion of reflection and expression
is determined by the spirit of the individual
and the needs of the local community, and is
also related to the needs of the wider
community.[30]

REFLECTION

One of the strongest needs of a community is the
capacity of each member to be open in communication
with the other. In the novitiate, a main task is to
awaken the sensitivity of each novice to the needs
(even unspoken ones) of those that are lived with and
served in the community. Overzealously, a novice may
think this means to be utterly honest and truthful with
the other novices or with the novice director. Through
trial and error she may soon realize that truth without
love is not really helpful because it can destroy the
other instead of showing love. Even though the other
novices in community are unique, and hopefully each one
is different according to one's own individuality, one's
efforts to form community, to respectfully communicate
with each person is an art that is learned over a lifetime.

Growth in sensitivity to each member of the community may also enhance one's prayer life and allow a
novice to walk the road of God's will for her. In
order to find God and be present to Him, each novice has
to be present to those met within the normal situations
of life. Awakening to the presence of God in each

person's life is an art that can only be mastered through everyday experience. The novice director is to lead the novices to a belief in community, for the call they have received from God invites them to follow Christ within a community life, by sharing respectfully and lovingly with others. Respect for the individual needs of each other will force the novices to come to grips with both the demands and the rewards of community life.

Respectful communication requires a patient putting aside of all preconceived notions of what community should be. It is a laying down of our images of a perfect and ideal community. It is a remembrance that we are always on the way, always trying to own the limitedness and possibility of each member of the community. Respectful communication means substituting concrete care and concern for feigned sympathy that doesn't really get involved in the lives of others. It is a shedding of our defensive doing to allow meaningful encounter and communication to take place. In other words, true communication is an ongoing growth in simplicity where each person can take a stand and allow others to take a stand that is most in tune with unique life calls. This may mean that time be taken to quietly listen to the concerns of another rather than doing some little nicety that would keep one safe from being rejected by the other. For another, taking a stand may mean that to actually "do" something concrete for another instead of pretending that one did not know another was really in need of her help may be the better option. Using Beha's words:

> Community is a union of responsible and
> responsive persons. The man who enters
> community must have enough responsibility
> to answer for himself. He cannot come to
> community just to be supported by it; he must
> be a contributing member. He must also have
> enough confidence in himself to value his
> contribution for what it is, his own unique
> response, and this without wasting his time
> in odious comparisons.[31]

Instead of wasting precious time in odious comparisons, each novice should waste time with alone and with God in prayer. One will only be able to give in community if a storehouse has been built from which to build care and concern for others. In finding time

apart from others a novice may grow in acceptance of
one's own unique situation. In sharing time with others,
a novice may become more sensitive to the uniqueness of
each member and value whatever that person can bring to
community. Through sharing life with others, one will
become aware that there is never a perfect community.
But through each person's individual efforts to be the
best possible person, in the true sense of the term,
the more likely will each person be drawn to a relationship of intimacy with Christ. The more Christ is the
center of a community, the more simple will be the
group's interaction.

Experiences in the novitiate will hopefully prepare
each novice to live a unique spiritual life within the
community. When one is sent out at the end of a novitiate experience, as Christ sent out his disciples
after sharing his message of love with them, the novice
will learn from personal experience how to carry on the
work of the Master, and how to get along with others in
community. Like the disciples, each person will find
that at times the message has been lost. By returning
to true roots in prayer and finding strength in community, the novice may simply try to bear witness to the
love of the Father for all.

Summary

The purpose of this Part was to show how the
particular time of the novitiate is a time of growth in
the spiritual life. Spiritual life, in the sense it is
understood here, refers to the integration of the
whole person, that is, vital, personal and spiritual
self dimensions.

Using van Kaam's theory, I first presented the
purpose of the novitiate experience as being one of
spiritual initiation. Through transcendent reflection
on life, a novice becomes awakened to the faith dimension of life. Paul Molinari presents ways in which the
novice director may lead the novices to a response of
faith. I concluded the first section by pointing out
the necessity of awakening the novice's sensitivity to
mystery. As the novice becomes more aware of mystery
in everyday situations, one may eventually be drawn to
experience the Mystery of all that is. Waiting upon
mystery in daily life will draw the novice into simplicity, becoming fully present to this deeper dimension of
life.

In the second section of this Part, I attempted to show that praying with an attitude of waiting leads to simplicity in prayer. Through the use of journal keeping and spiritual reading a novice may become more in touch with one's own experiences by reflecting upon the life experience of others who have searched for a deeper spiritual life. By this slowed down awakening to this spiritual dimension, the novice may sense a yearning, and a readiness to commit oneself to God through religious life.

To fully understand what it means to commit oneself, the novice must become aware of the distinctions between life call, fundamental life style and life form. Through this theory and reflection I stressed the necessity of initiating the never ending search for one's unique spiritual identity. I also pointed out the necessity of self-knowledge in order to substitute a fundamental life style in place of a defensive uncongenial style of life. These two fundamental dynamics, that is, a search for the unique life call and the unfolding on one's individual fundamental life style, must be incarnated within a particular life form. The more a novice is able to find all these aspects of life integrated into a harmonious whole, the more simple will life become.

To truly live religious life in simplicity, a novice must inwardly live the loosening process of mourning. Past and familiar person, events, and things are experienced in a new way, in a way that is closely aligned to the spiritual dimension of dependence upon God. When the novice outwardly becomes detached from persons, events, and things that no longer tie in with religious life and is able inwardly to let go of the introjected objects, this person is able to be fully present and responsible in a spirit of poverty. Without these introjected objects, responses to life may become more simple and transparent. In order for the novice director to aid the novice in the letting go process, the director must be in touch with personal life experiences and inner defenses.

In the final section we saw how community is a gift. Through one's taking stand in community, being responsible for oneself and for those with whom one lives, a novice will discover that community is never perfect. Through each person's acceptance of the limitations and the possibilities of people living community together, community becomes a place of living simplicity.

Conclusion

At the outset of this study I used the analogy of the folded bundle of cloth. This analogy stemmed from the etymology of the word simplicity, which means "without fold." Because of the anxiety stemming from certain life experiences, each person develops a way of being which is not simple, which can be a defensive protection from being hurt or feeling insecure. A person turns within oneself to keep from being overcome by feelings of lostness, aloneness and vulnerability. In the process, the unique beauty and individuality of that person's life is not allowed to show. Through the succeeding Parts of this study I attempted to show that the more I am in touch with my whole limited self, and the more I respond in the everday with that whole limited self, the more simple my life will become, and the more able I will be to live my unique spiritual identity. Through the process of slowing down to get in touch with the mystery of life that surrounds and permeates even the everyday situations of life, I will be able to give my limited response in tune with that mystery and to recover the lost childlikeness that is characteristic of a simple person.

Unfolding the "cloth of my life" in simplicty is a lifetime process. At times I may fear facing what I may discover about myself, or what surrender to God in simplicity might entail. At other times, the complicated world in which I live may tend to pull me off center as I try to answer all of its demands with my own strengths and weaknesses. By returning to Christ as my true center and as the ultimate concern in my life, my responses and interaction with others will unfold in simplicity, for He alone makes life meaningful, He alone is truly simple.

ENDNOTES

[1]Since the novitiate is a period that is devoted to personal spiritual formation, there are several presuppositions that will make this personal spiritual formation possible. Through a well-developed preentrance and postulate program the novice has attained a sufficient grasp of basic Catholic doctrine to be able, during the novitiate, to come to a more personal grasp of how this doctrine affects life. The novice has also been aided in the life-long task of discerning the difference between true self and a false self-image that may have substituted for the true self in an ego-functional society. This candidate has also been aided in solving personal problems, clarifying conflicting tendencies in life, and withstanding temptations to live on merely vital or personal level of life instead of delving deeply into the spiritual realm. This person has partially experienced the purification from earthly motives for entering a particular religious community, and through the process of self-clarification, has become more aware of what in life needs to be changed to become more ready for the living of a deeper spiritual life.

By the time the initiate advances to the novitiate, there should be some inclinations toward a need for silence and solitude in life. Also exhibited should be some signs of a longing to dedicate totally within the religious life form.

[2]Though for the most part I will be speaking about the role of the novice director, I do not mean to negate the necessary involvement of others in the formation team in drawing the initiates to a fuller living of the spiritual life. Formation of the total person in today's world necessitates a well coordinated program that will provide continuity for growth and development. A formation team will be better able to meet the individual needs of the initiates. It will also provide the opportunities for support, clarification of goals and ideals and the challenge to develop their own spiritual and personal lives.

[3]Adrian van Kaam, In Search of Spiritual Identity (Denville, New Jersey: Dimension Books, 1975), pp. 197-248.

[4]Paul Molinari, "The Pedagogical Viewpoint: Teaching How to Respond to God in Faith," Donum Dei No. 17 (1971), 37-64.

[5]Ibid., p. 38.

[6]Ibid., p. 54.

[7]Ibid., p. 42.

[8]Story of a Soul: The Autobiography of St. Thérèse of Lisieux TRANS. John Clarke (Washington, D.C.: ICS Publications, 1975), p. 238. (Italics in the Original.)

[9]Evelyn Underhill, Practical Mysticism (New York: E.P. Dutton & Co., Inc., 1943), pp. 10-11.

[10]van Kaam, op. cit., p. 229.

[11]William Johnston (ed). The Cloud of Unknowing (Garden City, New York: Image Books, 1973), p. 48.

[12]Keith J. Egan, What is Prayer? (Denville, New Jersey: Dimension Books, 1973), pp. 20-34.

[13]Ibid., p. 24.

[14]Ibid., p. 32. (Italics in the original.)

[15]Ibid., p. 33.

[16]William Johnston, op. cit., pp. 48-49.

[17]Ibid., p. 107.

[18]Story of a Soul, op. cit., p. 188. (Italics in the Original.)

[19]Susan Annette Muto, Approaching the Sacred (Denville, New Jersey: Dimension Books, 1973), pp. 9-78.

[20]Ibid., p. 49-50.

[21]Throughout this reflection I will attempt to draw together the benefits of both spiritual reading and journal keeping. These two spiritual exercises seem to be especially beneficial to a novice who is beginning the spiritual journey. To concretize this experience I will refer to the slowed down reading of a text that might be appropriate for the special novitiate situation.

All page references to this book will follow directly
after the quotation. Carlo Carretto, <u>Letters from the
Desert</u> (Maryknoll, New York: Orbis Books, 1972).

[22]Mary Caroline Richards, <u>Centering in Pottery,
Poetry and the Person</u> (Middletown, Connecticut:
Wesleyan University Press, 1969), p. 21. (Italics in
the Original.)

[23]Adrian van Kaam, <u>In Search of Spiritual Identity</u>
(Denville, New Jersey: Dimension Books, 1975), pp. 138-
171, 197-248.

[24]Ibid., p. 142.

[25]Adrian van Kaam, <u>The Vowed Life</u> (Denville, New
Jersey: Dimension Books, 1968), pp. 75-140.

[26]Ibid., p. 138.

[27]The reference for this reflection are taken from
Anthony Bloom and Georges Lefebvre, <u>Courage to Pray</u>
(New York: Paulist press, 1973), pp. 85-94. This text
may again be a possible source for the novitiate
spiritual reading program. Through this reflection I
hope to show the reader how a text of this sort may
ready a novice for a fuller acceptance of a limited life
call. (Page references will follow after the quotations.)

[28]Adrian van Kaam, <u>Religion and Personality</u>, (New
York, N.Y.: Image Book, 1972), p. 48.

[29]Marie Beha, <u>The Dynamics of Community</u> (New York:
Corpus Books, 1970), pp. 11-42.

[30]Ibid., p. 46.

[31]Beha, op, cit., pp. 29-30.

BIBLIOGRAPHY

Aldington, Richard. (ed.) The Portable Oscar Wilde.
    New York: Viking Press, 1946.

Andrews, Edward D. The Gift to be Simple. New York:
    Dover Publications, Inc., 1967.

Beha, Marie. The Dynamics of Community. New York:
    Corpus Books, 1970.

Bidney, David. Theoretical Anthropology. New York:
    Columbia University Press, 1953.

Bloom, Anthony and Georges Lefebvre. Courage to Pray.
    trans. Dinah Livingstone. New York: Paulist
    Press, 1973.

Bodo, Murray. Francis: The Journey and the Dream.
    Cincinnati, Ohio: St. Anthony Messenger Press,
    1972.

Bonhoeffer, Dietrich. The Cost of Discipleship. trans.
    R. H. Fuller. New York: The Macmillan Co., 1968.

Boros, Ladislaus. Meeting God in Man. New York:
    Herder and Herder, 1968.

Carretto, Carlo. Letters from the Desert. trans.
    Rose Mary Hancock. Maryknoll, New York: Orbis
    Books, 1972.

Cloud of Unknowing, The. trans. William Johnston.
    Garden City, New York: Image Books, 1973.

Dalrymple, John. Costing Not Less Than Everything.
    Denville, New Jersey: Dimension Books, 1975.

Dessauer, Philipp. Natural Meditation. trans. J.
    Holland Smith. New York: J. P. Kennedy, 1965.

Egan, Keith J. What is Prayer? Denville, New Jersey:
    Dimension Books, 1973.

Eisley, Loren. The Unexpected Universe. New York:
    Harcourt, Brace, Jovanovich, 1969.

Eliot, T. S. Four Quartets, New York: Harcourt,
    Brace & World, Inc., 1971.

Eller, Vernard. The Simple Life. Grand Rapids,
    Michigan: William B. Eerdmans Pub. Co., 1973.

Ellul, Jacques. Prayer and Modern Man. trans. C.
    Edward Hopkins. New York: Seabury Press, 1970.

Francis de Sales, Saint. Introduction to the Devout
    Life. trans. John K. Ryan. Garden City, New,
    York: Image Books, 1966.

Franck, Frederick. Pilgrimage to Now/Here. Maryknoll,
    New York: Orbis Books, 1974.

Frankl, Viktor. The Doctor and the Soul: From
    Psychotherapy to Logotherapy. trans. Richard and
    Clara Winston. New York: Random House, 1955.

Fromm, Erich. Creativity and Its Cultivation, ed. H. H.
    Anderson. New York: Harper and Row, 1959.

Fromm, Erich. The Revolution of Hope, Toward a
    Humanized Technology. New York: Harper and Row,
    1968/

Fromm, Erich. The Sane Society. New York: Fawcett
    World Library, 1955.

Goffman, Erving. Presentation of Self in Everyday Life.
    Garden City, New York: Doubleday and Co., 1959.

Hakenewerth, Quentin. For the Sake of the Kingdom.
    Collegeville, Minnesota: Liturgical Press, 1971.

Heidegger, Martin. Discourse on Thinking. trans.
    John M. Anderson and E. Hans Freund. New York:
    Harper Torchbooks, 1966.

Herrigel, Eugen. Zen in the Art of Archery. New York:
    Random House, 1953.

Horney, Karen. Neurosis and Human Growth. New York:
    W. W. Norton and Co., 1950.

Horney, Karen. The Neurotic Personality of Our Time.
    New York: W. W. Norton and Co., 1937.

Horney, Karen. Our Inner Conflicts. New York: W. W.
    Norton and Co., 1945.

Hyers, Conrad. Zen and the Comic Spirit. Philadelphia: Westminster Press, 1973.

Keen, Samuel. Gabriel Marcel. Richmond, Virginia: John Knox Press, 1967.

Kelly, Thomas R. A Testament of Devotion. New York: Harper and Row, 1941.

Kraft, William F. The Search for the Holy. Philadelphia: Westminster Press, 1971.

Levinas, Emmanuel. Totality and Infinity. trans. Alphonso Lingis. Pittsburgh: Duquesne University Press, 1969.

Lindbergh, Anne Morrow. Gift from the Sea. New York: Pantheon Books, 1955.

Lindbergh, Anne Morrow. Hour of Gold, Hour of Lead: Diaries and Letters of Anne Morrow Lindbergh, 1929-1932. New York: Harcourt, Brace, Jovanovich, 1973.

Luijpen, William. Existential Phenomenology. Revised edition. Pittsburgh: Duquesne University Press, 1969.

Marcel, Gabriel. Being and Having. trans. Katherine Farrar. London: The University Press, 1949.

Marcel, Gabriel. The Mystery of Being, Vol. I. trans. B. S. Fraser. Chicago: Henry Regnery Co., 1960.

Marcel, Gabriel. The Philosophy of Existentialism. trans. Manya Harari. New York: Citadel Press, 1956.

Maslow, Abraham. Toward a Psychology of Being. New York: Van Nostrand Co., 1968.

May, Rollo. Man's Search for Himself. New York: New American Library, 1953.

Merton, Thomas. Contemplative Prayer. Garden City, New York: Image Books, 1969.

Merton, Thomas. No Man is an Island. New York: Dell Publishing Co., 1955.

Merton, Thomas. <u>Zen and the Birds of Appetite</u>. New York: New Directions, 1968.

Metz, Johannes B. <u>Poverty of Spirit</u>. trans. John Drury. New York: Newman Press, 1968.

Muto, Susan Annette. <u>Approaching the Sacred</u>. Denville, New Jersey: Dimension Books, 1973.

Muto, Susan Annette. <u>Steps Along the Way</u>. Denville, New Jersey: Dimension Books, 1975.

O'Neill, David. <u>What Do You Say to a Child When You Meet a Flower?</u> St. Meinrad, Indiana; Abbey Press, 1972.

Pfuetze, Paul. <u>The Social Self</u>. New York: Bookman Associates, 1954.

Richards, Mary Caroline. <u>Centering in Pottery, Poetry and the Person</u>.

Schachtel, Ernest. <u>Metamorphosis on the Development of Affect, Perception, Attention and Memory</u>. New York: Basic Books, 1959.

Schutz, Alfred. <u>Collected Papers, I</u>. The Hague: Nijhoff, 1967.

Smith, Huston. <u>The Religions of Man</u>. New York: Perennial Library, 1965.

St. Exupery, A. <u>The Little Prince</u>. New York: Harcourt, World & Brace, 1943.

Story of a Soul: <u>The Autobiography of St. Therese of Lisieux</u>. trans. John Clarke. Washington, D.C.: Cistertian Publications, 1975.

Streng, Frederick. <u>Understanding Religious Man</u>. Belmont, California: Dickenson Publishing Co., 1969.

Thoreau, Henry David. <u>Walden and Other Writings</u>. New York: The Modern Library, 1950.

Tillich, Paul. <u>Dynamics of Faith</u>. New York: Harper Torchbooks, 1957.

Tzu, Lao. The Simple Way of Lao Tsze. The Simple Way of Lao Tsze. Fintry, England: Shrine of Wisdom, 1951.

Underhill, Evelyn. Practical Mysticism. New York: Dutton and Co., 1943.

van der Poel, Cornelius. Religious Life: A Risk of Love. Denville, New Jersey: Dimension Books, 1972.

van Kaam, Adrian. In Search of Spiritual Identity. Denville, New Jersey: Dimension Books, 1975.

van Kaam, Adrian. On Being Yourself. Denville, New Jersey: Dimension Books, 1972.

van Kaam, Adrian. Personality Fulfillment in the Religious Life. Denville, New Jersey: Dimension Books, 1967.

van Kaam, Adrian. Personality Fulfillment in the Spiritual Life. Denville, New Jersey: Demension Books, 1966.

van Kaam, Adrian. Religion and Personality. Garden City, New York: Doubleday and Co., 1968.

van Kaam, Adrian. The Vowed Life. Denville, New Jersey: Dimension Books, 1968.

van Zeller, Hubert. Leave Your Life Alone . Springfield, Illinois: Templegate Publishers, 1972.

von Hildebrand, Dietrich. Transformation in Christ: On the Christian Attitude of Mind. New York: Longmans, Green and Co., 1948

Wagner, Charles. The Simple Life. trans. Mary Louise Hendee. New York: McClure, Phillips, and Co., 1901.

Ziegler, Edward Krusen. Simple Living. Elgin, Illinois: Brethren Press, 1974.

PERIODICALS

Amoyt, Florette. "Listening and Responding to the Word of God," Open to the Spirit (Ottawa, Ontario:

Canadian Religious Conference, 1970), 40-46.

Feuer, Lewis S. "The Principle of Simplicity," Philosophy of Science XXIV (1957), 109-122.

Harvey, Arden. "The Pious Ones," National Geographic CXLVIII:2 (August, 1975), 276-298.

Karper, Mary Seraphim. "Be Still and Know," Spiritual Life XVII:4 (Winter, 1971), 247-253.

Masterson, Reginald, "Religious Life in a Secular Age," Cross and Crown XXII (June, 1970), 133-147.

Sister Miriam Louise. "Mary: Receiver and Witness of the Word," Review for Religious XXXI:5 (September, 1972), 765-769.

Molinari, Paul. "The Pedagogical Viewpoint: Teaching How to Respond to God in Faith," Donum Dei No. 17 (1971), 37-64.

McNamara, William. "The Recovery of Childhood," Desert Call X:4 (Fall, 1975), 1-3.

O'Shea, Kevin. "Enigma and Tenderness," Spiritual Life XXI:1 (Spring, 1975), 8-22.

Rapoport, Anatol. "The Search for Simplicity," Main Currents in Modern Thought XXVIII:3 (Jan.-Feb., 1972), 79-84.

Ruitenbeek, Hendrik. 'Mechanization Versus Spontaneity: Which Will Survive?" Humanitas II:3 (Winter, 1967), 261-269.

Smith, Herbert, "Prayer and the Maturing Sister," Sisters Today XLII:8 (April, 1971), 439-453.

Sullivan, Lawrence. "Therese of Lisieus and The Wisdom of China," Spiritual Life XIX:3 (Fall, 1973), 179-203.

Tillard, J. M. R. "The Theological Viewpoint: Religious Life, A Choice Rooted in Faith," Donum Dei No. 17 (1971), 13-36.

van Kaam, Adrian. "Dynamics of Spiritual Self-Direction," Spiritual Life XXI:4 (Winter, 1975), 261-282.

DATE DUE